**Praise for Aphrodite Jc
and Her Masterful Real-Life Thrillers**

"True crime legend Aphrodite Jones returns with a vengeance as she unravels the complexities of murder and deceit in Levi's Eyes. Smart and stunning, this is another classic from Jones. True Crime fans rejoice. She's back!"
     —**Gregg Olsen,** best-selling author of *The Girls Are Gone*

"Aphrodite Jones is one of the chief practitioners of the true-crime genre."
     —**Baltimore Sun**

\* \* \*

*A Perfect Husband*

"Marriage, murder, and manipulation—a classic true-crime page-turner only a writer like Aphrodite Jones could scribe."
     —**M. William Phelps,** author of *Kiss of the She-Devil*

"Jones uses an investigative style that puts her at the forefront of true-crime writers. Prepare yourself for a journey into a meticulous criminal mind."
     —**Corey Mitchell,** author of *Savage Son*

"In A Perfect Husband, Aphrodite Jones tells a richly detailed and deeply researched tale of a greedy, manipulative and sociopathic killer who uses his children as pawns to hide his wicked exploits: murder and mayhem!"
     —**Caitlin Rother,** author of *Lost Girls*

## Dog O' War
## (Formally known as Red Zone)

"The story that mesmerized and horrified the city and made headlines across the country. . . Jones blows the cover off the case."
 —*San Francisco Chronicle*

"Jones displays a remarkable ability to present an enormous amount of detailed information in a thrilling narrative that is neither sensationalistic nor maudlin."
 —*Publishers Weekly*

"In this riveting book, noted true-crime writer Jones goes behind the headlines and tells the whole story with simple, straightforward prose and plenty of close observation. It's a story that begins before the fatal attack and continues beyond its aftermath to embrace such hot-button issues as animal rights, the responsibilities of animal owners, and the legal rights of same-sex partners. This is no 'quickie' book released to capitalize on the headlines; rather, it's thoughtful, compassionate, unsettling, and enlightening."
 —*Booklist*

"Jones is a masterful investigator and writer who has pierced the heart of this tragic killing. Red Zone is a page-turning account that takes us deep into the relationship between man and animal.'
 —*Harper Audio Reviews*

*Michael Jackson Conspiracy*

"Aphrodite Jones provides the details that we never got in the news media and vividly captures the phenomenon that was the Michael Jackson trial. It's a deeply researched, intense account that keeps you anxiously awaiting the next scene."
   —**Roy Black**, NBC legal commentator

"To anyone who wants to learn what happened in the Michael Jackson courtroom, this is the book to read."
   —**Thomas A. Mesereau Jr.**, Michael Jackson's lead counsel

* * *

*The Embrace*

"Jones provides a good overview of the facts surrounding the murder and her prose glows with intensity"
   —*Publishers Weekly*

"Parents of teens may want to read *The Embrace* just to heed the warning signs."
   —**Denver Rocky Mountain News**

"Readers will get some sense of the shadowy fantasy lives of `kids fallen through life's crack.' "
   —**Kirkus Reviews**

*All He Wanted*
*(formerly known as All She Wanted)*

"Aphrodite Jones finds herself deeply affected by the cases she covers. . . The book grapples with sexual experimentation, murder, hate crimes, and the transgender movement. A page-turner!"
   —**The New Yorker**

## Other True Crime Bestsellers by Aphrodite Jones

   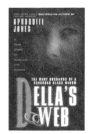

This book is dedicated to Cindy Best. Without her efforts, there would be no justice for Christina, no justice for Levi, and Karl would have gotten away with murder, *twice*.

LEVI'S EYES is published by

AphroditeJonesBooks

AAJ Productions, Inc.

Ft Lauderdale, Florida 33304

APHRODITEJONESBOOKS

# APHRODITE JONES

# LEVI'S EYES

**A Son's Deadly Secret and A Father's Cruel Betrayal**

APHRODITEJONESBOOKS
AAJ PRODUCTIONS, INC.
WWW.APHRODITEJONES.COM

## AUTHOR'S NOTE

I'm fully aware that there are folks out there who believe they already know this story inside and out. But trust me, just when you think you know it, there's more... And more... Much more.

It may seem odd to say, but writing a true crime book takes a village. In this case, law enforcement, witnesses, court clerks, and family members helped me gather 3,000 pages of documents, including court exhibits, diaries, photos, personal letters, depositions, police reports, and transcripts of the audio and video tape recordings which bring this story to life.

But the most incredible thing for me, was the unfettered access I had to the killer, Karl Karlsen, for over two years. I spoke to Karl every day from his jail cell in San Andreas and was able to explore the criminal mind beyond anything I've known in my thirty years as a true crime writer, producer, and host.

Part of this narrative is told from the killer's point of view, mainly because Karlsen's commentary is so outrageous, his point of view is so demented, I felt it had to be shared verbatim. There's also a competing narrative presented here, from the point of view of Cindy Best Karlsen.

There are those who might question the sincerity of her perspective, but I promise you that having been married to and threatened by this killer, she provides an essential context to this story, one that has not been told in any crime show, podcast, or news magazine show, ever.

There are a few other things I need to share with you, important elements of this story that did not enter into the main narrative, mainly because I've been saving them for this note.

The first thing I'd like you to know is just how "normal" the Karlsen household was for most of Cindy and Karl's eighteen-year marriage. As proof of this, the Karlsen family hosted a child from New York City via a program called "Fresh Air Kids," a boy named Brian Pestano. The Karlsens were not paid to do this. It was Cindy's idea to host a child who knew nothing of farm life. Brian stayed with the family in the summer of 2003 and then opted to return again in 2004.

That's a testament to how well Karl was able to hide his abusive ways, when he wanted to. And by the way, Brian was terrified of most animals when he first got to the farm, but he got better with time and came to love Karlsen's dogs and horses.

The other thing, a very important thing, that you need to know is that in the months before his death, Levi had found a new love in his life, a young woman named Jennifer Keefer, and the two of them were planning a future together. It gives me chills to think of this because it makes me feel heartbroken, yet I also feel joy in knowing that Jennifer was there for Levi until the bitter end. In fact, Ms. Keefer gave a sworn statement to police, stating that on the morning of November 20, 2012, at 11:30 AM, she received a text from Levi asking if "he could have me forever." Jennifer told police that she said "yes," and they exchanged the words "I love you" back and forth. Jennifer also stated that she sent a number of follow-up texts, and when Levi didn't respond to her, she thought he was playing "head games." But indeed, he wasn't. And unfortunately, we all know why.

There is one last item of business that I'd like to address here, and that's my unconventional writing style. I write in a novel-type style and create dialogue throughout this narrative, none of which I have made up. All dramatizations presented here are based on court transcripts, newspaper accounts, and personal interviews with the people who lived through this ordeal.

That said, for the purpose of narration, I have also condensed certain conversations, Facebook messages, and emails, in order to keep the flow of this narrative moving fluently. I have used this style of dramatization throughout my true crime writing career, hence this book is no different. If there are people who want to nit-pick and argue that one word is changed here or there, so be it.

I stand with the truth. And this is a true story, told in its entirety, using real names, dates, and places. I have written this book with the hope that Christina and Levi Karlsen's deaths will help all of us learn life lessons, that we will come to value the gift of human life, and the gift of animal life, just a little bit more than we think we do.

To you all, my dear readers, I write this with all my heart. You mean more to me than you'll ever know, I cherish each one of you and pray that together, we can figure out a way to make this world a better and safer place.

## ACKNOWLEDGMENTS

A book of this depth cannot be accomplished without the help and kindness of others. Members of law enforcement, particularly John Cleere, helped me understand the complexity of the Karl Karlsen case and supplied me with essential documents that made this book possible. I will always be grateful for his cooperation.

Throughout this book, I often speak of members of the press, both local and national, without naming any names. I did this because I had to pull from many media sources, not only to corroborate the hard cold facts in this saga, but to glean their perspectives as well. I do want to single out Glenn Coin, of *The Post-Standard*, Giuseppe Ricapito, of *The Union Democrat*, and Dakota Morlan, of *The Calaveras Enterprise*, who relentlessly covered every aspect of this case, reporting brilliantly about the courtroom antics that went on for years.

I also owe a deep gratitude to the many people whose lives I've represented here, perhaps most of all, to the brave firefighters and dedicated police investigators who never gave up in the fight for justice. There are too many of you to name here, but please know that you are my heroes. I hope that my respect for your hard work will somehow translate into the hearts of others. These days, there's a dangerous trend to commit violence against our public servants, and I think it's time to give props to them, to be thankful that we have people out there who are willing *to risk their lives* in order to keep the rest of us safe.

There are a number of people who I interviewed for this book, too many to list in total, but I want to single out Alex Karlsen, Allan Teets, Colette Bousson, Mike Karlsen, Dave Osier, Ken Buske, PI Steve Brown, and co-defense counsel, Leigh Fleming. I want all of you to know that, even though it might not seem blatant, your opinions and insights have made their way into these pages. Thank you for being generous with your time, I am truly grateful for your kindness.

Of course, this book would not have been possible without the cooperation of Cindy Best, who gave me unfettered access to her most personal diaries, financial statements, emails, and family photos. Her revelations and confessions permeate this work, as they should, because she lived this story more than anyone else. Cindy is a trooper. She went through hell with Karl. It's unfortunate that after Karl's arrest, rather than being heralded as a hero, she was ostracized and maligned by members of her own family who believed Karl's lies regarding the money from Levi's life insurance policy. I hope this book will set the record straight. I also hope this will show, once and for all, how integral she was in helping to catch a killer. I know it wasn't easy. I'm not sure that I could have done it.

I also want to thank George and Valerie Harris, two of my dearest friends, who have given me their utmost support for these past twenty years. George and Valerie, I couldn't have done this book without you. You've been behind this book all way, and because of your continued efforts and dedication, you have become indispensable to me. Indeed, the two of you have become my lifeblood, whether you realize it or not.

On another note, I wish to give a big thank you to my closest friends and closest family members (you know who you are) because you've believed in me, even when the chips were down. It's been because of your support and encouragement that I have been able to remain steadfast throughout this four-year process. You have brought me strength, courage, and most importantly, love. I don't know how I got so lucky to have you, but I know that I love you all dearly, and am eternally indebted to each and every one of you.

I must also give thanks to the love-of-my life, John, whose unwavering faith and support has gone beyond anything I could ever have hoped for. Not many people would be able to put up with me when I'm stuck at my computer and pulling my hair out, but you, my love, have the patience of *Job* and a heart of gold. There's a reason why my friends call you "Saint John." Sweetheart I want you to know that you mean more to me than anyone in this world, and I love you with all my heart.

Finally, and most of all, I want to thank my dear readers and fans, because YOU are the reason I keep writing, that I'm able to sweat bullets and tears, and find a way to squeeze out just one more page, even when I feel like I'm at my wits' end. Your support of my lifelong career makes it all worthwhile, because without you, I am nothing.

# ONE

There's something comforting about the thought of a yule log, with its slow burn and bright orange glow, and the woodsy aroma of a fireplace, with its pleasant crackling and occasional popping that can lull you back to cozy December nights, to feelings of olden days and Yuletide treasures, to the special celebrations of winter. Sitting fireside is hypnotizing. It takes you back in time. If you're lucky, it can take you back to the place you started from, to the warmth of your mother's stove and the smell of your mother's cooking, to a time when Mama's love was all the magic you ever needed.

Christina Karlsen was that kind of mom, the kind who baked everything from scratch and used patterns to sew her kids one-of-a-kind clothes. Karl was lucky to have a woman like her, so devoted to their kids, such a great homemaker. Even after seven years of marriage, the two of them acted like newlyweds, never missing a chance to sneak off for a quickie. Karl couldn't get enough of her, and in those early years, Christina was always game.

It was at a dance at a military base that Karl first caught a glimpse of Christina. She was a petite woman with a perfect hour-glass figure, someone he could easily imagine wrapping up in his arms. Karl would never forget the way she looked that night, floating around the dance floor in her flirty polka-dot dress and high-heel pumps. She looked like she belonged on the pages of a magazine, and just one smile from her -- made him think of what could be.

Their whirlwind romance landed them in Northern California, to a little town called Murphys, where Christina grew up. It wasn't the California people think of, with bright beaches and surfers and lush palm trees – no, this was the other California – the one with giant Sequoia trees and grizzly bears, with babbling brooks and secluded hiking trails.

Situated in the foothills of the Sierra Nevada mountains, Murphys was a hidden gem. The main tourist attraction was an ancient cave called Mercer Caverns, where people could marvel at multicolored crystals and massive rock formations, but Mercer Caverns, much like

Murphys, wasn't a place that people went out of their way to visit, not back then.

Being hours away from destinations like Yosemite Park and Lake Tahoe, Murphys was a spot on the map that most people passed through. It was a remote place where the land was still pristine, and for Christina, it was a paradise, a place where giant redwood trees and old wagon wheels were happy reminders of her youth.

In the late-1980s, when the Karlsen family arrived there, the town had a laid-back quietness about it. There was one traffic light, a gazebo in the center of town, and the Murphys Hotel, one of the oldest operating hotels in California. There were no billboards and no chain restaurants, it was almost like time passed it by. A century before, Murphys was a gold rush town, a bustling place with saloons and brothels and trading posts, but all that remained of that era were abandoned stone buildings, long-forgotten mining camps, and a rustic Main Street, which was just enough to give Murphys the feeling of the old wild west, and Karl fell in love with it.

He thought it was an ideal place to raise a family.

The Karlsens lived in a hundred-year-old house, an odd-shaped structure on the top of a hill that had once been a gold miners' chow hall. It was an isolated place on Pennsylvania Gulch Road, which had a dirt road leading up to it, a winding road that was narrow and steep. The house itself was in desperate need of renovating, but Karl made an arrangement with his landlord, who let him fix up the place in lieu of paying rent, and that gave the young couple the extra cushion they needed for Erin, Levi, and Kati, who, at ages of four, five, and six, had ever-growing demands.

It took them a few years, but Chris and Karl were able to improve the place and transform it into a home. Aside from the necessary repairs made to the roof and main water lines, Karl replaced the tile floor in the bathroom, created built-in closets, and wallpapered the kids' rooms. He'd become house proud.

As for Chris, she spent hours sanding and painting the main living area without needing any help, and over time, she found just the right fabric to replace all the curtains in the house, except for the bathroom window, where it was more practical to hang a plastic bamboo shade.

By the winter of 1990, Chris and Karl had successfully enmeshed themselves in the tight-knit community. The kids made friends at school, Chris reconnected with some of her cousins, and Karl was happy to be living an easier way of life, where the people were friendly and everyone looked out for each other. As the breadwinner, Karl had a good income working with Christina's dad, Art, (who'd made Karl a partner in his sheet metal business) and the two of them got along famously, Art being an easy-going man who trusted Karl implicitly.

The Karlsens had no complaints. For them, life was as good as it could get.

As Christmas approached that year, Chris went to special lengths, more than usual, to deck the house with angels and hand-crafted ornaments, stretching out the spirit of Christmas with cinnamon-scented candles and homemade spiced cider. Christmas was especially precious to her that year because Erin was about to turn seven, and she knew it would only be a matter of time before Erin would start asking questions. There was only a short window before the myth of Santa would end, before the notion of Santa would only be a pretense.

As always, the kids were eager to help their parents put up the Christmas tree. The three of them watched impatiently while their father adjusted the tree's position and strung up the last of the lights, placing the silver star squarely on top. The kids delighted in helping their mother hang bright red and silver ornaments, and then watched her finish trimming it with silver tinsel, placing each strand on separately, making sure the tree looked just so.

It felt like it took forever, but it was worth it because when their father finally turned the lights on, the bright shine on the tinsel made the tree look like it had infinite icicles. The shimmer always fascinated them.

It was bewitching.

# TWO

In the days leading up to Christmas, packages wrapped in brown paper arrived from their Grandma and Grandpa Karlsen back in New York, and gifts for Mom and Dad also appeared, building up everyone's hopes. The anticipation of Christmas was the best part of the whole thing, and of course the kids promised to be nice, and not naughty, something they would be reminded of whenever necessary.

"Erin, share your Barbie with Kati," Chris said as she passed by the girls' room and heard them squabbling. "Because If you don't, I don't think Santa's gonna bring either of you Barbies anymore."

The idea that Santa might be watching was always a good threat, and Chris would wink at Karl each time she invoked Santa because she knew it worked like a charm. This year, that little game worked especially well with Levi, who, among other things, wanted a special train set, a more expensive gift than he'd ever asked for before.

As had become a tradition, Chris's sister Colette would arrive in Murphys a few days before Christmas, bringing along her husband and their two boys, Blade and Rockio, who were close in age to their cousins. Colette had no problem making the three-and-a-half-hour trip from Red Bluff to Murphys; it was something she did so both families could spend quality time together.

Even though Colette was the younger sister, she had taken on a motherly role with Chris, especially after their parents divorced. It seemed strange to Karl that Colette was so overprotective of Chris, there was no reason for that, and he resented Colette's "mother superior" attitude. Though he didn't come out and say it, Karl couldn't stand Colette because she competed with him for Chris's attention. He thought she was controlling and arrogant, acting high and mighty because she had a job in the Air Force, but that Christmas, for some reason, Colette seemed to be on her best behavior, which was a nice change of pace.

Two days before Christmas, Chris and Colette took a drive to Sonora to do their last-minute shopping, catching up on family gossip while they listened to familiar Christmas tunes in the car. Back at the house, the two of them stayed up late that night to wrap presents, counting down the hours until Christmas Eve, anticipating the joy on their children's faces.

The plan was to spend Christmas Eve with Grandpa Art, who lived in nearby Douglas Flat, and then the following day, they would head to Sacramento, about an hour and a half away, to have Christmas dinner with their mom, Arlene, and her second husband, Randy.

It was odd that Karl agreed to spend Christmas at his mother-in-law's house, because visits to see Arlene had become a rare event. Karl wanted nothing to do with her because she'd become a born-again Christian, she was an over-the-top Bible thumper who drained the life out of him. Arlene and her second husband were so devout that they founded their own Christian ministry, and Karl couldn't stand their constant preaching.

After Colette left town, Chris would always get that sinking feeling, where the drudgery of life slowly seeped back in like the air going out of the balloon. She was always sad to see her sister go. The holiday seemed to fly by so quickly. They never seemed to have enough time.

With the excitement of Santa gone, Chris now had to deal with the Christmas aftermath which meant their new toys and Christmas clothes had to be organized and put away. Every year, she would methodically sort through the kids' closets, determining what should be stored in the attic and what needed to be given to charity, and that year, besides having her kids underfoot, the family had a new dalmatian puppy who ran around the house chasing the children, so she had her hands full.

The week between Christmas and New Year's was unusually cold that year. The temperatures at night had dropped below the freezing mark, so when Chris woke up and heard that the morning forecast was warning about a possible snowstorm headed their way, it made her nervous.

Logically, Chris knew that a snowstorm was unlikely, the average climate in Murphys was too warm for weather like that, but still, the threat of snow made her feel anxious about Karl driving on slick roads, so she decided to call him at work, thankful that she caught him there.

When Karl picked up the phone at Art's Sheet Metal shop, he only half-listened to Chris, who told him there was snow falling at their house already and she needed him to get milk and eggs and other basics. Having been raised in New York where there were *real* snowstorms, Karl didn't take Christina too seriously, but to placate her, he said he would make the stop, telling Chris he still had a few jobs to run to first.

"And can you stop and get a couple of movies?" she asked, just before they signed off.

"Tell me which ones you want," he asked. "You want stuff for the kids?"

"Yeah. Just get something that's animated. See if they have *The Little Mermaid.*"

Karl wasn't used to running errands for Chris, but since their house was a good fifteen minutes off the main highway, he figured it wouldn't hurt for him to placate her. It was snowing in Douglas Flat, and he didn't want Chris to take any chances, making an unnecessary half-hour round trip.

After he finished a heating job in nearby Vallecito, Karl was surprised to see large flakes of snow sticking to the ground, and he decided to cut his day short, thinking that perhaps Chris was right. He stopped off at The Sierra Hills Market to pick up the food supplies she wanted, and then loaded up on videos before he made the treacherous drive home.

Even in the best weather conditions, Penn Gulch Road is narrow and hard to navigate, but Karl made it home just fine, and after dinner was made and the dishes were done, all five of them piled up in front of the TV watching *The Land Before Time*, which Karl had managed to nab from Blockbuster.

The freak snowstorm that hit Murphys went through the night and into the next day, creating a snow globe for the Karlsens, a bubble where all the rest of the world didn't matter. For Erin, Levi, and Kati, this was their first time seeing their backyard covered in a blanket of white, and life couldn't have been more magical.

The three of them played outside in the snow and watched their favorite movies at night, and their mom put out fresh batches of her home-made cookies, real butter cookies that just melted in their mouths.

## THREE

On New Year's Day 1991, the Karlsen family would be taking down the Christmas tree, which was something Christina dreaded. It was a messy job, the weeks-old tree leaving needles everywhere, and it was a tedious chore for Chris, who had to wrap every ornament one-by-one. She slept in late that morning so Karl made smiley-faced pancakes for the kids, using M&M candies for the eyes and mouth, but even so, the three of them could feel the joy of the holiday season slipping away.

Before breakfast, Karl had taken down storage boxes from the attic and piled them up in the hallway; they were ready and waiting for Chris. It was unusual for her to sleep later than 7AM, but they'd been out late the night before, ringing in the New Year with their friend, Jeanette, who was like a second mother to Chris.

After she kissed the kids and had her coffee, Chris went to work taking the ornaments off the tree, handing the wooden ornaments to Erin and Kati to be rolled up in sheets of newspaper, placing the more delicate pieces on the kitchen table. The kids watched closely as their dad got up on a chair to untangle the string of lights, wrapping the green cord around his arm, trying not to entwine them. When he took the star off the top, the tree looked sad. The limbs were sagging from carrying too much weight, and the tinsel on it was now clumped together in a hodgepodge mess. It reminded Karl of a tired old woman who stopped doing her hair, who stopped wearing jewelry and make-up.

There was nothing much left to look at.

Karl plucked it from its stand and pulled the dried-out tree through the front door, dragging it as far away from the house as he could. He trudged through the wooded areas on the property, taking it to a large clearing where he kept bulky items, things that were waiting to be thrown out.

Once he got there, Karl decided to go back to the house to round up the kids. He wanted to show them something special. He told them he had a surprise.

Burning up the Christmas tree was a ritual Karl learned as a child.

He relished the days when his father took the big Christmas tree to their burn pile at the farm. He loved to watch it ignite…

Even though Karl knew it was illegal to burn anything that large in Northern California, that morning, with the snow providing a frosty blanket and the temperatures still freezing, Karl felt it was safe enough for him to try it. He wanted to show his kids what fun it was, and figured they were old enough now, to learn about fire.

With his three children by his side, Karl dowsed the tree with kerosene and told them to stand back. Karl knew the tinsel would act as an additional accelerant, and just as he expected, when he took his fire-starter to it, the tree was spontaneously set ablaze. The sudden burst of flames scared Kati so much that it almost made her cry, and it frightened the daylights out of Erin and Levi too, but Karl quickly calmed them down, pulling his kids further away from the blaze, promising them that nothing bad would happen.

"But why did you light it on fire?" Erin asked, frightened by the sight.

"I wanted to show you how fast a fire can start," he said. "Because if this tree was still inside the house and the lights got hot enough, it could have easily started a fire."

"I already knew that. I learned that from Smokey the Bear when he came to my class at school," Erin said, showing off in front of her siblings.

"Well, you can't *really* know about fires until you see them for your-self," he said, looking at each of his kids intently.

"Cause a house can go up in an instant. It can blow up," he said, snapping his fingers together, *"just like that."*

After the initial combustion, when the flames began to subside, the Christmas tree was doing nothing but blowing smoke, and the kids were getting bored.

"Is it gonna burn anymore?" Levi asked.

"No, it's only gonna give off smoke now."

"Are you gonna light it again?"

"Nah, I'll let it fizzle out."

It was no fun to watch anymore. The tree gave off a putrid smell and the smoke was getting in their eyes, so Levi asked if they could go play in the snow -- he wanted to make a snowman. There was barely enough snow for them to make a solid-packed snowball, but Karl was happy to see his kids making the best of it. They were throwing slushy snowballs around and chasing each other towards the woods, laughing with sheer delight.

Inside, Chris sighed as she finished boxing up the ornaments, placing the boxes marked XMAS near the other storage boxes, creating a cardboard mountain in the hallway. Normally, she would have stowed these boxes in the laundry room to keep them out of the way, but Karl bought a new waterbed for Christmas, and their old mattress and bedframe were still in there, taking up all the space.

Chris had to get on her tiptoes to stack the last of the Christmas decorations carefully. Those boxes held her home-made angels and her happy little nutcrackers, all of which would soon be hibernating among the kids' baby clothes and other sentimental things she kept in the attic, collecting dust until next year.

When she was finally done, Chris called to Karl and the kids to come in for lunch, telling them she would make their favorite, grilled cheese sandwiches with tomato soup. She wanted the kids to get cleaned up first because she'd made plans for them to spend the after-noon with her best friend, Tracy Carpenter. It was going to be a lazy kind of day for the two families. They planned to take it easy, to watch movies with popcorn and maybe order pizza for dinner.

After the kids finished the last of their tomato soup, Chris put them down for a nap. The three of them were worn out from all the running around, and she was glad to have that precious time to herself.

With her Walkman headphones on, Chris went to take a bubble bath. Chris loved to luxuriate in the tub, letting the rest of the world disappear for a while. That was her daily moment of peace. Out in the living room, Karl had dozed off while watching the Rose Bowl game, but something woke him up from his snooze, so he decided he had enough time to deal with a heating problem that was brewing.

Chris had been complaining that the heat wasn't strong enough in their bedroom, she was convinced that the heat was cut off to that side of the house, but Karl liked it cooler when he slept, which is why he'd been procrastinating.

Karl was experienced at this, he'd done so many heating jobs with Art over the years, and he was positive that there was something wrong with the insulation or the ductwork. Instead of wasting time, Karl went out to the garage and hauled his heavy ladder into the living room, certain he would need it to crawl his way up.

But after all the trouble he went through to unhook the ladder from the crowded wall in his garage, after he huffed and puffed and somehow managed to squeeze the thing into the house, it turned out that Karl didn't even use it.

When he stood up on a chair to pull the attic hatch open, he could see the problem right away. The insulation on one of the wires was damaged. It was an easy fix. All he needed was a stretch of insulated copper wire, and he went hunting out in the garage, scrounging around in his cubby holes, hoping to find it.

He couldn't have been out there for more than five minutes when he heard Chris yell, "Karl, get the kids!"

But at first, Karl didn't pay attention to it.

He was too busy looking for the wire.

# FOUR

*"KARL, GET THE KIDS!"*

Chris was shouting, and this time, there was absolute terror in her voice.

A million thoughts went through his head when he got outside and saw dark plumes of smoke coming from the roof vents. His heart was pounding as he launched himself onto the front porch, landing under Levi's window.

The window was double locked and it had a screen on it, so Karl scratched his way through the hot metal and then smashed the window, shattering it with his elbow. The room was already filled with smoke and Karl could see fire blazing in the hallway. Levi was covered by a veil of grey, and then all at once, a patch of smoke cleared, and Karl saw the faint outline of his son's figure.

Levi was curled up in a fetal position on the edge of his bed, clutching the new teddy bear his mom made. With one swoop, Karl grabbed the boy and pulled him out, but that swoosh caused the smoke to ignite. Suddenly, the fire was coming straight at them, breathing out like a dragon.

"It was like we were in the movie *Backdraft*," Karl would later say. "All I can remember is I grabbed Levi by the hair and pulled him out, and then a ball of fire came towards us and we were both blown back off the porch."

There were some minor scrapes on Levi, and what looked like a bloody nose, and Karl rushed the boy to his truck, yelling at the five-year-old like an angry drill sergeant.

"I want you to get on the floorboard and keep your ass there! You understand!"

Levi dropped down and cowered, crouching as low as he could.

"If you get out of the truck, if you pick your head up, *you're dead*! You hear me! You don't move! You stay where you are!"

With his father's voice still bellowing, Levi heard the car door slam.

"The last thing I wanted was for Levi to see his mother running out of there with her skin all burned up, with some part of her on fire," Karl would later explain. "I said a whole lot of things that I shouldn't, but I needed to put the fear of God in him."

When Karl reached the girls' room, the better part of their window was blocked. Karl had forgotten all about the new dresser he'd bought them. It was an expensive dresser that Chris really loved, it was a piece of Stickley furniture which Karl decided to buy as an early Christmas present … and now the fucking thing was standing in his way.

"Don't worry! Daddy's coming! Daddy's coming to get us!" he could hear Erin screaming.

"Get over to me!" Karl yelled over the top of the dresser. "Grab your sister and stand to the side!"

But the girls were too afraid to move.

"The dresser slowed me down a little," Karl would later recall. "I jumped up and kept trying to push the top over. And, I mean, it was really blocking me, but it didn't matter. I knew I was gonna go through it."

With one big push, Karl knocked the dresser over and found himself leaning halfway into their room, his legs dangling from the windowsill. The girls' closet was near the hallway, and he could see them hiding in there with a blanket over them. Luckily the smoke in their room wasn't as thick as Levi's, so Karl was able to motion to them, screaming for the girls to make their way to the window.

"Erin! Come on! Grab your sister and get over to me! I need both of you to come and try to climb up here!"

Their dresser acted as a make-shift ramp and Erin helped Kati climb up, protecting her little sister as best she could. The two of them grabbed their father around the neck, clinging to him for their lives, and Karl fell backwards off the window ledge, landing safely on the ground. His body acted like a cushion, shielding his daughters from the hard fall.

Little Kati wasn't really sure what was happening. She was shrieking because she only had one shoe on, crying hysterically about leaving her other shoe in the house.

"Don't worry, we'll buy you another pair," Karl said, as he scurried them to the car.

Karl's eyebrows were burnt off, his forehead was burning, but miraculously, from what he could tell, the girls didn't seem to be hurt. With his adrenaline working overtime, Karl practically threw the girls into the back seat, ordering them to stay put.

"You get down there with your brother!" he yelled. "You keep your heads down and you don't look up!"

Before Karl could slam the door, his Dalmatian puppy, Lydia, appeared at his side, her big eyes tugging at his heart. Without hesitating, Karl picked Lydia up and shoved her in with the kids. It was better that way, he thought, the last thing he needed was his dog running around, getting underfoot.

Karl then ran back to the house, hoping he'd find something on the ground, anything, that could help him break Chris out.

"CHRIS! *Can you hear me?*" he screamed, standing under the bathroom window.

But there was no answer.

The bathroom window had a piece of plywood boarded over it, which is why he was hoping he'd find a tool laying around. The window had gotten stuck a few days before, and Chris had accidentally broken it, shattering the glass when she tried to pry it open with a plunger.

But it was too late to worry about that now…

The bathroom window was higher up off the ground than the other windows in the house, and without a ladder, Karl found it impossible to reach. He scrambled around the yard and picked up a broken piece of fencepost which he used to rip the screen off. But the fencepost wasn't strong enough to knock the plywood out. He would need some type of axe for that.

He quickly ran around to the back door, thinking he could break his way into the laundry room, but black smoke was pouring out through the cracks. He attempted to kick it down, but the heat was too intense and decided his best chance was through the bathroom window.

"By the time I got back around to the bathroom," Karl would later say, "the whole front of the house had become a wall of flames. The house was caving in on itself and there was nothing I could do."

# FIVE

A pure flame, with its orange glow, is mostly opaque, almost see-through. The flame itself has no scent at all, so it's a myth that people can smell fire, because it's not the fire that people smell -- it's the gas it creates and the smoke that comes along with it.

The smell of smoke comes in all kinds of forms, from the earthy smell of incense burning to the sweet smell from a fragrant candle. Just like the unmistakable smell of burnt human hair, every burning object gives off its own unique odor, and to a trained firefighter, it's easy to distinguish.

But there's one type of gas that produces no smell at all. And that's carbon monoxide. When it comes to household items, this colorless gas is emitted from a variety of everyday appliances without anyone ever realizing it. However, this colorless phantom, if inhaled in large quantities, is quite deadly, which is why firefighters call it "the silent killer."

\* \* \*

When Karl ran back to his truck to check on his kids, he leaned on the hood for a split second, looking at the fire in disbelief. It was surreal, the tall flames pulsating from the roof. As he opened the back door, the kids popped their heads up, each with a look of terror. Little Kati seemed like she was about to cry, but Karl promised that everything would be okay, and then jumped into the drivers' seat, trying to determine whether or not he should take one last pass.

He knew his next door neighbor was out of town, he knew it would be a quarter of a mile drive, at least, for him to find a neighbor who could call 911, but after giving it some thought, Karl headed down the rambling road and was honking his horn, desperate to find help. When two little old ladies poked their heads out of their double-wide trailer, Karl was screaming at the top of his lungs.

"*My house is on fire!*" My wife is trapped!"

One woman ran to make the emergency call and the other offered to run to a neighbor for help, but Karl didn't have time for that. He was already making a three-point-turn, rushing back up the hill.

The orange flames were bigger now, there was fire blasting through the roof, and Karl threw the truck in park, shouting at his kids in a threatening tone.

"I need all of you to get down on the floorboard, NOW! And don't you dare look up!"

Karl approached the bathroom window for a second time, but it was useless. There was no way for him to reach Chris and in sheer disgust, he kicked at the concrete foundation. After a minute or two, he ran back to the pickup and decided to drive away. There was no use sitting there. He and the kids had been traumatized enough.

"Put yourself in my spot. Would you let your kids watch the house fall in on their mother?" Karl later said. "No, you wouldn't. You put the truck in gear and you drive away from it."

"What about Mommy?" Erin asked as they drove away.

"I think Mommy went to heaven," he said in a whisper.

It would be Ken Thurston, a volunteer firefighter, who was the first to arrive at the scene. Thurston had heard the call over the radio and had driven up in his personal vehicle, thinking he could locate a garden hose to contain the fire.

Thurston had passed a man and a boy sitting in a pickup truck, and upon reaching the house, realizing that he would need heavier equipment, he returned to the end of the driveway parked next to Karl, hoping to get some useful information.

Fire crews from two nearby towns were already en route, and as it happened, both the Murphys and the Vallecito fire departments arrived at the mouth of Pennsylvania Gulch Road in tandem. They had a tough four-mile drive ahead of them, they knew how twisted and narrow Penn Gulch was, and it was just as they got about halfway up the hill, that Murphys Engine 244 hit an ice patch and began to slide backwards.

The driver slammed on the brakes and was able to bring the truck to a halt, but with the sudden stop, all the hoses flew off the back of the engine, blocking the Vallecito team behind them. It was an unfortunate mishap that caused a precious five-minute delay.

Firefighter Bob Bliss and his team were planning to make entry through the front of the house, but when they finally made their way up the long dirt driveway, they saw that the fire was trying to force its way out through the front door. When Bliss jumped out and approached it, he caught a glimpse of a blue flame. The front of the house had already reached temperatures of 900 degrees; their initial plan had to be scrapped.

Bliss needed more hands, and the minute the second engine arrived, he started barking orders.

"Let's go, man! We need to get moving!" Bliss yelled. "We gotta go around the back!"

The Vallecito firefighters jumped to help Bliss and his men carry heavy fire hoses around to the back door, where the heat was less menacing. Bliss was hoping for a clean shot but when he tried to make entry there, there seemed to be something blocking him.

"Different people have different housekeeping standards," Bliss would later say, "and there have been times where I would run into stuff, but I was never totally blocked. I don't know what kind of obstacles I was encountering that day, but it was enough that we just didn't go any further."

Bliss and his men used all their might, but they couldn't push their way in beyond three feet.

Outside, around the front of the house, additional firefighters and equipment had arrived, as did the Incident Commander, Warren Wilkes, who gave the order for everyone to move into a defensive posture. With no fire hydrant to rely on, the Chief was concerned about running out of water. Wilkes needed the firefighters to defend the surroundings first, to get control of the perimeter before making further attempts to squelch the blaze coming through the roof.

The two teams of firefighters were now stationed about 25 feet away from each side of the structure and were waterbombing the ring of dark smoke that curled around the house. Once the surrounding area was stabilized, Wilkes gave the order to waterbomb the house, and within a matter of minutes, the firefighters turned the center of the house into a pile of ash, soot, and rubble.

It was Dennis Mills from Murphys and Mike Winn from Vallecito who were the first to reach the front porch. The men broke a large window and were about to make entry through the living room, and just then they heard Chief Wilkes yell out, "Hey, be careful, because we might have a body!"

The two men sprayed a gentle stream of water as they moved through the wreckage, knocking down little pockets of fire that were still smoldering around them. Dennis Mills walked through a door into what appeared to be a little boy's room. The heat had ravaged Levi's toys, including his new train set.

"I'm near the seed of the fire!" Mills yelled. "It's over this way! I need your help!"

The two men carefully broke away pieces of Levi's charred room, gently pulling away at the wall by hand. When they had created enough of an opening, Dennis Mills stepped through and came upon what looked like the white rim of a bathroom sink.

And it was there, in a *soot-filled cradle*, that Mills encountered a nude female body. The victim was slumped partially out of the bathtub, the head facing the ground. The skin was charcoal black. It was a gruesome sight.

With the sense of urgency now gone, there was no reason for him to dwell on it, but before he backed away, Mills took one last look at something he couldn't take his eyes off. There was a distinct mark on the victim's back, a bit of pink flesh peeking through the black charr -- in the distinct shape of a cross.

It was unnerving, that image.

It looked like it had been stenciled there.

# SIX

Having watched the flashing red lights of the firetrucks rush by, Christina's children sat helplessly in the back of their father's truck. They had no idea that hundreds of gallons of water had been pumped into their house, they had no idea all their earthly possessions had been destroyed, and the children certainly didn't realize, or comprehend in any way, just how dreadful it was, the way their mother had died.

Before they knew it, an ambulance pulled up and the EMTs loaded the family inside. While being examined, the children were giving short "yes" and "no" answers but as for Karl, the pain was hitting him hard.

"I couldn't talk, I couldn't catch my breath," Karl would later say. "When they put me in the ambulance, I was burned, part of my shirt was melted. I had smoke all over me, and I needed oxygen."

With a breathing tube wrapped around his face, Karl felt dizzy and nauseated. The back doors to the ambulance were not yet closed when Christina's dad pulled up. Douglas Flat was a stone's throw away, and he'd made it there in no time. Art fully expected to see firetrucks at the scene, but the sight of an ambulance unnerved him.

"I had two people come to my door that had scanners, and they told me, 'We think there's a fire at your kid's house' and when I went out in the front yard, I could see the smoke," Art recalled. "When I got there, I looked in the ambulance and Karl was in there and the three kids too, and I looked around and said, 'Well, where is Chris?' And one of them said 'She's gone to be with the angels.'"

Art's jumbled memories of that day were fuzzy. He thought it was Erin who told him about the angels, though it might have been Levi, but it really didn't matter who said what because in that moment, Art wasn't computing anything. It was impossible for him to believe that his beautiful Christina, daddy's little girl, was truly gone.

On the eternal ride to the Mark Twain Hospital, Karl remained silent. Art held on tight to his grandchildren. Because the kids weren't crying, Art was able to keep it together, but the minute they arrived at the hospital, things got real.

It took all of Art's strength not to break down.

Art watched over the kids as they were being examined. The nurses were concerned that they might have breathing problems, but their airways were clear. It was a miracle that none of them had any cuts or minor burns. Not one of them even asked for a band-aid.

For Art, the constant whirl of the emergency room, the beeping of the medical monitoring devices and the crying of an infant in the background, all of it was blurring together. When Art later tried to remember what happened that day, he realized he'd blocked almost everything out. Art didn't know what time he'd arrived at the scene, he didn't know how long they were at the hospital, he didn't even know how he got home…

Once the kids were officially cleared and released, the three of them were brought to an adjacent room by a nurse and were given ice pops and crayons. Under the watchful eye of EMT Pam Geidt, the children sat quietly, scribbling stick figures and coloring different shapes on blank sheets of paper. Pam Geidt had fully expected to see a meltdown, yet in the two hours she spent with them that day, not one of them cried, not one of them had an outburst.

It was odd.

They were completely buttoned up.

# SEVEN

It was about four in the afternoon when Art placed an emergency call to his friend, Jim Roberts, telling him that there had been a bad fire at his daughter's house, asking him to come down to the hospital. Art didn't want to talk about it over the phone.

"A fire? How bad was it?"

"The whole house is gone," Art told him. "I'll explain it when you get here."

"Is everyone okay?" Jim pressed, "is anyone badly hurt?"

Art said he was using the phone at the nurse's station to make the call.

He needed to hang up.

Jim and Art went way back, they'd been best friends for twenty years. They were like family, or even closer, and it didn't take more than a minute to jump in his car and bolt to San Andreas. When Jim arrived and asked for Art Alexander, he was directed to the second room off the hallway, away from the ER, which in his mind, made the situation seem less dire.

"I went down there, the kids were playing on the floor," Jim recalled, "and the way they were playing with their crayons, I started to think that everything was alright."

"My Mom's gone to heaven," Erin told him.

"Where's your Dad?"

"He's right in there," she said, pointing to the room next door where her father was behind a privacy curtain, getting some type of bandage changed. Jim popped his head into the other door and could hear a nurse behind the curtain, but her voice was muffled. He ventured a few steps into the room, trying to figure out what she was saying, and then swoosh, the nurse pulled back the blue curtain, and Jim saw Karl laying there with white gauze wrapped around his forehead, nodding at the nurse mechanically.

Karl seemed to be in another world. His head was slanted in the direction of the window, and it seemed like he was looking straight through the nurse, as if she was an unwelcome apparition. It was only when Jim's footsteps made a squeaking sound, that Karl turned his head to look.

"*What happened?*" Jim asked, taking a seat next to the gurney. "Can you tell me?"

Karl looked at Jim for a brief moment, but then turned his gaze down at the floor, unable to find the words. All Jim could see was the left side of Karl's face, which was beet-red and swollen. He looked for blisters, he looked for deep red marks, wondering how badly Karl was hurt.

"Are you alright?"

"It's just my face and hands," Karl said, holding up his right hand to show Jim.

"Where's Chris? Is she okay?"

"She didn't make it out," Karl said in a whisper. "I lost the best thing in my life."

Jim sat there stunned, trying to get a grip on himself. He'd known Chris since she was a child. She was such a sweet girl growing up. Jim had lost track of her when she moved to North Dakota, but for the past few years, after Chris moved back home with her kids, Jim had become much closer to her. He knew what a wonderful person she was – everyone did – and he knew how much Art loved his daughter. Chris had always been the apple of Art's eye.

"How did the house catch fire? Do you know?"

"It was around two o'clock this afternoon when I first saw the smoke," Karl said. "And I've been trying to figure out how it got started, but I can't think."

Karl wasn't really close to Jim, this was Art's buddy, from a different generation, but Jim was a friendly face, and Karl felt relieved to have someone who would just listen.

"The only thing I can think of," Karl said, "is that I was up in the attic just before it started. We had a small electrical problem, but it wasn't any big deal. I was just taking a look up there because I finally had the time to get to it."

"What kind of electrical problem was it?"

"Well, the house had faulty wiring, I always knew that," Karl told him. "And when I got up in the attic, I realized I needed a copper wire, and that's when I went outside to go look in my shed..."

Karl paused, trying to catch his breath, heaving a painful sigh.

"And the next thing I know, I hear Chris yelling, '*Karl, get the kids!*'"

Jim could hear the strain in Karl's voice.

The man looked devastated.

"Chris had just put the kids down for a nap and then she went in for a bath," Karl told him. "She likes to take bubble baths when the kids are sleeping, and I mean, when I first heard her yelling for me, I didn't even answer her, cause I didn't hear any panic in her voice."

Karl went through the harrowing rescue of his children, but his account of the events didn't quite make sense. It seemed peculiar, Jim thought, that Karl would run back and forth to his truck to bring the kids there one by one. But then again, as Karl spoke, he was slurring some of his words and Jim realized that Karl was all drugged up. He was jumping from one thing to another. Nothing he said was making sense. But that was to be expected. The man looked like he was off in another world.

Then, out of nowhere, Karl started talking about an earthquake that hit north of Murphys years back. Jim couldn't understand what an earthquake had to do with anything; it seemed pretty obvious that Karl was loopy.

"Do you remember that earthquake that hit up by Avery?" Karl asked.

"Which one?"

"That quake back two years ago," Karl said, "and what happened was, that quake shifted all the windows in our house, cause our place is a hundred years old, and it doesn't take much of a tremor to do damage to it."

Jim wondered why he couldn't recall the quake.

"It must have been a small one," Jim told him, "because I never heard of it. I never saw anything about it on the news."

"Well, after that quake, that window got almost completely jammed. You could barely open it."

"*What window*? What window are you talking about?"

Karl paused and then heaved out a heavy sigh.

"Chris was trying to open the bathroom window a couple days ago," Karl told him, "and God knows why she used the plunger handle to try to push it up a few inches, but anyhow, she wound up breaking it."

"What are you saying, Karl? I'm not following you."

"I think she got trapped behind it."

"You think she got trapped in the bathroom?"

"Yeah. Cause the windows in that house, I have to special order," Karl explained. "They're pocket windows and they slide different than regular house windows. And we had to do something real quick, so I found an old piece of plywood and Chris helped me board it up."

"When did you do that?"

"I'd say it was about a week ago. I can't remember exactly."

Jim sat in disbelief. He needed to hear more.

"We nailed it up from the inside," Karl told him. "We thought that was good enough to keep the cold out, just temporarily."

As Karl kept talking, telling Jim that he tried to knock the board out of the window, he began to wonder aloud about Chris, trying to figure out why Chris didn't run for it. The more Karl kicked it around in his head, the more he couldn't understand why Chris stayed in there so long. Why didn't she get out? It would have only taken a few steps for her to get to the laundry room door…

"You know, what I'm thinking is, Chris liked to play music on her headphones when she took baths, and that coulda been why she didn't hear anything. I mean, if it was something like the space heater that caught fire, she might not have heard it."

"But you said you heard Chris yelling, right? Where was she, do you think?"

Karl said it sounded like she was calling him from around the back of the house. He thought she was in the bath, then he talked about the space heater that she used which he had gone and unplugged because it was too close to the wall.

"Could it have been the space heater? If she decided to try to plug it back in?"

"I mean, I guess, but Chris wouldn't have done that, I don't think,"

Karl said. "One thing I remember was the smell of cinnamon in the house. I think she had candles going."

Jim realized he wasn't getting anywhere with Karl. The guy was confused and bewildered, he was speaking in hypotheticals, and he seemed to be getting himself worked up.

"Where's Art? I went and looked next door and he's not with the kids."

"I have no idea."

"Did Art get over to the house when this happened?"

"Yeah, he got there just after they put it out."

"And you think Chris got caught in the bathroom? Is that where they found her?"

"They haven't told me where they found her yet," Karl said. "But, you know, I kept jumping at that window and I couldn't reach it cause it's like, six feet off the ground. Cause that part of the house is up on stilts. You know what I mean?"

But Jim Roberts didn't know, at all, what Karl meant. There were no stilts holding up that house. Jim knew that. All he could figure was that Karl was in shock and didn't know what he was saying.

The guy was all over the map. He was like a flowing river, running off into tributaries, into countless streams and creeks.

# EIGHT

People tend to think that the brain stores memories accurately, that they can recall an event almost exactly the way it happened. But as vivid as an event may seem, particularly if it's something traumatic, each person recalls it through their own prism. Things that are real become entwined with things that are imagined, and in most cases, the memory is blemished.

In the aftermath of the fire, there were moments when the fire seemed to be something that happened in a far-away place, and there were other moments when it seemed like the fire hadn't happened at all. As Karl sat at his father-in-law's house gazing off into space, he didn't notice anyone around him. Close family friends had stopped by to check on the kids and to pay their respects, but for Karl, none of that mattered.

He was in shock.

When the doorbell rang at Art's house later that night, Karl assumed it was another friend of the family, but when he opened the door, he was surprised to see a man in uniform standing there. Karl could hear the words, but they seemed to be hitting him in slow motion. The man who had stopped by, unannounced, was Howard Stohlman, an investigator from the Ebbett's Pass Fire District. Karl was weary and disheveled, his clothes reeked of smoke, and he really didn't feel like talking to anyone, but the man assured him that he wouldn't be long, that he only had a few questions.

Why a fire investigator would be stopping by on the very night of the fire, Karl didn't know. He thought it was inconsiderate for anyone to be disturbing a whole household when their emotions were still raw. It was rude and intrusive, Karl thought, but he managed to keep his composure.

"I'm very sorry for your loss," Stohlman said, holding his hand out to Karl. "And I'm sure this is hard for you, but I need to clarify a couple of things."

Karl stepped outside with the fire investigator and began to re-live the tragic events of the day. He said he was out back in his garage when he heard his wife calling out to him, and at first, he didn't think anything of it.

"But the second time she called me, she used my full name. I heard her scream 'Karl Holger Karlsen, get the kids!' and that's when I ran out and saw smoke coming out of the vents."

The fire investigator was intent on reading the body language. The investigator made direct eye contact with Karlsen, trying to read him, listening intently as Karlsen explained that he'd gone outside to find a wire, that he wasn't out in his garage for more than ten minutes. He didn't know how the fire got out of control so quickly.

Karlsen seemed angry at himself for having to break his son's window, explaining that he vented the fire and made matters worse, but said he had no choice. He talked about the close call he had when he rescued Levi, and after he explained how he rescued his daughters, it seemed like Karlsen was out of words.

"Okay, so what you're telling me is that after you brought your son out to your truck, you ran back to get your daughters?"

"Yeah, I needed to get to the other side of the house, cause I was worried that the girls' room was about to go up in flames. When I got there, I could see they were sitting close to the flames in the hallway, and I had to knock over their dresser to get them out."

"And what did you do with the girls?"

"I ran them back to my truck."

It surprised Stohlman to hear that Karlsen had taken so much time running back and forth with his kids. It didn't make sense, but Karlsen said he was taking orders from his wife, telling the investigator that he thought Chris had already gotten out on her own. He explained that the reason he ran his kids out to his pickup was to prevent them from trying to run back into the house, fearful that they might attempt to rescue their cat, Lola, who was missing.

"I noticed a board covering your bathroom window. Can you tell me about that? Can you tell me why that window was boarded up?"

"We had to board it up temporarily because Chris accidently broke it the other day."

"How did she do that?"

"She was trying to pry it open with a plunger because the thing got stuck again and it only opened maybe an inch at the most. That window was always a problem because it was old and it got jammed all the time."

Karl elaborated about the board on the window, telling the investigator that he needed to nail a piece of plywood up there until he could get special-ordered glass for it. He explained that it was an odd-sized pocket window, that all the windows in his house were like that, but he didn't have the chance to order it because of the holidays. He said he was planning to call a glass shop downtown, that he'd already measured it, but in the interim, he and Chris decided it would be best to board it up.

"Do you have any idea what caused the fire?" Stohlman asked.

"Not really, because everything seemed fine before I went to get that wire."

"Can you think of anything that could have ignited?"

"I mean, I guess it could have been the space heater in the bathroom," Karl told him. "Cause I know Chris kept that on whenever she took a bath."

"I noticed a kerosene heater out on the front porch. How often did you use that heater in the house?"

"Oh, wait a minute," Karl said, suddenly recalling it, "you know, it's been so cold this week that we did use that heater. And we had a kerosene spill in the hallway, which is why I brought it outside."

"Do you remember what day that happened?"

"It was a few days ago. I'd say it was just after Christmas."

"Were both you and your wife home at the time?"

"Yeah, we were both home" Karl told him, "and what happened was, our dog and cat were chasing each other down the hallway and they knocked the jug over."

"Could you say how much kerosene spilled?"

"It was a lot. Maybe two gallons."

"*Two gallons?*"

"Yeah, it was a lot. But me and Chris got it all soaked up. We used towels and got it soaked up real quick."

"How much residue was left, would you say?"

"Not much, I don't think," Karl told him. "Cause we just kept soaking it up with whatever we could. And after we ran out of towels, we used Christmas clothes and whatever else was handy. Then we used Borax until we got the smell out of the carpet."

Karlsen was very confident, absolutely adamant, that he and his wife had soaked up every bit of the spill. He was all riled up, talking a mile-a-minute, trying hard to keep up with his own thoughts. At first, he was absolutely positive that the spill had nothing to do with the fire, but then suddenly, Karl stopped himself. He took a long pause and began actively re-thinking it, as if he had an "ah-ha" moment.

"You know, now that I think about it, there *must* have been traces of kerosene left. Cause even if you get the smell out, you probably can't get all of it, especially out of a carpet."

The idea that a woman would use new Christmas clothes to soak up kerosene seemed preposterous to Stohlman. The investigator would later try to cross-check that during his interview with Erin on January 4th, but the six-year-old didn't remember any smell, nor did she know what became of her Christmas gifts. All Erin could recall was that she and her siblings were playing leapfrog over a big pile of clothes in their hallway. The child didn't know anything about a spill.

"I'm curious about why you would keep so much kerosene inside the house?"

"Well, we normally don't. But Chris brought a big jug of kerosene into the house by mistake. She thought it was water."

"*Why would she mistake kerosene for water?* Can you tell me how she would do that?"

"Cause the jugs were both the same color. I had two five-gallon jugs out on the porch, and they were both blue. And Chris got them mixed up. She didn't realize that she'd brought in the wrong jug..." Karl's voice trailed off.

"Can you tell me why she would need to carry that much water into the house? Was it drinking water?"

"No, no, no. We didn't need it to drink. It was just whenever our pipes got frozen, that we had to haul in gallons of water for flushing the toilet and stuff like that."

"Okay. And she couldn't tell the difference between water and kerosene?"

"Well, whenever we needed water, I'd keep it in the same jugs as the kerosene because it didn't matter if there was a little bit of oil mixed in with it."

"Okay. So sometimes you'd have kerosene in these blue jugs and then you'd use the same jugs for water?"

"Right," Karl told him. "And there were times when I would bring those same blue jugs back down to the shop and refill them with kerosene."

"So, what you're saying is, these jugs were used multiple times? You would use them for kerosene, then water, and then kerosene again?"

"Yeah," Karl said, "but I did that only when I absolutely had to."

By this time, the questioning was going on much longer than Karl had wanted it to, and he was starting to get annoyed. Didn't Stohlman realize this was the same night his wife died? Couldn't it wait for a few days? But no, Stohlman was being an insensitive jerk.

"Okay. Do you know what kind of kerosene it was?"

"No, I don't."

What a stupid question, Karl thought to himself. What did this guy think it was? *Jet fuel?* Karl couldn't believe the nitpicking. He was angry about having to entertain stupid questions, and moreover he didn't feel that his privacy was being respected. He was just about to tell Stohlman that he needed to get some rest, that he'd have to come back the next day, but Stohlman had already jumped to the next question. The guy was persistent; he wasn't letting it go.

"Do you happen to know what became of the Christmas clothes? Do you know if they were thrown out?"

"No, Chris wanted to save them," Karl told the investigator. "It was mostly sweaters that she'd given me, cause I'm a big sweater guy. And I'd say she probably washed them four or five times, and they were okay after that."

"And those were the clothes that were in that hallway?"

"Right."

"And you're pretty sure that she got all the kerosene out?"

"I mean, there probably was *some* residue in them. Cause I know she put them in the dryer this morning and the house got all fogged up."

"Do you know, roughly, what time that was?"

"I think it was around noon. I remember I was cleaning up the kid's toys outside, and I think it was when I came back in for lunch, that the house was filled with white smoke."

"*White smoke*? And you say the dryer caused that?"

"Well, the dryer has been acting up lately," Karl said, pausing to think. "I mean, the house wasn't too smoky, really, it was just like a white cloud."

"How long has your dryer been acting up?"

"Well, see, our dryer isn't vented to the outside, so there's a lot of times when the house gets fogged up. That's just the way it is."

After about twenty minutes, Stolhman could see that Karlsen was getting antsy, so he decided not to press the matter further. He would wait for CAL FIRE investigators to arrive and get Karlsen's full statement on tape.

As the Ebbett's Pass fire investigator pulled out of Douglas Flat, turning onto the dark expanse of Highway 4, he considered the range of possibilities that Karlsen had brought up. Among other things, he said they had a wood-burning stove, he talked about the problem with the dryer, he mentioned that there could have been faulty wiring in the attic, and said he was using a droplight which he left in the hallway because it had a broken hook.

Stohlman would soon brief Bob Monson and the team from CAL FIRE when they arrived. Their investigation was just getting started. Everyone in the family would be questioned, all the wiring throughout the house, including every appliance and light socket, would be tested, and as for the droplight, Stohlman had already taken that into custody. It would be FedExed to a lab where the filament would be tested microscopically.

If that lightbulb got hot enough, if the droplight made contact with the carpet, that could be the simple answer. But as he drove through pitch-black darkness on the way home, the investigator couldn't get past two things:

The recent spill of so much kerosene.

And the very odd way the bathroom window got broken.

.

# NINE

The day after the fire, January 2$^{nd}$, 1991, Karl's older brother, Mike, along with his sister-in-law, Jackie, were on a plane headed from Rochester to Sacramento, where upon arrival, they would make the long trek through the unmarked roads that lead to Calaveras County. Both Mike and Jackie knew Christina well. Early in their marriage, before Kati was born, she and Karl had moved from Grand Forks to Upstate New York, where he was sure to find a good job.

At the time, Chris and Karl were still lovebirds and with two toddlers to take care of, Chris was delighted that Karl's family was there to help her. To the Karlsen family, Chris was a breath of fresh air. She was a happy person who always lit up a room and she fit right in with the whole clan.

All of them adored her. They thought Chris was the perfect match for Karl, so of course, in the aftermath of her death, Mike and Jackie were grief-stricken. Their drive to Calaveras County was solemn and the closer they got to Murphys, the more her death seemed impossible. She was only thirty, in the prime of her life.

Jackie could hardly believe Chris was gone. She'd had a heart-to-heart talk with Chris at one point, it seemed like ages ago. At the time, Chris asked her to be the guardian of her three children in the event that something should happen to both of them. Now that conversation haunted her.

It was a request that seemed eerie, but Jackie had agreed without mentioning anything about it to Mike. There was no need for that at the time. As she tried to absorb the shock, Jackie thanked God that Karl survived the fire, that the children did too. It was a blessing that they still had their father.

Over at Art's house in Ebbett's Pass, Karl was waiting nervously for them to arrive. He was worried about them getting lost, there were few road signs and even fewer stop lights in that area, and it was tricky to get there. Nonetheless, with Jackie navigating, using a road Atlas and her hand-written directions, she and Mike made it there just fine.

Karl was relieved when he saw the rental car pulling into Art's driveway and he rushed out to greet them. Mike was stoic, which was the "Karlsen way" but Jackie was visibly shaken, giving Karl a long hug, telling him how very sorry she was, choking out the words.

"Brother Mike," as Karl liked to call him, was the most level-headed person in the family. Karl was relieved to have him there for support. But Karl was miffed that no one else in his family had bothered to make the trip. The fact that his own parents didn't think enough of him to make the effort to get there, hurt him deeply. Their absence was a bitter pill that was hard to swallow.

It wasn't that his parents didn't care. Karl knew that. Everyone in the family knew that their father, who they called "Junior," was pragmatic and stubborn, that he only did what was sensible and didn't let his emotions get in the way. Junior didn't think it was necessary to travel to California, and his mother, Alice, had no choice but to go along with her husband. As for the other adult kids, Junior thought it would have been a hardship for them to travel three thousand miles away. Each of them had families of their own and bills to pay; they couldn't afford to miss work.

"My father got a call from Art the day of the fire," Mike would later say, "and he called around to each one of us, telling us to come down to the house, that Christina had died in a house fire."

"It was one of those things where he replayed the news about the house fire and told us about Christina not making it out," Mike recalled, "and there were probably fifteen to twenty people gathered around the table, and at that point, we all just tried to deal with the shock and disbelief. And then it was like, *now what do we do?*"

Now, as they stood looking at each other in Art's driveway, Mike could see his brother was full of nervous energy. Karl seemed to be in a rush.

Karl and his kids were no longer staying with Art, they were staying with close friends in Murphys, and Karl wanted to get a move on. He waited impatiently for Mike and Jackie to go inside to pay their respects to Art, letting them know that they shouldn't dilly-dally. The kids were staying at Bill and Pam Satterfield's house, good friends who were kind enough to open their home, not only to the children, but to

Mike and Jackie as well. The Satterfield's house, unlike Art's, was big enough to accommodate all of them.

When they finally arrived in Murphys, Mike having followed Karl through the Sierra Foothills, "Uncle Bill" and "Aunt Pam" were waiting to greet them.

Offering their deepest condolences, Pam told Mike and Jackie to relax, to make themselves feel at home. Pam had a pot of coffee ready and a plate of freshly made sandwiches on the table and told them to help themselves.

When Pam brought the children out to say hello to their aunt and uncle from New York, the kids were shy. It was painfully obvious that none of them truly recognized their distant relatives. Levi and Kati crouched behind their father, and although Erin managed to give her Aunt Jackie a hesitant hug, the three of them seemed frightened and mixed up. Within minutes, all three children retreated to the safety of their room, not having uttered a word.

Mike thought it was weird that the kids were dead silent, and even weirder that his brother didn't seem to be concerned about the kids. He knew Karl was a narcissist, but he didn't expect his brother to be so wrapped up in himself and his own loss. The fact that Karl never mentioned the kids that night -- had Mike baffled.

"It was like he put the kids on the back burner," Mike would later say.

The degree of Karl's self-absorption was shocking.

As for Jackie, who knew that her nieces and nephew were too young to completely understand the loss of their mother, the sight of them made her feel overcome and heartsick. Christina's death was permanent, but the children had yet to grasp that. For the moment, Pam was doing her best to take the place of their mother, feeding the kids and bathing them, doing whatever she could to make them feel like they were her own, but Jackie knew that Pam's efforts were only a temporary fix.

Pam Satterfield was a piece of tape that wouldn't hold for long.

Jackie was sure of that.

As they sat at Pam's kitchen table sipping coffee, Mike asked Karl about the funeral arrangements, but Karl had not yet done anything to start that process. Mike could see that his brother was in shock, but even so, arrangements had to be made, and as usual, Karl was shirking his responsibilities. It had been over 24 hours since Christina's death, and Karl had yet to set up a location for the memorial service, he had not placed an obituary in the local paper, in fact, he had not done anything at all. Karl was a child, waiting for instructions from his older brother.

"Are you going to look for an apartment for you and the kids?"

"I mean, eventually, yeah," Karl told him.

"Do you want me to go look at apartments with you?"

But Karl didn't answer.

It was too soon to think about *that*.

"Right now, I've got no clothes," Karl said. "I don't even have a toothbrush. I can't think about getting an apartment, I can't think about anything."

"If you want, I can take the kids out tomorrow morning and buy them some new clothes," Mike offered.

But Karl didn't seem to care one way or the other. He knew the kids needed new clothes because even if some of their clothing survived the blaze, it would all reek of smoke. Karl told Mike that the church community had already begun to take up a collection for the children, and while he thanked his brother for the offer, Karl didn't want to take charity from him. Brother Mike always acted like a big shot, and Karl didn't want to give him the satisfaction of feeling like a savior. He told Mike he was too tired to deal with anything right then, and started to head for the door.

"I guess we can figure all this stuff out tomorrow," Mike told his brother. "You really should try to get some rest. Give me a call when you get back to Art's, just so I know you've made it there okay."

"I'm not gonna stay with Art tonight. Cause I can't handle Art when he starts drinking. Especially at night, he starts to say things."

"Like what?"

"It's like he's trying to blame me for not saving her," Karl said. "And I mean, maybe I could have done things differently, but I did what I could."

"I don't think anyone is blaming you Karl," Mike assured him. "That's all in your head."

"I tried. I really did."

"It's out of your hands, Karl. You've got to stop blaming yourself."

The following morning, January 3$^{rd}$, Karl asked Mike and Jackie to ride with him over to the church so they could make arrangements for Christina's memorial, but when they got there, the pastor advised that the church was probably too small for all the folks who would be in attendance. Everyone in town had heard about the fire and were devastated by the news. Art was a pillar in the community and many people had already called to inquire about Christina's service, the church would be standing room only.

Karl was at a loss to hear this, he didn't have the faintest idea what to do, so when the pastor suggested that he might try the High School in nearby Angels Camp, which would be more suitable, Karl was glad to hear it. He rushed over to Bret Harte High School and thankfully, he was able to secure the gymnasium for Christina's memorial, which would be held on the following day, January 4th.

Before he left the high school, Karl used the principal's phone to call Colette, who was now staying at Art's house. He gave her the details about the time and place and asked her if she would arrange the flowers and the church music for the service. Of course, Colette was anxious to oblige. She was still in shock, she was in suspended disbelief, but she'd been waiting by the phone all morning, desperate to hear what Karl needed, desperate to hang on to whatever part of her sister that she could.

With that chore taken care of, Karl asked Mike and Jackie to take a ride with him over to the house on Penn Gulch so they could help sort through his belongings. Karl wasn't sure that anything had survived the fire, but he had to make the effort for his kids' sake. He was hopeful that he'd find something that belonged to Chris, some sentimental item that she might have kept hidden away, so he could have something of hers to share with his children - when the time was right.

Mike and Jackie were shocked when they arrived at the burned-out house and saw what a total disaster it was. They knew the fire was bad, but they didn't expect to see the place in such a state of ruin. All that was left was the shell of the house, and even that was breeched. As Karl led them through what remained of the outside walls, the three of them made their way through blackened pieces of furniture and burned-out pieces of sheet rock. With so much soot and debris, it was hard to distinguish what they were looking at.

It certainly didn't seem like there would be anything there that could be salvageable.

Jackie walked into what was once the bathroom where she was drawn to the mirrored medicine cabinet. When she opened it, Jackie could see that all the toiletries were still in place. They'd been protected by the thick mirror.

Next to the bathtub, Jackie saw a space heater covered in soot and ash, there was a lot of blackness in that small room – and then, Jackie noticed the plastic bamboo shade on the window that somehow had survived the fire.

The fake bamboo shade was ugly, in her opinion, it was a yellow and brown striped pattern that had been popular in the 1970's, but it looked like it was virtually untouched by the flames, which made her shudder. To think that *this was the shade* that concealed the boarded-up bathroom window, that this shade was still standing, pretty much fully intact, gave Jackie a sick feeling that she couldn't shake.

But Jackie didn't dare touch it. She didn't want to disturb anything.

After she made her way out of there and got down the hallway, Jackie saw a China cabinet that seemed to be in decent shape, and to her amazement, when she looked more closely, she discovered Christina's blackened and charred handbag - with all of its contents intact. She shrieked when she saw Christina's driver's license, and of course Karl and Mike came to see what was up, and then suddenly, the three of them realized that not far from the handbag was Chris's leather-bound Bible, which hadn't been scorched by the flames at all.

To Karl, this was a sign that Chris was looking down at them, that she was still with him, and always would be.

That thought gave him great comfort.

Holding Christina's *Bible* in his hands, Karl brought Jackie and Mike over to Chris's burned-out sewing area and pointed to her prized mannequins, bragging about the various ribbons Chris had won at county fairs, beaming with pride...

But the soot-covered mannequins were ghastly. Covered in charred fabric, the human-sized figures mortified Jackie, and by then, she'd seen enough.

Jackie told Karl it was time to get back to town.

Once in the car, however, with the house no longer in view, Karl suggested they take a ride up to the Big Trees Forest, which was only a quick thirty-minute drive north. Mike and Jackie had never been to California before and Karl wanted to show them this colossal redwood tree stump, a freak of nature, almost twenty-five feet in diameter. That stump was a sight that tourists flocked to from all over the country. It was a must-see.

On the drive there, Karl boasted that this particular tree was so gigantic, telling them that back in the day, people used it as a dance floor. He said he and Chris used to take the kids up to Big Trees often, and that once upon a time, Chris's mom, Arlene, had actually square-danced on it.

Karl was keen for them to see it.

"It seemed very strange to me that Karl wanted to go sightseeing, but then again, I don't know how different people react to that type of situation," Mike would later say.

While they were up there at Big Trees, marveling at the most ancient trees in the world, Mike noticed that his brother had a strange look on his face that was hard to describe. Karl's gaze was so far-off and distant, it was like he'd transported himself to another place and time. His eyes were glazed over, but then all at once, Karl snapped back to reality, and said it was time for them to get going.

"What do you plan to do, Karl?" Mike asked on the drive back.

"I don't know."

"Well, you've gotta have some sort of plan, don't you?"

"I just haven't been able to think much about that..."

"Are you going to keep the kids in school here? Do you know when their school will start up again?"

"You know, I have no idea," Karl said with a sigh. "Right now, all I can think about is losing Chris," he told her. "I mean, I just don't know how I'm gonna raise three kids by myself."

Just as they reached the first stop light near Murphys, Mike told Karl that everyone in their family wanted to help him get back on his feet, and with that said, Karl turned and looked over at Mike with puppy dog eyes, looking for Mike to say something further.

"What is it, Karl? *What is it you want to do?*"

And Karl, speaking under his breath in a whisper, said, "I just want to go *home.*"

"You mean, to *New York*?"

"Yeah," Karl told his brother, "cause there's really nothing left for me here."

# TEN

It was late in the evening, the same day as Christina's memorial service, that Bob Monson, the Battalion Chief of CAL FIRE in Calaveras County, knocked on the door of the Satterfield house, asking to speak with Karl and his daughter Erin.

There was a rumor going around that Karlsen was planning to leave Murphys, and, as one of the investigators on the case, Monson needed to move quickly.

and there were a couple of things that he needed to clarify with Erin.

Karl was polite to Monson. He had no other choice. But in truth, he resented the late-night intrusion. In the previous days, he'd fully cooperated with the investigation, he'd been questioned by both Bob Monson and Howard Stohlman, and Karl was now feeling the pressure of being under a looking glass.

He asked Monson if it could wait until the morning, explaining that Erin was fast asleep, but the investigator was insistent. Monson needed to speak with Erin very briefly, it couldn't wait, so Karl had to wake his daughter up at *ten O'clock at night* to answer questions. The thought of it was completely exasperating – it irritated Karl to no end.

In the wake of Christina's death, Karl had become very protective of his children. He didn't want them to feel overcome with grief, he didn't want them to be further traumatized. Karl wanted to keep them away from all the nosey people in the community, in fact, that was why he kept his three kids away from the memorial service, thinking it would scar them for life, being around so much sorrow and all those tears.

Nonetheless, Karl brought Erin out to the kitchen in her pajamas, encouraging his daughter to answer every question as best she could. Erin was still rubbing her eyes when she first sat down at the kitchen table. As she tried to size up the man in uniform, she seemed a bit dazed and confused.

But Bob Monson had a gentle way of speaking, he was a kind soul, and he was quickly able to make the child feel at ease.

With Erin now wide awake, Monson asked Karl if he wouldn't mind waiting out in the living room, explaining that he was following protocol, and Karl seemed to have no problem with that. Clearly, Karl felt there was nothing Erin could say that hadn't already been fully explained, and as he ducked out the kitchen door, he gave Erin a knowing nod, and then quietly disappeared.

"How did you know there was a fire? Did you smell the smoke?" Monson asked the child.

"No, I didn't smell anything. The first thing I heard was my mom screaming," Erin told him.

"Was your mom screaming a lot? Did it sound like she was hurt?"

"I think she sounded scared. I heard her yelling, and she was telling my dad to come get us."

"Erin, can you remember *exactly* what your mom said?"

"She just said 'get the kids,' and then I didn't hear her say anything after that."

"Where was the fire? Do you know what part of the house it was in?"

"Well, when I cracked open my door, I saw big flames in the hallway, so I shut the door and I got my sister."

"And what did you do then?"

"Then me and Kati stayed down on the floor in the closet."

"Can you tell me about how you and your sister got out of the house?" Monson prodded, "I'd like you to tell me what you can remember."

"Well, my dad broke the window out and he pushed our big dresser out of the way, and then we climbed up and he grabbed us."

Erin told the investigator that the dresser was new, that her mom and dad bought them a whole new matching bedroom set before Christmas, and then wanted to change the subject. She was off on a tangent, explaining that her parents bought new bedroom furniture for everyone in the family, and Monson wanted to steer the conversation back to the fire.

"Do you remember hearing anything that sounded like a burst or maybe a popping sound?"

"No, I didn't hear anything because I was taking a nap."

"But you said you heard your mom screaming, right?"

"Yeah, I heard her scream just one time, and that woke me up."

Erin told the investigator that she and her siblings usually took naps after lunch when they were home, explaining that even if they weren't sleepy, that was their "quiet time," that was their routine. Then suddenly, Erin started to cry – she was upset that her new bedroom furniture was ruined by the fire.

"I had just bought brand new beds for all of us for Christmas," Karl later explained. "It was expensive stuff, like $1,600 a piece. I think it was Stickley furniture. And my daughters were more worried about their beds than anything else, and it was like, so weird."

As Monson continued his line of questioning, he discovered that Erin wasn't aware of a kerosene spill in the house. The child didn't know that kerosene was soaked into the hallway carpet, but she did say that her mom and dad had piled up a bunch of towels and blankets in the hallway, explaining that she and her siblings had made up games and had fun jumping over the big pile.

Erin also remembered something else, telling the investigator that on New Year's Day, just after they had pancakes, their father had taken them outside so they could watch him burn their Christmas tree.

"So, that morning, you watched your dad light the Christmas tree on fire?"

"Yeah," Erin said. "It was really smokey."

"Did you ever see your dad do that before?"

"No, that was the first time he ever did that."

"Did he say *why* he was doing that?"

"Well, he wanted to show us how fast a fire could start," the child said, yawning.

"So, did the Christmas tree catch fire right away?"

"Yeah, it did," Erin told him.

"Let me ask you something. Can you remember if your mom was washing clothes or using the dryer that day?"

"I don't know," Erin said, yawning again.

Although Erin was just six years old at the time, Bob Monson was hoping for a more detailed account of the events leading up to the fire. The information about the Christmas tree was valuable, and the investigator wanted to circle back, but it was getting late, and the child was weary.

Monson decided to leave it alone for the time being.

He'd take another pass at Erin again, in due time.

## ELEVEN

Fire investigators were still in the midst of their job, making specific notes about what they found at the fire scene, examining photos of the victim, whose body had been found in a prone position, partially slumped over the bathtub, with her right hand holding a washcloth to her face.

The autopsy report on Christina Karlsen determined there was heavy soot on the upper torso, the back, and the posterior legs, that only the right side of the face was burned, that the trachea and larynx showed thermal damage as well. The cause of death was determined to be "simple asphyxiation" caused by the inhalation of smoke – but the manner of death was left "undetermined."

When the toxicology report on Christina Karlsen came back, it showed that the victim's blood alcohol level was .07 - a concentration just one point under the legal limit for alcohol intoxication. This was something that surprised Karl entirely, because Christina hardly ever touched a drink, no less got drunk. The high alcohol content the ME allegedly found in Christina's bloodstream, Karl believed, had to have been a mistake.

Colette too, was stunned by the toxicology report. The news that her sister was intoxicated at the time of her death - came as a complete shock to her. The only alcohol she'd ever seen Christina drink was something called a "Fuzzy Navel," a fruity cocktail consisting of peach schnapps and orange juice.

Colette had never seen her sister intoxicated – not even the slightest bit – and she wondered how this finding could be.

Did Karl coax Chris to drink on New Year's Eve?

Could he have gotten her drunk enough to be hungover and "out of it" on New Year's Day?

Colette was planning to confront Karl with these questions, but she never got the chance…

It was on January 5<sup>th</sup>, the day after the memorial, that Karl, without announcing it, without saying goodbye to anyone other than Bill Satterfield, had taken his kids to the Sacramento airport. By that afternoon, Colette discovered, the four of them were well on their way to Rochester, New York.

Colette couldn't fathom why Karl would rip the kids away from their hometown so quickly. He had cheated his kids out of being at their mother's memorial service, and now, he was spiriting them away to the other side of the country, where she would have a hard time maintaining contact with them.

Colette was only beginning to mourn the loss of her sister, and the sudden absence of her nieces and nephew, pained her greatly.

Karl would later tell Colette that it was his brother Mike's idea for all of them to fly back to New York together and made a point of telling Colette that it was *Mike* who had purchased the additional plane tickets, that *Mike* had gone down to the travel agency in San Andreas to arrange the trip, that brother Mike had bought the tickets very last minute, which is why no one knew about it.

In Karl's view, New York was the only logical place to take the kids. He trusted no one in California to help raise them. Not Colette, and especially not Art, who had a bad drinking habit.

"When I met with the reverend after the memorial," Karl would later say, lamented, "I told him there was nothing that could hurt me in California anymore, that I was done and I was ready to leave town, because what the hell else would I do?"

"I had just lost the best thing in my life," Karl later confessed, "and, I mean, I know there's God, or whatever, but I really got screwed over on this one."

It was on the second leg of their long journey from Sacramento to Rochester, after their long lay-over in Chicago, that the kids woke up and seemed rattled. Karl distinctly recalled that as he sat holding little Kati's hand after the plane took flight. His heart broke when Kati pointed to a star and asked, "Is that where mommy is?"

"Yes, that's where she is," he told her. "Mommy is right there looking down at us."

It's curious that Karl would have had that recollection since most people can't see stars while on a commercial flight, even on a night flight. In fact, if someone wanted to see a star from an airplane cabin, they would have to bend over and twist their neck up at an impossible angle, almost upside down, but perhaps Kati was just imagining the star, and perhaps Karl felt he should just go along with it...

Back in Murphys, it didn't take long for the expert team of fire investigators to collect all the evidence from the fire scene, they worked hard and worked meticulously, careful not to overlook anything.

On January 8[th,] the team from CAL FIRE, which was comprised of Bob Monsen, Kevin O'Meara, Carl Kent, and Scott McKinney, made their initial report, revealing what they had recovered at the scene, noting their most significant findings as follows:

- A slightly charred piece of plywood covering the bathroom window, which had been boarded up with 17 nails.
- A cardboard box in the hallway, filled with clothes that were saturated in kerosene.
- Four smoke detectors, the tops of which were adhered to the carpet in the hallway, the batteries having been separated from each of them.
- Burn patterns which indicated that the fire was centralized in the hallway.

# TWELVE

When they first landed in Romulus, Karl and his children lived with Junior and Alice in their log cabin house, where living quarters were tight. All four of them shared one small bedroom, sleeping on two sets of bunk beds, which wasn't ideal, but Karl assured the kids that it was only temporary.

Living there was a necessary evil.

Knowing the transition to Upstate New York would certainly add to their trauma, Karl's five brothers and his sister, Loretta, offered to do whatever they could to make their life easier. Brother Mike loaned his old station wagon to Karl, the rest of his brothers pulled together bags of clothes that their own kids didn't need, and Loretta took it upon herself to take the kids on day trips as often as possible, doing whatever she could to keep her nieces and nephew distracted.

There were many townsfolk in Romulus who also pitched in, making whatever cash donations they could, and those who couldn't afford it, humbly left boxes of used clothing and stuffed animals on the Karlsen's doorstep. Then there were Junior and Alice's closest friends, who often checked in on the family, stopping by with home-baked goodies and casseroles, encouraging the family to keep strong for the sake of the children, encouraging Karl to keep the faith.

But before long, as it always happens, the prayers and sadness over Karl's misfortune, along with the generous offerings from people in the community, would slowly come to an end. People had their own problems to deal with, their own complicated lives, and the unannounced visits to the Karlsen house began to fizzle out. With everyone getting back into their regular routines, Christina's tragic death became nothing more than a terrible reminder that life is short, that "tomorrow is promised to no one."

Even within the Karlsen household, slowly but surely, talk of Christina's death seemed to dwindle. But late at night, in the solitude of their own little bedroom, Kati would often have meltdowns, crying for her mommy, and as for Levi, there were times when he would wake up from a bad nightmare, having dreamt that something was burning. The boy had a recurring dream that he was running away from a fire…

Because Levi's nightmares were persistent and seemed to be getting worse, Karl decided to take his son for counseling. It wasn't something he put much faith in, but there was a free counseling service offered through the school system, so he decided to give it a try. Surprisingly, when he accompanied Levi to the initial counseling sessions, things were looking up. Levi was having much less trouble sleeping. His recurring nightmares seemed to subside.

But once Levi began going to the counseling sessions on his own, the child seemed to become increasingly withdrawn. Levi was always brooding. He didn't interact much with his sisters or even his cousins, for that matter, so Karl decided it was time to meet with the counselor to get some answers.

"Are you making any progress? What do you talk to him about? Does he still have dreams about the fire?"

"It's difficult for him to talk about it. I can't get him to open up. It will take time."

"Well, he still sits around the house sulking on the weekends," Karl said, "and when I ask him what's wrong, he just shrugs his shoulders."

The counselor admitted that Levi refused to answer any questions about his mother, saying that the child was despondent.

"Unfortunately, Levi often looks down at his feet, refusing to make eye contact with me."

Having heard that, Karl decided to put an end to the sessions. Just as he suspected, the mumbo-jumbo of counseling was a complete waste of time.

He had more important things to worry about, particularly his financial problems, which, having lost all his worldly possessions, put him in a precarious position. Money was tight and he was running out of funds. He'd been out hunting for a job, but until something solid came through, Karl decided to call Merle Lucken, his agent at the State Farm office in Murphys.

"I'm just hoping this goes through soon, and as quickly as it can," Karl told the insurance agent

"Well, it has to go by the book," Lucken explained. "And right now, your claim is still in review."

"I hate to put it this way, but the insurance policy is there for a reason," Karl told him. "I just spent *six thousand dollars* on plane tickets for me, my three kids, and my brother and sister-in-law, and I'm flat broke."

"I'll check on it for you. But this claim has gone up to headquarters. It's out of my hands."

"I've got funeral expenses and to be honest, it's a bitch raising three kids by myself."

According to Karl, it was Chris who suggested they take out life insurance policies on each other as an additional safety net. Chris wanted to be sure, in the event that both of them died in an accident, that the kids would have nothing to worry about.

"It wasn't *my idea* to take out those policies," Karl would later say. "It was Chris who made that decision because she wanted a security blanket."

In the aftermath of the fire, with State Farm stalling, Karl took the civil service exam in Seneca County, certain that his years in the Air Force, along with his father's government connections, would make him a shoo-in for a government job. After all, Junior Karlsen was the Superintendent of Highways in Seneca County, a job that yielded a lot of power, and Karl was counting on that.

Karl put in an application at the Seneca County Sheriff's Office, having taken the required written exams, he was anxiously waiting for a response. But it was not meant to be. It wasn't that Karl lacked the intelligence or the physical ability to do the job, it was that, for whatever reason, Karl failed the *psychological* part of the test.

Feeling downtrodden, Karl looked to his father for financial help, but giving handouts wasn't something Junior thought kindly of. It had already been a month that Karl was living off the fat of the land, and Junior had no patience for it.

"If you're just sitting around waiting on insurance money," Junior told him, "you really should be ashamed of yourself."

"I'm not waiting on money! Why would you even *think* that?"

"That's *unearned money!*" Junior howled. "And you shouldn't be counting on it."

"I'm waiting on a job with Seneca County. There's plenty of jobs I could do, and you have the pull."

"What makes you think I could get you a job after you *failed* the damn test? There ain't nothing I can do about that. You need to *get up off your ass* and get some kind of work *now*. I don't care if you have to dig ditches."

But Karl wanted to wait for the right position. He knew his worth and besides, if he really needed to, he could always get his old job back at the Seneca Stone Quarry. He could start working there in the spring, as soon as the weather broke.

As it happened, Upstate New York had a particularly bad winter that year and as more inches of snow accumulated, Karl, having halted his job hunt, decided to introduce his kids to his favorite winter activities. The four of them made snow-angels and rolled up giant snowmen, using carrots for a nose and black buttons for the eyes. Karl was being a full-time dad, bundling his kids up in thick wool scarves and hats, getting them outside in the fresh air. He took them for rides on snow mobiles, he taught them how to ice skate, and was happy that they started to embrace their surroundings.

All three of them were amazed by the incredibly tall snowdrifts and the foot-long icicles that hung from the barn roofs. They were laughing and having fun in a world that didn't exist in Murphys. That type of winter wonderland was exciting. It was something they'd only seen in movies. But there was no amount of snow, no snowman or snow angel, that could make up for the loss of their mommy.

# THIRTEEN

Back in Murphys, CAL FIRE Investigator, Carl Kent, was proceeding with the criminal investigation against Karl Karlsen, collecting witness statements to present to the Calaveras County District Attorney to support a murder charge. He wanted to know the exact date that the Karlsens had taken out life insurance policies, and he paid a visit to Merle Lucken, asking to take a look at the signed documents.

Fumbling through his papers, Lucken pulled out the file, looking for the Life Insurance policy he'd written on Christina Karlsen and, according to the agent's detailed notes, he told Carl Kent that Karl had made inquiries about life insurance in October of 1990, that he hadn't met Mrs. Karlsen until November of that year, when Mr. Karlsen returned with his wife to make further inquiries.

"Isn't $200,000 considered a large policy?" Kent asked.

"No, not particularly," Lucken told him. "I had an office in San Jose before I moved up here, and I would sell a lot of policies in that range, anywhere from $100,000 to $500,000."

"And do you check to see if the person buying life insurance can afford the premiums?"

"Salary-wise, we do get into that, and yes, there was a question in my mind as to whether or not he could afford it," Lucken said. "But we don't delve too far into someone's finances, because they could have a chunk of money sitting in a bank somewhere, and, well, that's not our business."

"So, according to what he provided to you, Karl Karlsen could afford that amount of insurance."

"Yes, that's right."

"Was there anything about Karlsen's request to buy life insurance on his wife that caused you concern? Being that she wasn't the main breadwinner of the household?"

"You have to understand that Mr. Karlsen was also purchasing life insurance on himself at the time," Lucken said. "So that didn't raise any eyebrows."

"What about their demeanor? Did either of them say anything, or act odd in any way, when they were signing these documents?"

Merle Lucken couldn't answer that because he was out of the office on the date that the policies were signed. The Karlsens finalized their policies with his employee, Bobbi Jo Vallerga, and unfortunately, Miss Vallerga was away on holiday. The investigator would have to wait a few days before he could speak with her.

"Okay, but while I'm here, I'd like to ask you a few basic questions about how life insurance policies work in general. I just need you to clarify some things for me."

"Well, the process is pretty simple," Lucken told him. "As soon as the applications are filled out, the paperwork is then submitted to an underwriter and the person being insured has to pass a medical exam."

"And while the applications are on their way to underwriting, are the policies actually in effect?"

"Yes. They go into effect from the moment the application is signed and paid for," Lucken told him. "When the Karlsens made the first payment, they would have left here with a conditionally binding receipt."

Carl Kent asked for whatever documentation that Lucken had on file and was quite stunned when the agent handed over a total of five insurance policies, three of which were written on their young children, Erin, Levi, and Kati Karlsen. Even more significant was the fact that Karl and Christina Karlsen had signed the final documents for all five policies on December 19, 1990, just two weeks before her death.

"And just so I'm clear on this, who was the beneficiary on the children's policies?"

"I believe it was Christina," Lucken told him.

"And can you tell me what a conditionally binding receipt means? In practical terms?"

"Well, if the client satisfies all the criteria to ultimately have the policy issued, if they pass the medical exam, State Farm will issue a final certificate of approval."

"But the policy is effective on the date of signing?" Kent asked.

"Yes, it immediately goes into effect. However, it can be nullified if something untoward is found later on. In other words, if the under-writer finds a medical issue with the person being insured, that would be a reason to nullify it."

As Kent walked out of the State Farm office, he questioned why Christina Karlsen, a thirty-year-old woman, had signed a life insurance policy on herself and wondered what could have possessed her to purchase policies on her three children. It was *Christina's* signature on the kids' policies, who were ages of four, five, and six at the time.

Other witnesses had described Christina as a doting and caring mother, as a woman who was always talking about her children's future... but something didn't add up.

Under the guise of having new information to impart to Mr. Karlsen, Kent placed a call to Romulus the following day, informing Karl that he would soon be hearing from Darin Luttrell and Heather Gower-Small, two of State Farm's investigators. He explained that State Farm would be holding off on the payment until their investigation was concluded.

"What made you think to take out insurance on Christina?" Kent asked, "I'm just curious."

"It wasn't a matter of *me* thinking about it," Karl told him. "It was something *Chris* wanted. She was the one who brought it up. She was the one whose name was on the life insurance policies for me and the kids."

"Okay. I didn't realize that."

"You don't have to take my word for it. All you need to do is go down to the State Farm office. I'm sure they have a record of when Christina first went in, because she was the one to fill out all the paper-work, not me."

"Do you know what her reason was?"

"Because when we talked to Merle Lucken we didn't know what amount to put on anyone. And so, for the kids, he started spitting out figures on what it would cost to raise the kids. I had no idea that it would cost $9,000 a year to raise a kid."

"So, let me clarify. You're saying that it was Mr. Lucken who suggested that you take out life insurance on the kids?"

"Yeah, he ran the numbers," Karl said, "But at first, I was the one who made out applications to take out $50,000 policies on each kid."

"So, wait a minute. You're telling me that it was you who first applied for life insurance on your children?"

"Yeah, but then it was Chris who went back and re-wrote the applications."

"Do you know why she did that?"

"Because we were both looking at it as an investment for the kids," Karl told him. "I mean, my parents had life insurance on *me*, so when Chris called from the State Farm office and said she wanted to raise it to $100,000 on each kid, I didn't question it."

"Okay. So your *wife* went into the State Farm office on her own to sign for the kids' policies?"

"Well, yeah," Karl said. "She went in because she wanted to up the policies. I mean, the way Chris put it, she said that when the kids reached the age of 21, they'd have thousands of dollars for college."

"So, to be clear, you didn't go in with Christina to sign the policies on the children?"

"Well, I mean, Chris already had all the paperwork done. And then afterwards, when I got there, that's when we signed all the papers."

"And you were there to finalize the kid's policies?"

"No, no, no, no! If you ask Merle, he'll tell you that *he* was the one, he was the guy who put this whole thing together for us."

"Okay. I guess I'll take a quick ride over there, just so I can confirm everything."

"Well, I know it doesn't look good. I know that," Karl told him. "But we figured what the hell, we'd get the insurance on all of us, cause we didn't have any other bills to pay and we could afford it."

# FOURTEEN

Unbeknownst to Karl, Kent had already interviewed a string of witnesses and the investigation was moving along quickly. Extended family members had come forward to report their suspicions of Karl, claiming that by the end of 1990 there seemed to be trouble in their marriage.

No one reported that Christina had been physically abused by her husband, but there were indications that Karl was controlling and would lash out at her when she stepped out of line. One such report came from Christina's cousin, Jan Starr, who seemed to be quite afraid of Karl, telling the investigator that she'd seen Karl fly into a rage just weeks before Christmas.

Karl didn't allow Chris to have visitors when he wasn't home, but Jan had snuck over one day to bring the kids some Christmas cookies. It was not long after Jan arrived, just after she and her cousin sat down to have a cup of tea, that Karl came home unexpectedly and barged into the house, all red-faced.

According to Jan Starr, Karl walked in and slammed his hand down on the kitchen table so hard, he practically knocked the teacups off the table. Jan said she saw her cousin's eyes well up as the children ran to the other side of the room in fear, telling Kent that was the last time she saw her cousin.

After a few days passed without Kent giving him an update, Karl was getting antsy. Their brief conversation weighed heavily on him and he couldn't quell the urge to call Kent again, checking to see if there was any news. He hoped they'd figured out what caused the fire.

"We're waiting on lab tests," Kent told him. "We sent the trouble light and the kerosene heater to the DOJ. But with all the red tape over there, it could be eight months before we get the results."

"Eight *months*? Are you kidding me?"

"We don't have that lab capability in our offices here, so we're at the mercy of the DOJ. There's no telling how long it will take," Kent claimed. "We're still waiting to get a finding on the trouble light. Can you remember if you turned it off before you went outside?"

"I was just running out for a minute, so I probably left it on. I know I was gonna put it on the China cabinet, but there was a damn bowl on it."

"Did you attempt to go inside the house to get Chris at any point?"

"No, because the house caught fire real fast, and right after I got my kids out, I already knew there was too much smoke."

"Let me ask you, was there ever any trouble between you and Chris?"

"No. Cause we were best friends. We could tell each other anything."

"Well, I'm asking you because when I spoke with Colette, she mentioned that you guys had argued a few times."

"Oh yes, but that was because of my bullheadedness."

"Your bullheadedness?"

"Well basically, yeah. We had a rough time about a year and a half ago, and I don't remember exactly why, but I pushed her off a chair. That's the only thing I can think of."

"You pushed her off a chair?"

"Well, not exactly. Chris was sitting in a chair and I pushed her, and the chair went back."

"Was it a rocking chair?"

"No, it was a regular four leg chair."

"Okay. And you don't remember what that was about?"

"Well, sometimes I have a hot temper. A real hot one. So we must have been having a disagreement about something. It was probably something stupid."

"Okay."

"One of our cardinal sins was, you didn't argue, you talked it out."

Before their chat ended, Karl suddenly recalled what that incident was about.

"I was cooking chili on a hot plate that day," he told the investigator. "And when I reached up to get it, the whole thing tipped over and that's when I pushed Chris off the bench. I wound up pushing Chris and Kati away cause that chili was so damn hot."

## FIFTEEN

Whether we like to admit it or not, everyone lies, typically to benefit themselves in some way. But Karl is not like other people. His level of deceit goes so deep, it's hard to characterize. He lives in an upside-down world where he can disappear and reappear, distorting all reality around him.

Lies become truths, and truths become lies.

He takes pleasure in confusing people.

* * *

After the hot chili story, Kent steered the conversation back to the subject of kerosene. Karl recalled that he'd purchased a five-gallon jug the week before the fire, which seemed strange. Earlier in their conversation, Karl insisted that the kerosene heater in the house wasn't working. After Kent called him on the discrepancy, Karl explained that he'd bought the jug of kerosene for his father-in-law's business, not for use in his home. But Kent had already reviewed a year's worth of receipts and back invoices from Art's Sheet Metal, and no such purchase for the business had been made.

"Have you been getting the checks and things from people in Murphys that have donated stuff?" Kent wondered.

"Yeah, I've gotten one lump sum so far, but that only paid for the plane tickets. I'm just hoping this goes through as quickly as it can, because let's put it this way, I'm flat broke," Karl paused. "There's just no way I could start back up again, not on what I'm gonna make."

Carl Kent sympathized with the man, promising to do whatever he could to move the investigation along. Then just as they were about to sign off, Karl blurted, "I could *kick myself in the ass* because I could have made more effort for my wife."

"What do you mean by that?"

"It's just, I knew at the time, I knew she was dead."

"How did you know she was dead?"

"Just by the smoke."

"Was she still calling for you, or anything?"

"No. I never heard anything once I got to the porch," Karl sighed. "There was no screaming, no yelling. There was no pain, I guess, if that's what you want to hear."

Kent sat on the other end of the phone, absolutely stunned, waiting for Karl to clear his throat.

"I mean, to put everybody's mind at ease," Karl said, taking a pause, "I guess, it's going to be stupid to say, but if I wanted to kill her, *why the hell would I have saved the kids?*"

To that, Kent had no comeback.

"I mean, let's face it," Karl continued, "I had a hundred-thousand-dollar life insurance policy on all three of them and, in my opinion, if I was gonna do it, *I'd have to let them go too*, because then, I wouldn't have to be a mommy."

"Okay. I see what you're saying."

"You know, if I didn't give a *shit* about her, I wouldn't have given a shit about the kids. So why would I *bust my ass* to get the kids out?"

"Did any of your children see you trying to get to the bathroom window?"

"I think Levi did, but I'm not sure. But I mean, *why the hell would you kill your best friend?* We were more than husband and wife."

"You're making sense," Kent told him, "but I still need to ask you these things."

"You know, if Chris had *done* something to me, if I was gonna get a divorce and she was gonna *take* everything from me, then maybe I could think about knocking her in the head..."

Karl was making a joke, a bad joke, but Kent wasn't laughing.

"We were happily married," Karl told him, "and I mean, how could I have killed her? Her policy wasn't even accepted yet. Did you know *that?*"

"I'm not sure if we checked on that," Kent lied.

"I mean, two hundred thousand dollars isn't gonna buy you a damn thing, hardly. It isn't gonna buy you shit," Karl said, his voice raising to a high pitch. "And you know, if I was in it for the *money*, how would I have killed her without her policy being accepted?"

"Why wasn't it accepted, do you know?"

"Because she still needed to get a medical exam," Karl explained. "So, in plain and simple words, this is just me telling you *that I didn't kill her*. That's all I can say."

## SIXTEEN

Heather Gower-Small, an ambitious young woman who worked her way up the corporate ladder at State Farm over the course of fifteen years, was a member of their Senior Investigative Unit at headquarters. Gower became the person tasked with analyzing the evidence at the Karlsen scene, and because of the severity of the fire, she decided to hire a forensic electrical engineer, a top expert in the field of arson by the name of Ken Buske.

Ken Buske (pronounced Bus-kee) had an impressive resume. Among other things, he'd worked for the U.S. Navy for five years, where he built sonar systems for Naval war ships that could detect a nuclear submarine fathoms below in the sea. The man had an IQ at the genius level, and she trusted his finding one hundred percent.

Her first order of business was to send Ken Buske the trouble light found at the scene, asking him to perform testing on it. If Karlsen's trouble light was in use at the time of the fire, that would be significant.

The particular trouble light that Karlsen had was unusual. It had a rare bulb in it, so to make certain that his testing would be absolutely accurate, Buske ordered a case of the bulbs and performed a series of tests on them. He specifically compared the filament inside the test light bulbs with the filament inside the bulb from the fire scene, which remained intact. The expert took his time, it was an elaborate process, and his final conclusion was that Karlsen's trouble light, which still smelled of kerosene, was not turned on at the time of the fire.

As for the fire scene itself, it was more complicated than most. It remained active for almost a week before being released by local authorities, and much of it had been disturbed and compromised. On the day that Buske made his way up there, on January 8, 1991, he walked through the burned-out walls and doorways, and had a hard time determining the layout of the house.

The level of disruption, the layers of burnt ash that had crusted over every appliance at the scene, also made his job more difficult. Nonetheless, he was able to identify a U-shape pattern of kerosene in the hallway, a distinct horseshoe shape which Carl Kent had also made note of, indicating that there had been a *second pour* of kerosene.

When Buske was finished at the scene he headed to Gavin's Restaurant, a convenient meeting point, where he would explain his findings to Gower-Small. Once there, he drew a quick diagram of the Karlsen house on a paper napkin so he could simplify his findings.

"The second kerosene pour is right here," he said, pointing to the U-shape in middle of the diagram.

"Are you sure of that?"

"Oh yes, because of the wicking pattern I saw in the hallway," Buske assured her. "If you look closely you can see, right in this area, there's less wicking."

Ken Buske ran through a broad range of potential scenarios that caused the fire to ignite, and he believed he could calculate the exact time of ignition based on the quantity of fuel that had been poured in that U-shape.

"How can you be so sure of this?" Gower-Small wanted to know.

"Because I correlated the spill area with the wicking and burn patterns."

In Buske's expert opinion, the second pour of kerosene occurred *just minutes* before the blaze ignited.

## SEVENTEEN

Just days after Ken Buske's official report was submitted to State Farm headquarters, Heather Gower-Small got the green light to fly to New York for a sit-down with Karl. By that time, she had gathered all the CAL FIRE reports, including hundreds of photos of the fire scene, and she'd interviewed most of the witnesses, and had already spoken to Karl on the phone, who had been very cooperative.

It was on March 8th that Gower-Small arrived at the Karlsen residence in Romulus, and Karl couldn't have been more welcoming. He seemed like a normal dad who was concerned for his kids' welfare more than his own. As he held out his hand, he seemed very happy to see her. He asked how her flight was, he offered her something to drink, and at first, they engaged in the convivial conversation that strangers have, talking about the weather and how cold it was in New York, just idle chit-chat.

Karl appeared to be upbeat, but he was nervous. He was dreading the serious talk about his wife's death and hoped the woman wouldn't run him through the ringer. Gower-Small had implied that this would be his final interview, and being optimistic, Karl was hoping to sign the final paperwork.

"I'm so very sorry for your loss," she told him. "I'm sure it's been rough on you."

"Have you made progress on the investigation? Have you figured out what caused the fire?"

"We're still trying to determine that," she told him. "There are certain electrical items that have come into play, and I need to clear up a few things."

She then pulled a tape recorder out of her briefcase and placed it between the two of them, asking Karl to spell his full name, asking if he gave his consent to have the conversation recorded, which he did. She also handed Karl a blank piece of paper, asking him to draw a diagram of the house and asked him to mark the locations of the doors, windows, and all the appliances.

"This is where the washer and dryer were," Karl showed her, marking the diagram with a "D" and a "W" in the laundry room. He then pointed to the center of the hallway, showing her where he had access to the attic, placing a mark directly underneath it, marking a "C" for the China cabinet that stood there.

"What was up there in the attic?" Gower-Small wondered.

"It was a huge mess. There were a bunch of 55-gallon drums up there and about 30 boxes of our stuff."

"Okay. And when you came down from the attic, what did you do?"

"I came down the steps, got on the chair, and put the trouble light on."

"Did you ever go in the bathroom while Chris was in there that afternoon?"

"Yeah, I did. Cause I saw the heater was on and I moved it away from the wall. Cause if that thing got within a foot of the wall, it would burn the wall up. That's how hot it would get."

"Have you ever carried a life insurance policy before? Before you got the policy with State Farm?"

"Just through the military when I was out there," Karl told her. "And I had it once before with a company called Nationwide, that was when we first moved back here to New York, maybe six or eight years ago."

"And do you still carry those?"

"No, I cancelled them out a long time ago."

Knowing that Karl had changed the amount of insurance on himself and his wife just before they signed the policies, upping the coverage from $100,000 to $200,000, Gower was interested in hearing about Karl's financial affairs, asking who paid the bills, wondering if he and his wife had a joint bank account.

Karl was proud to tell her that he was the breadwinner, that it was only *his* name on the checking account. "Chris was just a housewife and she liked it that way," he told her, "because I was the one who paid all the bills."

"What was your income at that time? What did you earn yearly?"

"It varied," Karl said. "I could bring home $700 a week, or I could bring home $1,000 a week. It depended on what type of jobs I was doing, cause I got paid different amounts."

"And do you remember when you first gave Mr. Lucken any money for the policies?"

"It was the same day all the paperwork was done," Karl paused. "I believe I wrote a check sometime in the first part of December."

"Okay, and you told me when we last spoke, that you could afford the payments because you didn't have any bills? "Can you explain that? Because for me, that's kind of hard to understand."

"It's called *bankruptcy*," Karl said, "I filed for it about four years ago."

With that, Gower-Small stopped to jot down a note.

She seemed to be checking off items on a list.

"Oh, and I forgot to ask you, again, about your past. Have you ever had a fire before?"

"Yeah, I had a car burn up about six years ago. Actually, it was in 1986, now that I think about it."

"How did that happen?"

"They don't know," he told her. "The car was a lemon."

Karl only had a vague recollection of the incident. He said they bought a two-door Dodge Charger when they first moved to New York and complained that he'd had problems with the car from the get-go, that he could smell fumes every now and then.

"Exactly where did that fire happen?"

"Over in our driveway when we lived near Seneca Stone," Karl told her. "I came home one day and went inside to ask Chris what she needed from the market, and next thing we knew, Chris looked out and saw flames. And that was the end of that car."

"Oh, and I meant to ask you, where did you keep your life insurance policies? Did you keep all your paperwork in the house?"

"*All my paperwork?*"

"Yes. I'm wondering if you had a safe deposit box."

"We had a safe box out in the garage. That's where we kept all the birth certificates and everything else."

"Can you tell me why you chose to keep your safe box out there, rather than in your house?"

"Yeah, I can tell you exactly why I did that. Because normally, if your house burns, your garage doesn't burn."

## EIGHTEEN

When Gower-Small got back to her hotel room later that day, she placed a call to Carl Kent to ask what he knew about the 1986 car fire, but that was the first Kent heard of it. The following day, he decided to take a drive to Sacramento to find out what Arlene Meltzer knew. Not just about the car fire, but about her daughter's financial situation.

"They were always struggling very very hard for money," Arlene told him. "I remember when we went out to New York to see Chris and the grandkids, this was before they moved to California, and the leather on one of the kid's shoes had come off... And that was one time I saw Karl get real angry. He was furious that the little tennis shoe bottom had fallen apart."

Arlene said she offered to give Chris money from time to time, but her daughter refused to accept it. She recalled her daughter saying, "Karl would be angry mother, if you gave me anything to help." She was aware that Karl challenged every penny Chris spent, but her hands were tied. There was nothing she could do about it.

She also revealed that a few months before the house fire, Chris and Karl had been talking to Art about buying a piece of land he owned in Douglas Flat. She said her daughter was excited about it, that she and Karl planned to put a trailer on the land and eventually build a house there.

"Chris was a daddy's girl and she wanted to stay close to Art, but they never went through with it. And when I asked her what happened, that's when she told me about the bankruptcy. She said something about not being able to buy a trailer for the next five years."

"The bankruptcy? Did she say anything else about that?"

"Not really. She just called to ask me to pray for her."

"Can you recall if Chris ever said anything about a *car* going on fire?"

"I know she mentioned something about an engine blowing up when they were back in New York," Arlene told him, "but she didn't know why."

"Is that all she said?"

"She called me a couple of times and sounded worried. She told me the insurance company didn't believe Karl."

"And I remember asking *how they could think that Karl would set fire to a car?* Because that's the last thing I would think of."

"Is there *anything else* I should know about their marriage? Because I've talked to a lot of people, but I'm not sure I'm getting the whole picture."

For a minute, Arlene sat silent.

She seemed torn.

"The only thing that really blew me away," she finally said, "was what happened on the day of the memorial..."

"I've never told this to anyone, because I was so numb that day, but I heard Karl say, '*Third time's a charm.*'"

"And what did you take that to mean?"

"Well, he was standing by himself when he said it, and at the time I didn't think much about it. But when I got home, all I could think of was... there's a fire in a car back in New York, and then there's a fire here. And I said to myself, *My God,* what about my three grand-children!"

Later that day, Kent placed a call to Nationwide Insurance to follow up on the car fire. An investigator there told Kent that the car fire was very suspicious, explaining that the brand new vehicle somehow combusted while sitting in Karlsen's driveway. Looking back at his notes, the insurance investigator saw that Karlsen had removed his kids' car seats just days before the fire and had removed a box of tools from his trunk as well.

But apparently, they decided to pay the claim anyway.

"I got screwed by Nationwide because I didn't have insurance to cover the replacement cost, so I had to take a loss on that car," Karl would later say. "It was a brand-new car, a teeny little hatchback, and I think I paid around $11,000 or $12,000 for it because it had sporty tires and louvers on the back window."

With the paltry sum Nationwide paid him, Karl was forced to downgrade to a used Ford station wagon which he "dragged out to California" when the family moved there the following year.

Karl thought he was cursed.
He had the worst luck in the world.

## NINETEEN

It was two weeks before Thanksgiving, at a local bar in Seneca Falls called JR's, that Karl first laid eyes on Cindy Best. He picked her out of a crowd while she was line-dancing, and as he sat at the bar with a beer in his hand, he caught the cute blonde's eye and gave her a wink.

Cindy had gone there to meet up with her aunt, Sheila, who had convinced her to get out of her funk and mingle. Cindy was going through a painful divorce and she was leery of men, but she'd agreed to go, telling her aunt that all she wanted was someone she could let loose with, someone with no strings attached.

When Cindy got off the dance floor and approached the bar, Karl couldn't take his eyes off her. He moved himself closer and gave her a nod, offering to buy the ladies a drink. As he waved over to the bartender, he turned around and teased Cindy about her tiny little waist, telling her she could use a little meat on her bones, and Cindy thought he was cute. She found herself blushing.

Karl was a good-looking guy, maybe an eight on the scale of ten, maybe even a nine. He had a great physique, a very strong build, and he was well dressed, looking confident in his cowboy boots and leather jacket. Still, even with that going for him, Cindy was ambivalent. The guy seemed nice enough, he was likeable and funny, but at first, she didn't feel any chemistry. Karl, on the other hand, felt an instant spark. He seemed to be completely enamored with her.

"She sat at the bar, and she was wearing some type of soft white sweater," Karl would later recall. "I could see her belly button and that's what stuck in my head. For some stupid reason, I don't know why, that's what drew me in. And I couldn't stop looking at her."

Cindy was definitely his type, a petite woman with perfect little features and crystal blue eyes, and her carefree attitude, her nonchalant manner, made him want to impress her all the more. There was something about her, something inexplicable, which made Karl feel like they'd been together in another life. She was exactly what he wanted. She had an innocence about her that reminded him, very much, of Christina.

It was like déjà vu.

Cindy and Sheila sat at the bar and listened intensely when Karl began to open up about his young wife who recently died in a horrible house fire. He explained that he was struggling to raise three young children on his own and talked about how hard it was to lose his wife to such a tragedy. He explained that he was able to rescue his children before the house became an inferno, but he was devastated because he'd been unable to save his wife...

Cindy and her aunt felt so sorry for him, but Karl didn't want their pity. He told them the kids were lucky because in addition to having their grandparents nearby, they had gobs of aunts and uncles who spoiled them to death.

As the hours flew by, even though Cindy didn't want to admit it, there was something about Karl that grabbed her. She'd been up front with him, telling Karl she was still married, that she was in the midst of a divorce and wasn't ready to start dating. But in the back of her mind, Cindy thought this could turn into something meaningful.

When the bartender announced the last call at JR's, Karl offered to take Cindy and Sheila to his favorite place for breakfast, but her aunt quickly bowed out, already feeling like a third wheel. He took Cindy to an all-night diner, a converted railroad car that had definitely seen better days, but once they got inside, Cindy was surprised at how cute the place was. With its checkered floors, swivel stools, and old-fashioned soda fountain, Cindy understood why Karl liked it there. It felt very homey. It reminded her of younger days.

After the two of them slipped into a red leather booth, they ordered pancakes from a very friendly waitress and sipped on coffee. Karl had a lot of questions for her, he wanted to know everything about her, about her hopes and dreams and plans for the future.

Cindy had already told him that she was a waitress, but now she was confiding that waitressing was only a temporary job, that she needed to save up her own money until her divorce got finalized. Cindy was already attending night classes at Finger Lakes Community College and was hoping to land a good job in the field of health care.

Of course Karl was curious about her divorce, he wanted to know what happened to the relationship, and Cindy explained that her husband, Tim, wanted her to be a stay-at-home mom.

"The minute we got married he wanted to have kids... but it wasn't meant to be."

"Why not?"

"Well, we tried to get pregnant and couldn't. So I went to a specialist and found out there was a problem with my fallopian tubes. The doctor said I might not ever be able to carry a child."

"But, you know, doctors can be wrong," Karl told her.

"Oh, I know. I was told it was *possible* but it sounded like the chances of me getting pregnant were very slim. And Tim really wanted to have his own biological child."

Karl encouraged Cindy, telling her she shouldn't give up on the idea of having a baby, but deep down, Karl was already picturing Cindy as a makeshift mom. Maybe he'd finally found *the one*, he thought to himself. He needed someone to share the burden of his children.

Karl wasn't sure he could make it without his wife. He told Cindy he was being unfairly punished, insisting that it should have been *him*. That he wished *he* was the one who died in the fire.

"To lose her that way, it's something I'll always have to live with," Karl said, getting choked up. "My wife was like Betty Crocker. She did special things for the kids and always went out of her way for me. That was just her. Being a homemaker was something that came naturally to her."

"How are your kids handling it?" Cindy asked. "It's got to be really tough on them. I can't imagine how they must feel."

"Well, to tell you the truth, I think they were too young to completely remember the fire," Karl told her. "My little one, Kati, was only four at the time, so I doubt she has any memory of it at all. And then, my older two, Erin and Levi, they were five and six when it happened. I know they remember some of it, but they never bring it up anymore."

"It must be awful to lose a mother that young..."

"My kids are troopers," Karl said. "I mean, they miss their mom but they're good kids and they seem to be pretty happy here."

"Well, thank goodness for that."

"Yeah, you're right. I'm lucky that way."

Karl went into detail about how bad the fire was, telling Cindy that a kerosene heater was knocked over by their dog, that kerosene had soaked into their carpet. Firefighters weren't sure exactly why the kerosene ignited, they could only guess.

"And I mean, it happened so quick. It happened while my wife was taking a bath, and she got trapped before I could get to her..." his voice trailed off.

By the end of their midnight breakfast, Karl asked to see Cindy again, and that same weekend, he took her to a trendy place in Geneva, a college hangout, and the two of them spent hours talking about everything and nothing.

They clicked on every level.

For the first time in a long time, Cindy felt butterflies.

When Karl asked if she'd like to meet his children, Cindy was flattered, but she didn't want to jump into things too quickly. Then again, with Thanksgiving just around the corner, with Karl asking her to join him and the kids for Thanksgiving turkey, Cindy was considering it.

"You think your kids would be okay with that?"

"To be honest, I think they're ready to meet someone cause I think they're tired of me being 'mister mom,' you know what I mean?"

A few days later Cindy agreed to meet Karl's children and of course, she thought they were the cutest kids in the world. Erin and Levi were so polite and well-mannered. Their shy little smiles and uncertain eyes really tugged at her. And then there was little Kati, who was missing her two front teeth, which made her the most adorable one in the bunch.

And Cindy felt herself melting.

## TWENTY

When Cindy first arrived on the scene, it had been almost two years since Christina's death. To be upfront, Karl told her about the insurance money he'd collected from State Farm, telling her that he received a lump-sum payment after Christina died which he used to pay for his house in all-cash.

Karl wanted his kids to feel safe, they needed a home, and he was lucky to get a steal on a quaint little three-bedroom house which had previously belonged to one of his siblings. It was a far cry from the dream house that he and Chris had once imagined, it wasn't anything great, but Karl planned to buy a farm of his own eventually. And in the meantime, it was serving its purpose.

In the weeks following Thanksgiving, Cindy quickly became embroiled with Karl's children. She adored them more than she ever imagined. The children made her smile, they made her laugh and also gave her a few scares along the way, and Cindy relished every moment. She was forming a bond with them that would last a lifetime.

Karl was making good money working double shifts at a nearby cosmetics factory at the time, and with Cindy being there every night to feed the kids and get them ready for bed, the situation worked out perfectly. Karl no longer had to shell out $300-a-week for a babysitter. He could spend that money on things he needed for himself and Cindy was none the wiser.

But it seemed Karl couldn't pacify himself with material things. The fleeting moments of happiness were replaced by dark thoughts and there were many nights, after the kids were fast asleep, that Karl would fret and vent for hours to Cindy, angry about his bad luck, angry about his failure as a husband. To Karl, life was so unfair. He became riddled with anxiety and there was no medication (though he tried a few) that could relieve his angst.

"Without Chris, I had to look at things differently," Karl would later say, "I knew Cindy was good with the kids, but that didn't help me deal with what happened to Chris. I always felt I was going to lose it."

Karl talked about Chris nonstop, telling Cindy that he and Chris were 100% ready to move to New York, that the fire had robbed them of their plans. Cindy had heard all of this before but she indulged him because, in a strange way, Karl's venting was something new to her. Cindy's first husband was the type who kept everything bottled up inside, and Karl made her feel needed. Between his good looks and his solid family background, Cindy felt she'd landed a prize.

## TWENTY-ONE

It was in early May that Karl got a call from Colette. She and Art wanted to come visit the weekend of Memorial Day, and she was bringing her kids. Karl wanted everyone to stay at his place, he said he'd make room, but Art planned to book a hotel room in Geneva. He needed his own space.

When Cindy got home from work and he informed her about the visit, he didn't expect pushback. But Cindy bristled. She wasn't ready to meet Christina's family but Karl wouldn't let up. He was adamant about having Cindy by his side. He needed her there.

Karl was taking time off from work and promised it would be a mini vacation for everyone. They could go fishing in the lake, they could rent paddle boats or maybe something bigger that could fit all of them. It was going to be fun.

Cindy helped Karl prepare for the visit, putting away toys so the kids could camp out in the TV room, cleaning the house from top to bottom, stocking the fridge with juices and sodas and special goodies from the good bakery in Geneva. Even though Kati had no memories of Murphys at all, even though Erin and Levi's memories of California had largely faded, they were excited about the visit. Erin and Levi remembered Aunt Colette, and they remembered their cousins too. And they couldn't wait to see them.

Cindy was happy for the kids, she was happy for Karl, but she felt it wasn't a good idea for her to stay at the house. There would be too much hub-bub, she told Karl, but he tried to convince her to stay. Karl wanted Cindy by his side. He needed her to be there. But Cindy felt, out of respect to Art and Colette, that she shouldn't flaunt her relationship with Karl.

"What difference does it make if you're staying here? I already told Colette all about you," Karl insisted., "she knows you're helping with the kids."

"I just feel funny about it. I don't want anyone to think that I'm trying to take Christina's place."

"You're being paranoid! The kids want you here. And I want you here. And I know Chris would want you to meet them."

"I'll meet them," Cindy told him, "but I don't want to start off on the wrong foot. I'm pretty sure Colette won't like the idea of me sleeping in your bed."

"You know what? It's been almost *two years* since Chris died, so at this point, I really don't care what Colette thinks. Because, let's face it, she's always going to hold a grudge against me"

"Why?"

"Cause she's like that. Cause I guess she has nobody else to blame, so I get to be the scapegoat and get blamed for not saving Chris."

Cindy sat quietly for a minute, thinking about how raw Colette's emotions would be, seeing Karl and the kids for the first time since her sister died.

"Believe me, Colette's going to be very nice to you," Karl told her. "It's *only me* that she has a problem with. And if she wants to beat me up some more, I can take it. Cause I know I didn't do anything wrong."

As it turned out, just after they arrived, Karl changed his mind about Cindy spending nights at the house. He thought it was better for her to keep her distance, and Cindy was happy to hear it.

She decided to wait at the house so she could greet Christina's family and was pleasantly surprised when she met Colette, who was as friendly and polite as could be. Of course Colette and Grandpa Art were completely focused on the children, giving big hugs to each of them. Colette couldn't believe how beautiful the girls were, she couldn't believe how tall Levi had gotten. The three of them looked so grown up.

When Grandpa Art opened up his carry-on bag and pulled out the gifts he'd brought, the newest gaming toy for Levi and beautiful dresses for the girls, his wide-eyed grandchildren thanked him and kissed him on the cheek, then promptly ran off to play with their cousins.

Colette followed Cindy into the kitchen where the two women sat down over a cup of tea and tried to get to know each other. Cindy was telling Colette about the children, bragging that the girls had good grades, explaining that Levi needed a little extra help with his home-work, which she worked on with him as much as possible.

Colette was glad that Cindy was helping out with the children and Cindy assured her that, for the most part, the three of them were doing just fine. Even Kati was getting to be a big girl by then and Cindy was happy to report that she'd recently taught Kati how to ride a two-wheel bike, which impressed Colette.

Outwardly, Christina's sister seemed to like Cindy. Cindy believed she'd won Colette over by sharing some cute stories about each of the kids, she thought Colette appreciated that.

"You certainly seem to be doing a good job with them," Colette told her, "Much better than Karl could do on his own."

"Well, when I'm not around, I think Karl can be a little tough on them," Cindy confided. "When I first met the kids, I thought he was acting like a drill sergeant, making them all stand at attention and I'm glad I put an end to that!"

"Karl still thinks he's in the Air Force," Colette told her. "I've always told him that he should just let the kids be kids. He always gave them too many chores, practically from the day they were born."

"He's stuck back in a time warp, and I always have to remind him that things are different these days," Cindy said. "Because sometimes, he's backward thinking. I always tell him to try to be more open-minded."

"Like about what?"

"Well, like, just a few weeks ago, I was painting the girls' fingernails and Levi wanted to be included, so I painted his nails purple, and Karl just went crazy. He said I was trying to turn Levi into a girl. He's so nutty."

"I'm sure he was pissed about that!"

"Oh yeah, he acted like it was the end of the world. And finally, I took the nail polish off, just to get him to shut up!"

The two women had a good laugh about that, which helped break the ice, but when Cindy asked Colette a question about Chris, wondering if Chris dealt with the same kind of issues, Colette's eyes welled up and she looked away. She was unable or unwilling to respond and Cindy felt bad that she'd brought it up. In time, she thought Colette would be able to share a few things about her sister, but to her dismay, the two women never talked about Chris -- at all.

Cindy decided to work extra shifts at the restaurant and was happy to have time of her own at her apartment in Geneva. She thought it was good for the kids to have quality time with their mother's family. The only time she joined them was for dinner at a Chinese restaurant one night, and she was delighted to see that Colette and Karl were getting along. There was no inkling of bad blood. Cindy thought Karl had blown things out of proportion.

Karl's girlfriend had no idea that the only reason Christina's family came to visit, the *real* reason they were there, was to check on the kids in person. They needed to see for themselves -- that the kids were alright.

On the last day of their visit, Karl asked Colette if she'd like to take a quick ride over to his family farm. Karl had always bragged about his horses and he wanted her to see them, so Colette decided to take him up on it, eager to find out if anything that Karl ever told her – was real.

"I remember my dad buying his first team of horses when I was probably seven or eight," Karl said on the drive over. "So, ever since I was a kid, they've been in my blood."

"Do the kids ever get to ride? Do you bring them to the stables?"

"Oh yeah. I take them on rides around the farm when I can, cause it's good for the kids to get used to 'em. I'm hoping Levi will carry on the family tradition."

Colette was surprised to see how vast the acreage of the farm was. It was far greater than she'd imagined, and Karl puffed up with pride as he drove her beyond the horse barns to show off the peacocks that roamed freely on the property.

No doubt, the farm was impressive and the horses were beautiful creatures, but Karl was ruining the whole thing with his incessant boasting. He carried on about his horses like they were winners of the Kentucky Derby. She'd forgotten how delusional he was.

When Colette told Karl that she'd better get back to the house, that she still needed to pack, Karl insisted on keeping her there, painstakingly walking her through every barn on the property, acting high and mighty about his "well-to-do" family.

Colette couldn't stand how self-aggrandizing Karl was and having had her fill of his line of bullshit, she decided to take him down a notch. She decided to burst his bubble.

"These barns are *so old*," she told him, pointing to a pile of hay that was rotting under some old farm equipment. "You've got so much *junk* piled up in here... I'd be surprised if there weren't a lot of *rats* running around."

"Yes, we have plenty of rats. I see rats running around all the time because they come out from under the hay. You know, that's where they live."

By then, Karl was standing in the doorway, blocking the exit of the barn, and he gave Collette the most ungodly glare.

"Do you know how an arsonist *gets away with a fire*?"

"How?"

"You douse a rat in kerosene and then light it," Karl told her, "And it always runs back to its home."

## TWENTY-TWO

Cindy never had a chance to say her good-byes to Art and Colette. She'd asked for time off at the end of her lunch break so she could run over to see them off, but instead she found Karl sitting in the living room by himself.

"Where is everyone?"

"The kids are next door playing frisbee, and Colette decided take off for the airport early because there's a big storm brewing out West and she's hoping they can take an earlier flight."

"Why didn't you let me know? You could have called the restaurant instead of letting me rush over here. I wanted to give Colette my number so we could keep in touch."

"Colette already said they'd be coming back next year so don't worry about it," Karl assured her.

But Colette didn't return the following year.

Or the year after that.

Not long after Memorial Day Karl started bugging Cindy to get rid of her little apartment in Geneva and move in with him officially. But Cindy wasn't sure she should take him up on it. The last thing she needed was another failed relationship, and she didn't know Karl well enough to take that chance.

"You're here most of the time anyway, and it would be better for the kids," he insisted. "And if you were living here, you wouldn't have to be running back and forth to Geneva all the time."

"Let me think about it..."

But Karl didn't want her to think. He kept hounding her day after day. And ultimately, she decided it was easier to give in.

It was a hot summer day in mid-June, the day that Karl helped Cindy move out of her apartment. It was a quick and easy move, being that Cindy's rental came fully furnished. The only piece of furniture she owned was a small dresser that once belonged to her grandmother. It wasn't valuable, but it was a sentimental piece, and Karl had no problem getting it into his pickup.

As for the rest of her things, Cindy's jewelry box, her family photo albums, and her collection of CDs, those were things Cindy wanted to transport on her own. She let Karl handle the bulky boxes full of her clothes and shoes, except for her wedding gown, which she placed carefully in her back seat.

Between the two vehicles, they only needed to make one trip, and once Cindy got settled, it seemed the children were more comfortable with her, so she'd made the right choice. Kati and Erin liked to be around Cindy whenever possible, especially when Cindy baked chocolate chip cookies. Even Levi, who had a hard time showing emotions, was coming around. After years of being told she was barren, Cindy finally had the children she'd been praying for.

Her life seemed complete.

At first, Karl was doing all the normal things a father does, taking the kids  to their sporting activities on weekends, making sure they were tucked in every night, but over time, he seemed to be leaning on Cindy to handle most of the parental duties, choosing to spend much of his free time with his beloved Belgian horses.

Whenever she asked him to help with the kids, Karl was full of excuses. He would complain about how tiring his work week was, reminding her that he was working extra shifts to keep the household running. He would also remind her he'd made an agreement with his father, who let him board his horses in the big barn in exchange for extra work that needed to be done around the farm.

"Whenever your father says '*jump*,' you go running over there," Cindy argued, completely fed up.

"Well, they're my horses, and I can't just leave them for my father to deal with!"

"You say that, but you know it isn't just the horses, Karl. You wind up doing all the work around his barns and you say they're your horses, but we both know that only three of them belong to you. All the others, you take care of for your father, without pay. He's taking advantage of you!"

But as usual, Cindy's argument with Karl went nowhere. He would agree to get more involved with the children, but after a day or two of being on good behavior, Karl would go back to his first love, his magnificent horses.

Cindy knew Karl was eccentric, she thought she knew what she was bargaining for when she moved in, but it became clear that the horses were more important to Karl than his children were. For the life of her, she couldn't understand why Karl was ignoring his kids' needs.

To help him make ends meet, Cindy had gotten a waitressing job at Connie's Diner in Waterloo, a town much closer to Romulus, but between working lunch shifts while the kids were at school, then helping them with their homework and fixing dinner every night, it was becoming too much. Cindy was so busy, she didn't have time to think, and she was feeling run down.

It was about six weeks after she moved in with Karl that Cindy woke up one morning with a huge headache, feeling queasy. She thought it was the flu, but something made her go to the drugstore to get an at-home pregnancy test, which to her amazement, came out positive... Karl seemed ecstatic when he heard the news, and by the time Cindy's pregnancy reached the third month, he started talking about marriage.

Karl hadn't proposed yet, he hadn't bought Cindy a ring, but he made it known that he was ready to take the plunge. Cindy agreed that it was only right for them to be married before the child was born, and the two of them started kicking around some possible dates. But in the midst of their wedding plans, Cindy began to have severe abdominal pain, and late one night, she woke up to find that her side of the bed was covered in blood.

Karl rushed her to the nearest emergency room, but it was too late.

Cindy not only lost the baby, her health was in jeopardy. The attending ER doctor explained that she'd had an ectopic pregnancy and there was possible damage to her organs.

Cindy had lost a tremendous amount of blood. Her condition was so serious that she had to be hospitalized for three days. And while she lay there feeling helpless, the doctor made it worse by telling her that she couldn't risk having another ectopic pregnancy, that it could be life-threatening.

On the day she left the hospital, when Karl arrived to fetch her, Cindy broke down in tears. She felt helpless. She told Karl that the only way she could get pregnant was through in-vitro fertilization, and even then, the doctor warned, she'd be taking a substantial risk.

He tried to console her.

But it seemed he was only making her feel worse.

"Let's get married anyway," Karl suddenly said.

"Let's just go ahead and do it. What do ya think?"

## TWENTY-THREE

Women in every culture view their wedding day as a fairy tale, and for new brides, the importance of the wedding gown, which serves as a symbol of that special day, becomes a search for perfection.

But second weddings are different.

In most cases, the party tends to be smaller, and even though the bride often wears white, she makes sure that her dress is nothing like a flowing ball gown, nothing that would evoke the image of a princess.

It was on an extremely hot day in August, a sticky and humid day, that Karl and Cindy tied the knot. Their wedding was without frills, really, but Cindy made sure that the kids felt special, dressing the girls in identical flowery dresses, dressing Levi in a button-down shirt and blue necktie. Cindy and Karl had professional photos taken to mark the occasion, and she beamed in her simple white dress and single strand of pearls. She thought Karl looked more handsome than ever, she'd rarely seen him in a suit and tie, and just after they said their vows, she found herself hugging and kissing, not just Karl, but also the kids.

She felt like the luckiest woman in the world.

The newlyweds held their reception at the Varick firehouse, where Karl had once been a volunteer many years before. It was attended by immediate family and the closest of friends, and it was a down-to-earth party, which was just how she wanted it. The dance music came from a boom box, the meal served was a pot-luck dinner, and Cindy was quite satisfied with that.

There was love in the air, and everyone there had a good time.

Cindy didn't care about a honeymoon all that much, but Karl promised to take her on an "official" honeymoon cruise as soon as he could. In the interim, a quick trip to Niagara Falls would do, where the newlyweds spent two passionate nights making their own rainbows. Rainbows that were better than any natural wonder on earth.

In between love-making, Karl was opening up to Cindy more than he'd ever done before. He revealed that their honeymoon cruise had to wait because he'd been battling an ugly civil lawsuit in California that was draining all his savings. With venom in his voice, Karl confided that the owners of the house he'd rented in Murphys had the audacity to sue him for $200,000. It was not because they deserved anything, Karl told her. The homeowners were "greedy, "they were looking for easy money.

"Can you believe it?" Karl asked. "*They* are the ones who are negligent. *They* are the ones who rented me a house that couldn't be insured because the place was over hundred years old!"

"But why would they sue you? Wouldn't it be their loss if they didn't have homeowner's insurance?"

"Well, that's just it. They rented me a shack that turned out to be a tinderbox, and now they're trying to collect on it."

"But why would you have to pay for a house that wasn't even yours?"

"Because that's the way things are these days. People can sue you for anything, even if what their claiming is totally nuts."

Karl told Cindy they didn't deserve a dime. However, because Karl had mounting legal bills that he couldn't afford to pay, his attorney recommended that he reach a settlement. He confided to his new bride that he'd paid the Murphys homeowners a lump-sum of $60,000 to get rid of them, claiming that the settlement had completely drained him of his savings.

Of course, Cindy had nothing but sympathy for him.

How could people kick a man when he was down?

But Cindy wasn't too worried about it. Karl owned his house outright and their expenses would be minimal, she thought. Together, they managed to make ends meet. Cindy pulled extra shifts on weekends and Karl created a side business, building horse carriages from scratch which he sold to folks who used them for county fairs.

Together, they saved up a small nest egg, and that November, true to his word, Karl left the kids with his parents and took Cindy on a week-long cruise to the Bahamas. It was the first time Cindy had ever been to the Caribbean. It was the first time she'd ever been on a cruise. And she was blown away by the aqua blue waters and all the luxuries that the cruise ship provided.

Karl was an upstanding man. He wasn't everything she'd ever dreamed of, but he was as good as it would get.

Cindy somehow managed to make everything she was doing for the kids look effortless, juggling their schedules, the housework, and her weekend shifts at the diner. But as weeks turned into months, Cindy realized that Karl didn't share a common goal with her. He didn't seem interested in creating special memories with her. If anything, Karl had gotten more complacent, expecting her to keep up her "wifely duties," without bothering to make anything romantic.

By Christmas time, the kids started calling her "mom," which was very gratifying, especially because Cindy made it clear that they didn't have to. Cindy never wanted the kids to forget Christina, and when she came across a glamour shot of Chris, she framed it and placed it on the mantle in their living room.

Like all kids at Christmas, Erin, Levi, and Kati had their hearts set on the hottest toys, things that were propped up by perpetual advertising, and some of those items were impossible to get. Still, Cindy managed to snag at least one toy on each of their wish lists, spending her time hunting for the specific requests that Levi and Kati made, both of whom believed in Santa.

But Karl ignored her efforts. He was taking her for granted, making her feel "less than" Christina, who he idolized as the perfect wife.

"Do you realize how much you talk about Chris?"

"What do you mean? I never talk about her."

"That's not true, Karl, and you know it. You're always telling me that she was the best at *this* and the best at *that*. And how do you think that makes me feel?"

"I don't compare you to her," Karl argued. "I would never do that."

"Maybe you don't even know you're doing it, and maybe I'm not the perfect Betty Crocker, but you don't need to keep reminding me about her…"

"I'm not comparing you! You're dead wrong about that."

"Well, maybe you can't see it, but you brag about her all the time, and you know what? It really hurts my feelings."

It was within 24 hours of that conversation that Erin went to Cindy, promising that she wouldn't talk about her mother anymore, and Cindy was shocked.

"Where did you get an idea like that?" Cindy asked her step-daughter.

"Daddy told me not to. He said I can't talk about my Mom in front of you anymore because it makes you mad."

"Well, that's just not true. I've never said you can't talk about your mom. I like hearing about your mom. I don't know what possessed your father to say such a thing!"

But Erin believed her father. That was clear. Instead of looking at Cindy and agreeing, Erin fixed her gaze on the floor.

"You can talk about your Mom *all you want*, okay?"

"Okay," the child whispered.

"I never want you to forget her. Okay? I hope you understand that."

Later that night, Cindy had a huge fight with Karl. She was livid that Karl brought up her personal insecurities, furious that he'd twisted her words around, making Erin think she should erase the memory of their mother.

But Karl didn't understand what the problem was. He told Cindy it was no big deal, that he'd talk to Erin again to make sure she didn't take it to heart, but the damage had already been done.

From that point on, Erin began to pull away. She was no longer confiding in Cindy. She was no longer seeking advice. The ten-year-old had become rebellious, treating Cindy like she didn't count. It was the beginning of a wedge between Erin and Cindy that would continue to get wider with time.

## TWENTY-FOUR

Something that Cindy kept hidden from the kids was her life-long struggle with alcoholism. It ran in her family, and Cindy thought she had it under control, but a year into her marriage, she snuck a few bottles of wine into the house and that kicked off a drinking binge. Karl wasn't a drinker, he never cared for it, and she expected him to get on her case, but surprisingly, Karl didn't mind it.

This was early in their marriage when Karl had not yet realized that his wife had a serious problem. In his view, Cindy was able to hold her liquor and on weekends, he'd join her for a glass of wine or a beer. Karl liked her better that way. When Cindy was drunk, Cindy was more passionate in bed.

It came as a shock to him that in October of 1994, Cindy got pulled over for Driving Under the Influence. She tearfully admitted that she was facing a court date and was afraid she'd lose her license. She figured Karl would read her the riot act. After all, he was trusting her with his children, and now she'd blown it.

"It's not the end of the world," Karl said at the time, "but if you get another one, you'll be in deep shit."

"I know. And I'm going to stop drinking, I promise."

The following day, Karl went to see his father. He knew his father could probably make the DUI go away, but Junior flat out refused to get involved. His dad asked why he would bring "someone like that" into the family and told his son to get control of his wife. The only thing Junior cared about was the family's reputation. None of his kids had ever been arrested, they all had a clean slate, and he was mad as hell.

Cindy had just been accepted into the family and already she was tarnishing the Karlsen name. Junior told Karl he wouldn't tolerate having a drunk in the family. As the Supervisor of Highways, Cindy's DUI was a big embarrassment for him.

When Karl came home later that day, rather than reassuring Cindy that everything would be okay, Karl was now taking his father's side.

He was suddenly furious about the DUI and was making a big deal of it, telling her she needed to go to AA, that she needed to get help.

Luckily, Cindy didn't need Junior's connections to help sort the matter out. This was back in the 1990s, when people didn't think twice about drinking and driving. Back then, the laws weren't as stringent and after she faced the judge, Cindy was put on probation and was issued a strong warning, and she thought that was that. But it wasn't.

But Karl now used the DUI on Cindy's record to badger her every chance he could, threatening to tell the children she was sneaking alcohol into the house, threatening to leave her if she didn't straighten up and fly right.

Karl was hard on her but the tough love saved Cindy because it forced her to swallow her pride and join AA.

Cindy was proud of herself for getting through the twelve steps. She had taken the vow of sobriety, which she thought Karl would be happy about, but he didn't seem to care. He never gave her a pat on the back, he never gave her support. Karl wasn't the man she thought he was, he was cold and callous, and Cindy was having second thoughts.

Jumping into marriage so quickly was a big mistake. Karl was no longer affectionate, he expected sex on demand, and Cindy became resentful. Her marriage to Karl slowly began to degrade. As it was, Cindy had to fight an uphill battle as a stepmother, and it didn't help that Karl was pitting her against the children, forcing her into the role of disciplinarian.

Cindy had quit drinking, she was giving the kids her undivided attention. But it didn't matter. Karl had forced her into wearing the black hat and the kids seemed to resent her more each day.

"You 're not my mother!" Erin screeched at Cindy, "so don't think you can boss me around!"

Erin was ten-going-on-twenty, and she'd decided to be obstinate, and suddenly Levi and Kati were taking her lead, retreating to their bedrooms every chance they could. Feeling totally inadequate and downtrodden, Cindy mustered up the courage to tell Karl that she wanted to try in-vitro fertilization. Now, more than ever, Cindy wanted a child of her own. And her biological clock was ticking.

"Do you know how much that costs? How are we going to afford it?" Karl asked, clearly annoyed by her suggestion.

"I know it's expensive, but I've been saving up my tip money..."

"Okay already, if that's what you really want, I guess we can look into it."

Cindy had her heart set on it and Karl wasn't too thrilled, but before he knew what hit him, he found himself sitting down with an infertility specialist who was running through a check list with his wife.

The fertility doctor was upfront, telling the couple that the process of in-vitro fertilization would be strenuous. They would have to administer daily injections of hormones, there would be multiple eggs implanted, and in the end, there would be no guarantee of success. But Cindy was ready to go.

Karl had gone with her to a fertility clinic to placate Cindy. He was hoping that this idea would be squelched, but here it was, on their very first visit, that things got *real*. And Karl couldn't find a way to back out.

However Karl changed his tune after the in-vitro process got underway. He suddenly relished the idea of starting a "new family" with Cindy. He was tolerant of her mood swings and did whatever he could to alleviate Cindy's fears about losing the baby.

It was on August 5th, 1995, that Cindy gave birth to a beautiful baby boy, Alexander Thomas Karlsen, and Karl would forevermore brag about his youngest son, who he called a "miracle test tube baby."

When she and baby Alex got home, the kids were all excited to have a baby brother. They seemed to gel as a family with Alex in the picture, and Karl was like a new man. She was surprised by how much he helped her with the baby.

Erin and Kati loved playing "mom" with baby Alex. They were amazed by every stage of his growth. And Levi, who'd never dreamed that he'd have a baby brother, became incredibly attached to Alex. Once his brother became a toddler, Levi would playfully wrestle with him, always letting Alex win. In those early years, the three older kids enjoyed teaching Alex how to ride a tricycle, how to ride a horse. Everything they did with Alex gave them a thrill.

By 2001, Karl and Cindy decided to make an offer to buy a piece of the family farm, offering Junior a good price for the quaint country house and a substantial number of acres it sat on. By the time they moved in, Alex had just turned six, and being around him was a delight. He was big enough to handle himself, he was full of wonder and mischief, and he brought a sense of levity to Karlsen family, something they'd been missing for a long time.

Levi would carry Alex around the farm on his shoulders, parading him like a trophy, and the girls would play outdoor games with their little brother, thrilled to watch him evolve into a full-blown person.

In those early years, Alex's life was idyllic.

His parents spoiled him. His siblings adored him.

He was the apple of everyone's eye.

# TWENTY-FIVE

It was at 2AM on November 3rd, 2002, almost a year to the date after they had moved to the farm, that Cindy was awakened by Karl's shrill voice.

"Cindy, WAKE UP!" Karl was yelling, "Oh my God! Call 911!! The barn is on fire!"

Cindy launched herself to the back bedroom window, looking at the red glow in disbelief. Karl was out on the driveway, screaming for her to get some clothes on.

"Come help me!" he yelled up to her, "Ginger's in there!"

It was freezing cold outside so Cindy pulled a sweater over her head and ran out there. By then, Karl had reached the barns and she watched Karl making an attempt to push the barn doors open, but the intensity of the heat was too great. As he pulled away from the barn doors, Karl watched in horror as a second barn caught fire.

At that point, Karl already was running back towards her, telling her to stand back, telling her that all they could do was wait. The firefighters arrived within minutes, but it was too late to save the horses. The fire had gotten out of hand quickly because there were so many bales of hay in there and Cindy was heartbroken.

"I tried to get to them but the metal door handles were too damn hot, "Karl told her. "The metal on the hinges were already melting. There was just no way..."

By that time, the fire had spread to their garage and Cindy raced to the house to wake Alex up, running her seven-year-old to the next-door neighbor's house. She got back just in time to see the firefighters removing the badly burned remains of Ginger, Buddy, and Star and was horrified at the sight of their charred bodies.

It was ghastly.

It was gruesome.

The fire occurred when Junior and Alice were away on holiday in Las Vegas and the minute they heard about it, the two of them flew back on the red eye. The following morning, after Junior surveyed the damage, he wanted answers. Not only were two of his colts in that barn, but his custom-made harnesses and bridles were in there too. Junior's prized collection could never be replaced, and he gave Karl a look that was deadly.

"*What the hell happened?*" Junior asked Karl.

"I don't know. I left a radio on overnight but that couldn't have been it."

"Do you realize how much we lost? Those harnesses alone cost a small fortune! And they were one of a kind. They can't be replaced!"

"The harnesses weren't in there."

"What do you mean? Where did they go?"

"I was cleaning out the barn while you were away," Karl told his dad, "and I temporarily moved them to the shed behind the house."

Later that morning with the clean-up fully underway, Cindy went to Karl asking him to bury Ginger's body far in the back of the property where Alex couldn't see her. Karl nodded in agreement but that same afternoon, he hoisted Ginger's corpse into the bucket of his tractor and drove right past the front of the house.

"I specifically remember seeing Ginger's body on the front of the tractor," Cindy would later say. "I saw *Ginger's leg* dangling out and that image is ingrained in my mind."

Karl claimed he was trying to figure out exactly where to bury her. He told Cindy he'd taken her to the front of the driveway because he needed to take clear pictures of her for insurance purposes, promising to clear her out of the way before the insurance adjuster showed up.

"The insurance guy told me he needed to see the horses for himself," Karl recalled. "He said pictures weren't good enough and we argued about that for a while."

Apparently, the insurance company needed proof that three horses died in the fire, explaining that he'd have to write death certificates on each of them, which Karl thought was crazy. He couldn't believe his ears. Who'd ever heard of such a thing?

"Me and my brother already buried 'em way back in the woods," Karl told the insurance investigator, "so if you really need to see 'em, I'll give you a shovel!"

Karl was angry that the insurance company forced him to dig up the horses, later stating that he had dug up as much as he could, but was only able to find "two baby heads and one big mouth."

He never found Ginger's head...

It was about a week after the tragic barn fire that Alex and his dad were playing hoops out in the driveway, and suddenly, Alex caught a glimpse of Ginger's hoof. The boy happened to spot it because the sunlight made her horseshoe glimmer, and when he went over to examine it, Alex started to cry.

"Alex kept asking and asking me about Ginger," Karl would later say, "cause Ginger was the one he thought of as a pet... And after we found her hoof, I had to explain to the kid that it was easy for her to come apart because she got cooked, and then the coyotes got in there..."

## TWENTY-SIX

What an investigation would later reveal was that three weeks before the blaze, Karlsen increased the insurance coverage on his barn from $20,000 to $60,000 and added two Belgian colts to the policy, insuring them for $10,000 a piece...

It was two days after the fire that William Ostrander, a fire investigator hired by Wayne Insurance Company, went out to the Karlsen farm to access the scene. After photographing the two structures destroyed by the fire, the main barn and a second building which housed farm equipment, he sat down with Karlsen and conducted a quick interview, recorded on audiotape.

After giving his consent, 42-year-old Karl Karlsen answered a series of "establishing" questions, confirming that he was the owner of the property, confirming that he'd been living on the farm for over a year, confirming that he'd lost three of his horses in the fire.

"And who actually discovered the fire?" Ostrander asked.

"I did."

"Okay. And how did you come to do that?"

"By looking out the bedroom window."

"Does your bedroom face the barn and the other buildings involved in this fire?"

"No. The bedroom faces the road," Karl explained, "but I could see the orange glow on the ground because we had a little snow coverage, and it was reflecting off that."

"Did you try to remove the horses once the fire was discovered?"

"Yes, I went around to the two big sliding doors and I opened up one of them, but there was just too much smoke and it pushed me back."

"And the large Belgian mare, Ginger, what was she used for?"

"Mainly breeding, but also for hayrides."

"Have you updated the wiring in the main barn since you've owned it?"

"No, I have not."

"Do you have any idea what the cause of the fire was?

"We still had the old cloth-coved type wire in the one barn, so I don't know if that could have been it."

"I noticed that there was a radio inside the main barn that was plugged in. Could that have been a source of the fire?"

"I guess anything is possible..." Karl's voice trailed off.

"And the radio that was plugged in, what did you use that for?"

"We'd keep the radio on at night so the small horses wouldn't cry for their mother. Everyone with horse farms does that."

But there were suspicions raised after Ostrander interviewed Karl's brother, Kristin Karlsen, who maintained that the large Belgian mare, Ginger, had been deemed infertile and therefore was not worth much to anyone.

But whatever suspicions there were -- didn't matter.

The point of origin couldn't be established and the cause of the barn fire remained "undetermined."   After all was said and done, Wayne Cooperative forked over about $115,000 to Mr. Karlsen, a jackpot he'd kept hidden from everyone, including his wife.

## TWENTY-SEVEN

In the months leading up to the barn fire, life at the farm became difficult for Levi, who was now 17. His teenage rebellion had reached new heights. He was caught stealing $400 from his sister's cookie jar, he was caught smoking pot, and when things like that happened, Karl hit the roof.

"I am God to you!" Karl told his son during a heated argument.

"No you're not!" Levi howled. "You're nothing to me!"

From Cindy's vantage point, Levi was doing whatever he could to defy their rules, intentionally trying to make his father angry. Karl wanted Levi to fit in with "normal" teens, he wanted his son to check all the right boxes, but instead Levi chose to become a Goth. Suddenly he was wearing spike chokers, heavy chains, and a strictly black wardrobe.

When Karl confronted Levi about it, things only got worse. Levi went out and got a few more piercings and paid for tattoos that ran up and down his arms. As for contributing to the household, Levi had become obstinate and refused to lift a finger.

There finally came a day when Cindy found herself cursing at the top of her lungs, insisting that Levi unlock his door and face her, but instead, he jumped out his second-floor bedroom window, fracturing a bone in his leg.

The incident devastated Cindy. After she took Levi to the emergency room and brought him home with his leg in a cast -- she proceeded to have a complete nervous breakdown. By the time Karl got home from work, Cindy had gotten herself so worked up that her bladder let loose. Karl was telling her to calm down but she couldn't. She was shaking and crying hysterically as urine came running down her legs.

After she went upstairs and changed, Cindy managed to compose herself somewhat, but she still needed to vent.

"Now that Levi's old enough to drive he doesn't need me anymore. That's why he makes me the enemy!"

But Karl didn't comfort her.

He liked the idea that Cindy wore the black hat.

"*What else do I have to do* to prove I love these kids?" she asked, completely frustrated with the situation. "I've been taking care of them for almost ten years now, and they don't respect me. Do you realize that?"

"Is it that long?" Karl said, "I can't believe it!"

"We already know that Erin hates me, and Levi seems to be heading in the same direction."

"Well, Erin is another story," Karl told her. "You can't compare the two because she's nothing like Levi. Believe me, Erin would have flown the coop no matter what, because she's bullheaded."

"But why is Levi turning against me?" Cindy asked. "It's like he despises me, yet he says nothing to you!"

"Well, that's how teenagers are. It's not cause he hates you, it's just when you're that age, you don't care about anyone else but *yourself.*"

When Cindy complained about all the effort she'd put into these kids, about how she scraped together her tips so she could pay for extras, Karl had to agree that the kids didn't seem too appreciative. Cindy had used her own money to help pay for family getaways to places like Niagara Falls, Marine Land, and even Disney World, but none of that seemed to count.

"Kids these days expect everything to come to them easily," he told her.

"And Levi's just going through a phase. Eventually he'll grow out of it."

But Levi never did.

If anything, he got worse.

Cindy could sense a pent-up rage in him.

Levi needed professional help, and Cindy, who was determined to get him into some form of counseling, discovered a new program called PINS (Persons in Need of Supervision) which sounded promising. She'd spoken to someone on the phone there and was expecting a return call regarding what steps she needed to take. She was surprised when two days later, two men in uniform came knocking at her door. She thought they were from PINS but the men identified themselves as members of the Seneca County Sheriff's Department, telling Cindy they were there to respond to a distress call made by Levi Karlsen.

Cindy could hardly believe it. She had no idea why Levi would call the police. A few minutes later, Levi came down and spoke privately to the sheriff's deputies, claimed that his father had physically abused him. Furthermore, Levi claimed that Cindy knew about it, and did nothing to protect him.

"My father was hitting me in the head and ears, he was punching me in my shoulders and my lower ribs, saying I was making up stories about him," Levi claimed in the incident report. "He was pushing me and slamming me down, and he asked me if I wanted to die. He said that if I ever told lies about him again, that he would take me outside and I would not live through it..."

The matter was turned over to CPS who came to the farm to question Karl, who categorically denied laying a hand on his son. Upon further investigation, a social worker discovered inconsistencies in Levi's statement. The young man had specified the date of the alleged abuse and was adamant that his stepmother was there to witness it...

But Cindy was in Canada on that date, and she'd handed over her passport to a CPS worker which proved it. After six months, with nothing further being reported by Levi Karlsen, CPS determined that Levi's allegations were unfounded.

## TWENTY-EIGHT

Levi moved out of the house not long after that, choosing to stay with his Aunt Donna and Uncle Curtis who lived down the road. Things were better that way. He had little reason to go to the farm and he kept his distance. However, when Erin decided to visit home for Thanksgiving that year, Levi joined his family.

At first, everything seemed fine, but right after their turkey dinner, Levi and his father got into a huge fight. He was confronting his dad about the barn fire and then questioned him about the fire in California. Cindy and Alex witnessed the argument, as did Erin, and the next thing they knew, Karl put Levi in a headlock and slammed him down on the floor.

The two of them struggled. Levi was kicking so hard, he was knocking into furniture, but somehow, Cindy managed to pull the two of them apart.

As soon as Karl released his grip, Levi ran out and jumped in his car, but minutes later he could see the headlights of his father's pickup in his rearview mirror. Levi was the first to reach his aunt's driveway, he was the first to make it to the threshold, but Karl was already out of his vehicle.

"Levi ran toward my house and made it inside," Donna would later tell police in an incident report filed in November of 2002. "My oldest son tried to lock the door but Karl forced it open. And the minute he got into my house, Karl grabbed Levi by his throat. He was trying to choke him. He was using both hands and he pinned Levi to the wall."

According to Donna Karlsen's statement, she and her son tried to pull Karl off Levi, each tugging at one of his arms, but Karl was too strong. When Donna saw Levi's face begin to turn red, when he started gasping for air, she yelled for someone to call 911.

But the minute Karl heard Donna's screams for help, he let go of Levi's neck and stomped out of the house. Before the cops got there, Karl had disappeared into the night. There were no injuries to report, there were no bruise marks around Levi's neck, but Levi would tell police that his father tried to run him off the road…

## TWENTY-NINE

It was in late January of 2003 that Levi met Cassie Rood, a like-minded seventeen-year-old who was heavy into the goth scene. The two of them seemed to be made for each other and it didn't take long for Levi to move in with Cassie and her mom, Terri, who lived in a double-wide trailer in Clifton Springs.

Levi landed in a peaceful community that was a half hour drive from Romulus, far enough away for him to feel safe. The accommodations were snug, but Levi was made to feel like family. He was finally being accepted unconditionally, which was all he ever wanted, telling Cassie that his parents never loved him.

It was true that Levi had a strained relationship with his dad. It was also true that Cindy was tired of dealing with him, that she'd given up on him at that time. But Cindy never washed her hands of Levi completely, not at all. She still loved her stepson, she just didn't approve of his lifestyle.

"Levi told Cassie's mother that we kicked him out and claimed he was living in his car, which was a total lie," Cindy would later say. "At the time, he was living with his aunt and uncle and he just wanted an excuse to move out."

Levi was good at making up stories. He'd done that all his life. To Cassie, he painted a picture of his father as a tyrant, of his stepmother as a task master, asserting that the only kid she ever cared about was his seven-year-old brother, Alex. Even so, Cassie wanted to meet his parents so Levi waited for a Sunday, calling over to the house, telling Cindy they'd be stopping by.

Cindy was anxious to meet the girl, but when the two of them arrived, wearing black from head to toe, Cindy wasn't too happy about it. Nevertheless, Cindy thought Cassie was well-mannered, she could see the puppy love in Cassie's eyes, and she was happy for her stepson. But Karl didn't care about the girl's googly eyes. He was old school, and he didn't approve of Cassie, not one bit. To him, the dark make-up around her eyes and the whole black getup she wore, made her look stupid.

Karl never could wrap his head around Levi turning "goth." To him, it was a cult. Cindy tried to explain that being goth was primarily a fashion statement, but Karl didn't want to hear it. In his view, this creepy girl was encouraging Levi to become even more of an outcast, which could only mean trouble. He'd hoped Levi would find himself a "normal girl," a girl who could help him "pull his head out of his ass..."

Levi's new "look" was an embarrassment. Karl was concerned about his family name. He worried about what other people would think. To him, *image* was everything. There could be hell going on in his house, but as long as no one knew about it, Karl was all good. But now, with these two kids looking so morbid and out of place, Karl had a problem. He knew Junior would throw a fit if he ever saw Levi wearing a spiked dog collar, he knew his father would blame *him* for not being able to control his son, that his father would look at him as a failure.

Not only were Levi and his girlfriend wearing matching dog collars, Levi went and got his tongue pierced and kept adding more piercings. Levi was a small-framed kid, he was so scrawny, and now with his metal jewelry and black nail polish, he looked like a girl.

His son looked ridiculous.

"He looked like a freak and I was disgusted with him," Karl would later say, "and I could see he was going down a bad road."

Dressed like *that*, Levi would never find a good job, Karl was certain. He wanted to rant at his son for carrying on with this gothic bullshit, but Levi was on his own now. And there was nothing he could do about it.

Cindy, on the other hand, wasn't as concerned about looks. During the brief time she spent with Levi and Cassie, she'd noticed a shift in her stepson. She thought Levi seemed more confident, but all Karl saw was defiance. Levi was acting like the king of the hill, while relying on total strangers to support him.

The kid was living in a fantasy world.

And Karl was waiting for that bubble to burst.

"When I found out that Cassie and her mother lived on food stamps and whatever, I knew Levi was going to run into money problems," Karl would later say. "It was no surprise to me when he came asking for a handout cause the kid couldn't even hold down a minimum-wage job. His first job was cleaning stores and banks at night, he was basically cleaning toilets, but he lost that. He couldn't handle changing toilet paper."

Karl saw nothing but a train wreck ahead, and in a way, he was angry at himself for failing his son. He'd done his best to help Levi with his emotional problems, he'd done his best to coddle the kid throughout the years, and this was the thanks he got. Levi got himself tangled up with "white trash."

Levi was going to screw up his life.

Karl predicted it.

"I knew as soon as they started living together, I knew that Cassie was gonna get herself pregnant, and right away, that's *exactly* what she did," Karl would later say. "I was pissed that her mother wanted to shout it out to the world and celebrate. Cause I knew there was nothing to celebrate. I knew they'd wind up getting a divorce."

But Terri wholeheartedly disagreed. Cassie's mother was busy making wedding plans, and had a list of people to invite. Terri wanted a church wedding, she wanted the kids to get married right away, before the end of the summer and Cassie followed her mother's lead. Levi wasn't sure about the church, he didn't want the wedding to become a whole big deal, but Levi knew how easily Terri could twist people around her finger. He'd learned that whatever Terri wanted, she would find a way to get.

Since the wedding plans were beyond his purview, Levi stayed out of it. The only thing that mattered was that they had a baby on the way. He was about to become a father and couldn't wait to start a family of his own.

Although things were still rocky between him and his dad, Levi was willing to let bygones be bygones and drove over to the farm to share the good news. He was sure that once his parents heard that they were about to become *grandparents*, whatever problems Cindy had with him, whatever fights he'd had with his dad, would be left in the past.

But Karl had a big scowl on his face when Levi broke the news.

Cindy was equally disappointed but she could see Levi's face drop, so she managed to smile and give him a hug. She had no idea that a wedding was in the works so when Levi announced that he and Cassie were planning to get married before her October due date, Cindy's heart sank.

"There's no saying that you have to get married right this minute," Cindy said, trying to dissuade him. "You should really think about it and hold off because you and Cassie don't know each other that well."

"We do!" Levi insisted. "We've never been apart since we met, and we're like, inseparable. It's like we've known each other all our lives."

"But how long have you really known her? Isn't it only a few *months*?"

"It doesn't matter... I love her!"

"What's the rush? Why don't you live with her first?"

"I just told you. We're going to have *a kid*. Why can't you be happy for me, for once!"

"I'm happy that you found someone, and I'm happy that you're in love, but I still think you need to wait."

At that point, she looked to Karl for backup, but his eyes had glazed over. "I'm sure your father agrees that you're too young to be making this kind of decision," Cindy told him.

"If you don't want to come to the wedding, that's fine. I don't care."

"I never said that!"

Apparently, there was no use arguing. Levi had his heart set on marrying the girl, he was angry that Cindy was questioning him, and he stomped out of the house in a huff.

"Terri called me about having a church wedding," Cindy later recalled. "She asked me to put together a guest list and I told her that we were not going to support a big wedding or anything like that. With Cassie being seventeen and Levi having just turned eighteen, I thought the marriage was doomed."

But Terri won out and as planned, the wedding took place that summer.

Cindy and Karl still disapproved, as did their daughter, Kati, who thought Levi was stupid for dropping out of high school, but she and Erin joined the celebration, hoping that everything would work out.

As for eight-year-old Alex, who certainly didn't know it was a shotgun wedding, the boy didn't notice Cassie's baby bump, he didn't realize that Cassie was seven months pregnant because really, it hardly showed. All Alex knew was that he idolized his big brother. He was happy to be part of the celebration.

The weather was perfect that day.

There was everything to be happy about.

The bride wore a thin spaghetti-strap dress with a layer of white chiffon flowing over it, and she carried herself well, her face glowing with the radiance of a mother-to-be. Cassie had a silver band holding her hair in place and she wore silver platform sandals. She looked elegant. She had transformed, it seemed, overnight.

As for Levi, who had taken out most of his piercings for the occasion, the young man looked more handsome than ever. Sporting a cool hairstyle that made his hair stand up like a crown, Levi's eyes sparkled, and he was visibly gleeful. It was probably the happiest day of his life.

As it turned out, the wedding was short and sweet. There was no church involved, and no grand list of guests. Those in attendance were immediate family, and after the short ceremony the reception was held in Terri's small backyard. They had a down-home barbeque with chicken and hamburgers being served, and that was just the way they wanted it.

When the bride and groom cut the white layered wedding cake, their gold wedding bands gleamed in the sunlight, and everything was looking up.

# THIRTY

In the first year of their marriage, Levi and Cassie proved their naysayers wrong. Both had moved on from the goth scene, their perspective had changed, and they were looking toward the future. Levi had secured a decent job at a nearby factory, and by October of that year, when their daughter, Elletra, was born, their bond was stronger than ever.

Elletra absolutely lit up their world, but like all newborns, she also made things more complicated. The three of them were living with Terri, who helped out as much as she could, but the sterilizing of bottles, the night-time feedings, and the middle-of-the-night crying that went with it, brought the stress level in the household to a boil.

Through one of his co-workers, Levi learned that he might be eligible to qualify for a mortgage through the HUD program, the government's Housing Urban Development plan, but Levi had no money saved. The idea seemed preposterous, but incredibly, the timing was right.

In 2003, President George W. Bush wanted to help low-income families become homeowners and in December of that year, he signed the "American Dream Down Payment Act" into law. The new federal policy not only enabled Levi and Cassie to get approved for a mortgage, it also provided them with financial assistance for the down payment and the closing costs as well. Levi and Cassie were literally being handed a piece of the American Dream, and they didn't have to pay a dime.

It was in July of 2004 that Levi and Cassie Karlsen signed the final paperwork for a mortgage on a three-bedroom house that sat on an acre of land in Clifton Springs. It was more than they'd ever dreamed of, not that it was perfect. Nothing ever is.

The house was almost a hundred years old and they'd later discover a score of hidden problems that came with it. The place was in drastic need of improvement, but Levi was brimming with pride on the day he took possession of it. He was certain that his father would be impressed.

The bones of the house were good, which was the most important thing. In time, Levi planned to replace the wood floors and the old appliances, and at some point, he would clean up the neglected basement, covered in layers of filth. As for the kitchen, Cassie couldn't live with it. The walls that were splattered with grease, so at her request, Levi painted the kitchen a bright salmon color which spruced things up quite a bit.

The kids had no money for furnishings, but their credit was good, and thanks to a rent-to-own furniture business, they rented an entertainment center, a couch, two end tables, and two matching recliners. In order to keep their payments low, they decided to rent the bare necessities, renting a mattress and dresser for their room, and a crib and changing table for Elletra.

For the time being, that was enough.

Levi didn't want to tell his father about the house until the cleaning and painting were finished but Karl heard about it through the grapevine. He was annoyed that his son had confided in his Uncle Mike, rather than him, it was quite an insult, but eventually, Karl and Cindy were invited over to take a look at the place.

Unfortunately, rather than being impressed, Karl expressed his doubts about Levi being able to handle the payments. Frankly, he was shocked that the government helped them get any kind of mortgage at all. Levi and Cassie were clueless. They were two kids playing house.

"The minute we got there, I noticed that Elletra was crawling around on the kitchen floor which had dirty footprints on it," Cindy recalled. "Levi was only nineteen at the time and he was more concerned about his pet iguana and his pot-belly pig than anything else. He let the pig run all over the house, that's how immature he was. It was crazy."

After Karl inspected the place, he chastised Levi for taking a mortgage on a house that, in his opinion, needed to be torn down. It wasn't worth anything. Levi had bought himself a headache.

"The first time we showed up at Levi's house, I saw a big old stove sitting outside on the back porch," Karl later said. "They had it rigged up through the back entryway, and I couldn't believe it. I chewed Levi out about that."

Karl would later talk to his brother Mike, who worked as a land surveyor in Seneca County. The house wasn't safe, Karl insisted, telling Mike about the old wiring and the rigged-up stove that were definite fire hazards. Karl wanted a second opinion but Mike believed that his brother was blowing things out of proportion. He assured Karl that HUD wouldn't let anyone buy a house that was unfit for living.

## THIRTY-ONE

It was about a year later, at 2:30 AM on June 17, 2005, that a neighbor saw a big orange glow coming from the direction of Levi Karlsen's house and dialed 911. At the same time, two teenage boys had also seen the blaze and one of them called an emergency dispatcher from his cell phone. As they got closer to the house, the teens saw two cars parked in the driveway, a GMC Blazer and some type of Datsun, and were afraid that the family was trapped. Nineteen-year-old Clayton Keller bravely approached the living room window and broke it, yelling to see if anyone was inside.

It was too smokey for Clayton to see anything, and when he heard no response, he ran back to the car. When he turned to look back, the front porch was on fire, there were two power lines down on the driveway, and sparks were flying. In a panic, the teens decided to drive around the area to find help, but at 2:30 in the morning, their search was useless.

When Clayton and his buddy returned to the scene, the house fire was in full force. Huge flames were flaring out of the broken window but there was nothing they could do but wait. The first person to arrive was a volunteer fireman, and by then, huge flames were bursting through the roof.

"Is anyone in the house?" the volunteer yelled, jumping out of his pickup.

"We don't know!"

It took another ten minutes for the Clifton Springs Fire Department to arrive and by then, the shingle roof had collapsed, the whole left side of the house was ablaze, and two of the exterior walls were compromised.

Laying lines from two separate hydrants, attacking the flames through voids in the roof, it took firefighters over an hour to get the fire under control. After the smoke cleared, firefighters discovered a charred electrical service panel and degraded electrical wires on the north wall. They confirmed that no residents were inside, however, the two-story house was completely destroyed.

Clayton Keller would later give a voluntary statement to the Ontario County Sheriff's Office, telling law enforcement that he knew Cassie Karlsen because they worked at the same convenience store some years prior, but said he'd lost touch with her. Still, because Clayton lived down the road from the Karlsen home, he'd observed that "every once in a while, they would have a small bonfire in their backyard." Beyond that, Clayton knew nothing else.

Two days later, on June 18, 2005, Levi Karlsen was contacted by a Clifton Springs investigator, James Minute, who asked if Levi would come down to the station to give a recorded statement. And Levi was very forthcoming.

"Can you tell me what you were doing from 5PM on Thursday evening, June 16th, through the morning of June 17th?" Minute asked.

"I went to bed about 8:30 AM and slept until 4:40 PM because my wife, Cassie, and her father, Guy Getz, were coming to pick me up at 5PM," Levi told the investigator. "They didn't come into the house, I went out to them, and then we drove to my in-law's place on Prestige Drive in Clifton Springs. And I had dinner there."

"Did you leave your in-law's house at any point last night, other than to go to work?"

"Yes, I did. I had to be at a traffic court appearance at 7PM, so my father-in-law drove me to the Manchester Town Court and waited for me. We got back at about quarter to eight and I stayed there the rest of the night until I went to work."

"Did you drive yourself to work?"

"No. My father-in-law drove me. I punched in at 10:53 PM."

"Okay. And how did you hear about the fire?"

"The cops came to my work around 5AM to tell me about it and then they took me to see my house."

"Do you have *any idea* how the fire started?"

"Not really."

"Did you have smoke alarms in the house?"

"We had one in the basement but I don't know if it worked. We also had one in the kitchen and another one in the hallway, and I think we had one upstairs, but I'm not sure."

"Where were Cassie and Elletra at the time of the fire?"

"They were sleeping at my mother-in-law's house. They stayed there because Cassie is pregnant, and she was having stomach pains," Levi explained. "And also, Cassie doesn't like thunderstorms and it had been storming all week."

"Do you have insurance on the home?"

"Yes. That was required when we got the house. I think it's for $70,000."

When asked if he had anything else to add to his statement, Levi said he did not. He'd told the investigator everything he knew.

## THIRTY-TWO

Later that morning, just before 9AM, an Ontario County Fire Investigator knocked on the door of Terri Getz's home asking to speak with Levi Karlsen. The investigator needed Levi to sign a document giving permission for law enforcement to enter his home and Levi quickly signed his name. The twenty-year-old was exhausted, he hadn't had *one minute* of sleep at all. He was too tired to answer any questions but Investigator Jeff Harloff wouldn't let him off the hook.

"Have you ever had any electrical problems in the house?"

"No. Not that I'm aware of. We had a few outlets that didn't work, but that's all I can think of."

"Did you have any recent home repairs? Or any electrical work done in the house?"

"No. We haven't done anything like that."

"Let me ask you, are you a smoker?"

"Yeah, I smoke, but I only smoke outside," Levi said, "never in the house."

Before he left, the investigator asked Levi to draw a diagram of the layout of the first floor and asked him to mark where each piece of furniture was placed.

When Jeff Harloff returned to the fire scene later that morning, crossing yellow barrier tape with three other investigators, he had a list of things to accomplish:

1) Clear the debris from the first floor living space.

2) Examine the electrical service in the house.

3) Run an accelerant detector test.

Photos were taken of the molten copper wires on the two exterior walls. Electrical wires on the North wall were fused together and beading was evident in the electrical panel box. In the basement, Harloff and his team discovered multiple code violations, including unsecured electrical wires and unprotected junction boxes.

After removing the roofing debris from the living room by hand, investigators came across large holes in the flooring and eventually uncovered the metal frames of two recliners and the metal frame of a couch. Apart from that, there was nothing left to find. Most of the furnishings on the first floor – had turned to ash.

The charring was most severe in the living room, the dining and kitchen areas were less damaged, and when investigators got to the second floor, they found that the bedrooms were basically intact. However, there was plenty of black soot and just underneath it, they found a few things that concerned them.

The sheets and blankets had been removed from two mattresses.

In the primary bedroom, the large dresser was empty.

And the closets in all of the bedrooms had been cleaned out.

With the cause of fire under scrutiny, Harloff checked around and discovered that another member of the Karlsen family had been involved in a fire. He learned from Charles McCann, the Seneca County Fire Coordinator, that a barn fire in 2002 caused the death of a breeding horse on the Karlsen farm. Looking through the files, McCann found a report stating that the Romulus Fire Chief had ruled the fire "accidental."

Approximately a month later, Investigator Jeff Harloff submitted a seven-page report detailing his findings, concluding that the Clifton Springs house fire seemed to be "accidental in nature." However, the actual ignition source remained "undetermined."

## THIRTY-THREE

Less than four weeks after Harloff's investigation concluded, Cassie Karlsen wrote a letter "To whom it may concern" requesting a copy of the fire report. Cassie panicked. She and Levi had learned that even though their house had been destroyed, the remaining balance of the mortgage was still due.

She needed to sort it out with HUD.

She needed the report ASAP.

Cassie's next step was to apply for disaster relief funds from the government, which FEMA immediately approved. With that money in place, Levi didn't feel the need to reach out to his parents. Their relationship was more strained than ever, and the last thing he needed was to hear his father say, "I told you so."

Two days after the fire Terri placed a call to Cindy, admonishing her for being a bad parent.

"I don't know how you can just *sit there*," Terri said in a huff, "and do nothing, absolutely *nothing* to help the kids!"

"What are you talking about? Help them with what?"

"Don't play dumb with me, Cindy. The whole area knows about the fire. Don't you read the newspaper? They lost their whole house!"

When Cindy hung up, she immediately called Karl at work, telling the front office that it was an emergency. When she told Karl what happened, he was shocked, but relieved to hear that the kids were okay. It was a miracle that none of them were home when the fire broke out.

"How bad was it?" Karl wanted to know. "Do you know if they were able to save the house?"

"I have no idea. All I know is that it happened in the middle of the night and they're staying with Terri for now. Do you think I should drive up there?"

"Nah, cause if it was really that bad, I think Levi would have called. I'll go take a ride over there when I get off from work."

But Karl didn't drive to Clifton Springs, not on that day.

# THIRTY-FOUR

Cindy was hurt that Levi hadn't called the house to ask for help, that he hadn't even bothered to call her to tell her about the fire until days after it happened. She couldn't understand, for the life of her, why Levi and Cassie had become so distant, why they seemed to be harboring bitter feelings. She thought she and Karl had mended fences with them, especially after the birth of Elletra, but apparently, something had gone wrong.

"What happened with Levi?" Cindy asked Karl. "Why did he stop calling?"

"Levi's mad because I gave him hell. I told him that house wasn't safe and I warned him about it being a powder keg. I chewed him out because he put his whole family in jeopardy!"

"Why would you tell him that? Why would you make him feel worse and blame him for a fire that happened when he wasn't even home?"

"Because he knew better, that's why. That place had *hundred-year-old wiring* in it. It was an accident waiting to happen."

"Well, no one got hurt, that's the main thing."

"He should never have bought that damn house in the first place!"

Cindy tried to reason with Karl. She asked him not to be so hard on Levi, but Karl was stubborn. He muttered something about the rigged-up stove that Levi never bothered to fix and was absolutely furious with his son. Cindy tried to change the subject. She reminded him that they were about to be grandparents again, that for the sake of the children, he should let it go.

But Karl had no interest in making peace.

In the wake of the fire, Levi and Cassie received an insurance payout somewhere in the neighborhood of $110,000, of which $70,000 was paid to the bank, leaving the kids with a $40,000 windfall.

Karl thought Levi would use the cash to rebuild his life, but rather than renting a house and buying new furniture, he and Cassie opted to stay with Terri temporarily, which was absurd. Karl could just picture the two of them with their baby trying to squeeze into the back room of the double-wide.

He argued with Levi, chastising him for not taking care of his family, and was disappointed that Levi chose to rent a run-down trailer that sat next to Terri's place. Karl couldn't understand it. The thing was a piece of junk...

When Ivy Phoenix Karlsen was born on October 21, 2005, Cindy and Karl were invited to the hospital, but that was about it. Levi was aloof, as was Cassie. It was obvious that Terri had taken over, and Cindy had to wait for six months before she was allowed to spend time with her new granddaughter. And even then, Cindy was only able to spend time with Ivy at the trailer park, and her visits were truncated.

All along, Cindy reached out to Levi and encouraged him to bring the girls up to the farm anytime, but Cassie didn't want that. She was still resentful of Cindy and Karl, both of whom tried to put a damper on the wedding – both of whom had a negative attitude toward her.

Cassie thought Karl treated her like trailer trash. And she blamed Cindy as well. It would take almost a year for Cassie to ask Cindy to babysit. And Cassie allowed it, not because she liked her mother-in-law, but because the girls were now toddlers and she needed a break from the chaos.

Cindy loved the idea of being a grandmother, she was happy to re-live those days of innocence. Baking cookies and playing "pretend" with Ivy and Elletra reminded Cindy of the old days, of the times she played "pretend house" with Erin and Kati, back when her stepdaughters still needed her.

By that time, Erin was long gone, she was married with two children of her own, and Kati was away at college, living on campus most of the year. Cindy still had Alex at home, but he was about to turn twelve and was at that age where his friends were the most important thing in his life – not his mom.

Thankfully, the bond between Cindy and her granddaughters grew quickly, and by the summer of 2007, Levi was bringing the girls to the farm every other weekend. Cindy spoiled them every chance she got. She always had a surprise up her sleeve, and the girls couldn't wait to see her.

The minute Elletra and Ivy arrived, Cindy would change them into cute little outfits she'd purchased for them, which was their little secret. And Grandma Cindy always had milk and cookies waiting for them, animal crackers which the girls lined up one-by-one, picking out each animal with care. Elletra and Ivy loved being with their grandma and they loved everything about the farm. The horses, the peacocks, and the giant pond full of fish, were absolutely magical.

But back at the trailer park, things weren't as rosy.

Just before Ivy turned two, Levi went to his father and confided that his relationship with Cassie was on the rocks. He said that he'd lost his job, that Cassie had threatened him with divorce, and admitted that they were having huge fights about money.

"What about all the money you got from your insurance?" Karl asked. "What happened to that?"

"It's all gone."

"What the hell did you do with it?"

"Well, you know, I loaned a bunch of money to my friends. And then I also got my Datsun 280Z..." his voice trailed off.

"I told you not to buy that crappy sports car. How many times have you left it here because it wasn't running right? That piece of junk shouldn't be on the road!"

"Well, I got a very good deal on it."

"You know, money doesn't grow on trees. And I mean, what were you *thinking*? You're a father now. You should be putting your kids first!"

Karl told Levi he and Cindy were willing to help with Elletra and Ivy on weekends, that he'd pay for whatever the girls needed when they were at the farm, but he made it clear that no money was going to be handed over. Levi and Cassie would have to fend for themselves.

"Right from the start, I told Levi that he should use that insurance money to get a nice apartment and make sure his family was all set," Karl would later say. "But did he listen? NO! He just sat back and got lazy. He didn't care about his kids cause if he did, he wouldn't let them live in that rat hole!"

## THIRTY-FIVE

Like a character from a Shakespearean tragedy, Karl had numbed himself to the darkness of his own mind. To Cindy and Alex, he feigned compassion for Levi, but deep in his soul, Karl took pleasure in Levi's crumbling life.

It was a tragic waste.

When Levi first split up with Cassie, he was living in a broken-down camper in his friend's backyard that had no heat. Karl had to go out and buy Levi a space heater, which annoyed and disgusted him. Levi had a crappy job where he was making peanuts. The kid wasn't even trying, and Karl just didn't get it.

"You keep coming out here asking me and your mother for a hand-out, but that's not gonna cut it when your divorce papers come through," Karl told his son.

"I'm trying to get my GED. I need to get that first."

"That's just another excuse! You gotta learn a skill, you gotta get experience. A high school diploma ain't gonna help you."

"Well, it's on every job application..."

"Okay, get your GED if you think that's gonna make a difference, and then go out and get yourself a *real* job cause you're gonna be stuck paying child support. And Buddy, we ain't helping you with that!"

Levi sat staring at his father, looking completely dejected.

His father always made him feel like he wasn't good enough.

And he had no comeback.

"Look, we've all been young and stupid," Karl told him, "but it looks like you're not gonna change until you hit the bottom of the barrel."

"I'm already there. I've got nothing left. Cassie won't let me see my kids!"

"Well, I knew that was coming. So, what else is it gonna take? You need to get your act together."

But Levi just stood there with his head hung low.

"In your case, I guess the barrel's gonna have to *fall* on you. I guess the barrel's gonna have to *hit you in the head*, cause that's the only way you'll learn!"

But apparently, Levi didn't learn.

Trouble followed this kid. It always had.

Karl encouraged Levi to spend more time with him. He wanted them to get closer. He told Levi he would help him get through the rough patch. It was the least he could do. And Levi was happy about that, spending every other weekend with his dad, helping out with minor chores.

In no time, Levi became a fixture at the farm.

Being there helped him perk up.

However, during one of those weekend visits, Alex came running to the back barn, screaming something about a fire. Apparently, Levi's 280 Z was smoking up the garage. Alex said he saw thick smoke and Levi took off running, hoping to get there in time to save it.

But it was too late.

When the smoke cleared, the exterior of the car was in good shape, but everything in the interior, from the seats to the door panels, from the headliner to the dashboard, was trashed.

Karl got there just a few minutes after Levi and surmised that an electrical short might have caused the fire. It was typical with these cars, Karl told Levi. It was either that, or perhaps Levi left a cigarette smoldering in the ashtray. Could Levi remember? Whatever the case, the sports car would have to be scrapped.

It was really a shame.

Levi couldn't catch a break.

Not long after the car fire, in fact, within a matter of weeks, Levi called his father with another problem, and this time, Karl wasn't taking delight in it. In fact, he was mad as hell. Levi confessed that he'd met a new girl and had just been told that she was pregnant. And before Levi could say anything else, his father flew into a rage.

"I mean, how *stupid* can you be! *What the hell were you thinking?*"

"It was an accident."

"Who is this girl? Do I know her?"

"Her name is Lisa, you never met her."

"And you think she's telling you the truth?"

"I don't know. She says she hasn't been with anyone else."

"How old is this girl?"

"I think she's nineteen."

"Well, if the kid turns out to be yours, then you're in *real* trouble, buddy. Cause if Cassie's mom ever finds out about it, there's gonna be holy hell to pay!"

"I know."

"It's gonna turn into another reason for Cassie to keep the girls away from you!"

"It was an accident," Levi insisted. "And, I mean, I don't even know this girl. I was just with her for a couple nights, and then *this* happens."

"You're gonna get hit three ways from Sunday when this kid is born," Karl said, sneering at his son. "Cause you're gonna be handing over your whole damn paycheck!"

"She doesn't want anything from me. She wants to keep the baby for herself. She says her parents are gonna help."

"If you think this girl is gonna let you off the hook, *you're dead wrong*. You better hope you can get a DNA test that comes out in your favor, cause if it doesn't, you're in deep shit!"

According to Karl, Levi's illegitimate child, another girl, was born in late 2007, at a time when Levi and Cassie's tumultuous divorce was still in process. Levi made his father swear that he would never say a word about the baby, not to Cindy, not to anyone. And even though Karl loved to blab about bad news, this time, he kept quiet.

There was never a whisper, not a fleeting word to anyone in the Karlsen family, about Levi's love child. No one, other than Karl and Levi, knew this child existed.

## THIRTY-SIX

Child custody is usually the biggest issue in a divorce, and in Levi's case, after his divorce from Cassie was finalized, he wound up with a raw deal. Cassie had done her homework. In open court, she told the judge that Levi was a heavy pot-smoker, that her children's welfare would be endangered if they were left alone in his care.

Her accusation was enough to tip the scales.

Cassie was awarded full custody of Elletra and Ivy.

And Levi would be restricted to "supervised visitations."

Which were ordered to take place at his parents' farm.

It was a devastating blow, and to make matters worse, Levi discovered that Cassie had already found herself a new boyfriend and had moved into his house. She was already thinking about marriage and during one of the supervised visits with the girls, Levi overheard Elletra saying that she had a "fake dad." Levi went to his father, asking what he should do, but that was a mistake.

"Why are you worried about that *fat tub of lard*?" Karl asked. "Believe me, he's no prize. Whenever I go over there, I see him spread out on the couch playing Nintendo with a big bowl of chips on his belly. The girls are never gonna take to him."

"Elletra says they live in a very big house."

"Are you kidding me? It may look big, but I've been in there. The place is a dump!"

But Levi wasn't convinced.

He worried that he would lose his girls for good.

"Look, all the judge needs to see is that you'll be a good parent," Karl told him. "You got to be working somewhere steady. You got to prove you've living in a decent place. No one's gonna let you have kids when you're living in a tent."

"Stop calling it a tent. It's a decent trailer and the only reason I can't have the girls is because of Cassie. She's a liar!"

"Just get your head right," Karl told him. "Cassie's never gonna last with this guy. There's no way. He must weigh 400 pounds!"

Within months, however, Cassie had moved on to yet another

boyfriend, and this time, it was serious. She eventually married the man, giving birth to another two children, and ultimately, Karl felt she made the right choice.

"I hate to say it, but I think she deserved better," Karl would later confide. "I give her credit for putting up with Levi for as long as she did."

# THIRTY-SEVEN

Throughout 2007, Levi was struggling in every way possible. He hadn't landed a job, he was still living at the trailer sitting in his friend's backyard, and on Christmas Eve of that year, he would learn that his closest friend, Brett Werner, was killed in a car accident. The news was devastating. His friend's car was T-boned and then crashed into a steel pole on the driver's side, killing him instantly.

"You know, I've lost good friends over the years," Karl told his son, having a heart-to-heart talk with him on Christmas Day. "But this is what happens in the real world. I mean, Brett made a mistake, he pulled out in front of that car. And it's no one's fault..."

But Levi couldn't be consoled.

His best friend was taken from him for no reason at all.

Nothing in the world made sense.

"You got to try to remember the good times," Karl said, "cause you can't change it. Just try to remember all the times Brett tried to help you out. You know what I mean?"

But Levi couldn't hear a word his father was saying.

"In a way, this should be a wake-up call," Karl told him, "and all you can do at this point, is honor his memory. You should try to make him proud of you, cause that's what he would want."

Of course, Levi could never make peace with it. Brett had become a staple in his life after Cassie was out of the picture, and there was no way to fill that void. And the timing of it all, the fact that Brett died so closely to the anniversary of his mother's death, caused Levi to sink into a full state of depression.

In an effort to make things better, Karl talked to him about getting him a job interview at Guardian Glass. He said he'd be willing to stick his neck out, but Levi would have to get rid of his earrings and all other body piercings. That was non-negotiable.

"Guardian won't hire you if you've got piercings," Karl insisted, "so that's got to go."

"That's not legal, that's job discrimination. *They can't do that.*"

"Levi, you don't get it. Guardian will come up with another reason about why you can't work there. They're not gonna tell you it's because you look like a punk!"

"But nobody cares about guys wearing earrings anymore!"

"Look kid, I'm not gonna let you make me look like a fool," Karl insisted, "and if you *do* get a job there, they're gonna take you into the furnace room, and that furnace runs at just under *three thousand* degrees. And if you're anywhere near it, those metal earrings are gonna start to burn right into your ears!"

It was only after Levi relented that his father helped him get the job.

Levi started at Guardian Glass in the spring of 2008, and he was grateful for the opportunity because Guardian Glass was big-time. The company dominated the glass market in the Western world and it offered great pay and incredible benefits. The plant Levi and his dad worked at produced over *700 tons* of glass a day, and it operated 24/7.

Even though Levi got stuck working the graveyard shift, for the first time in his life, he was proud of himself. He was handling giant robotic machines, loading large sheets of glass onto trucks for transportation, and he was quite good at it.

Having become more practical about things, Levi bought himself a used truck for work, keeping his prized Datsun 280-Z at the farm, and after he saved up enough paychecks, he found himself a decent apartment in downtown Seneca Falls, just a short commute to the plant in Geneva, and about twenty minutes from Clifton Springs.

Levi was on an upswing.

By the summer of 2008, he'd gotten a new lease on life.

The pendulum was moving in his favor.

## THIRTY-EIGHT

Levi was intent on getting his girls back, he believed he'd be granted shared custody, but until then, he made the best of his visitations at the farm. Grandpa Karl would take the girls to see the horses, he'd take them for rides on his tractor, and Alex would join the fun. Levi was glad to see the girls whenever he could, and Cindy was a great care-taker, making sure the house was equipped with whatever the girls needed.

One of Elletra and Ivy's favorite things to do was to play "dress-up" and put on dance performances for the family. Cindy bought glit-tery outfits and cute little wigs for them and every Saturday after dinner, the two of them would dress up in costumes and pretend they were pop stars, holding invisible microphones while singing along with the newest hits. Both Elletra and Ivy were able to imitate stars like Brittany Spears and Miley Cyrus, and it was always a hoot to watch the show, especially for Levi.

Levi considered the summer of 2008 to be one of the best times in his life, because it was then that he bonded with his father in a different way. Karl had lightened up on him, he'd stopped pointing out faults. Levi was killing it at work and Karl was very proud, treating Levi like an equal. Karl was impressed at how capable Levi was, he could see that the job meant a lot to Levi, and his son was excelling.

"Levi found a minuscule defect in a sheet of glass one day," Karl would later brag. "It just caught his eye on the computer and he wound up saving the company a lot of money. I'd say he saved them *millions*, cause they shut down production for three days and got rid of the whole lot."

Levi beamed with pride when his supervisor told him how incred-ible it was that he'd caught the defect, saying the chances of that were one-in-a-million. Karl later learned that Guardian rewarded his son for it, handing Levi a substantial bonus that summer. Finally, Karl thought, his son was on his way.

But unfortunately, as soon as Levi had some extra cash in his pocket, he couldn't spend it fast enough. Levi started bumming around with his old crowd again, a bunch of ne'er-do-wells as far as Karl was concerned, and had reverted back to his old ways.

"Levi wound up wasting a lot of that money on God knows what," Karl would later say. "And I asked Cindy about it, cause I suspected Levi was spending money on pot, and she agreed with me. We both thought Levi was wacked out half the time."

Since Karl couldn't prove it, he decided to take a ride over to Levi's apartment, unannounced, ready to read Levi the riot act. But Karl found Levi home alone. He was getting ready for the night shift, and other than a pile of pizza boxes and some crumpled soda cans, nothing seemed amiss. There was no marijuana out in the open. There wasn't a whiff of it in the air.

"All these little 'friends' of yours are gonna take you down," Karl warned him. "And you know why these so-called friends have come back around? It's cause they take you for a *sucker*. If you don't get rid of them, they're gonna stick on you like flies on shit, until all your money runs out!"

"That's not true!"

"If you get yourself in trouble with these dumb asses, *I'm* the first one you'll ask to bail you out and I'm not gonna do it. Just know that right now."

Not long after that brief confrontation, Levi's apartment building was condemned. There had been a fire that originated in one of the corner units and it was thought to have been caused by a careless cigarette smoker.

It was unfortunate that firefighters weren't able to salvage the building, but thankfully no one got hurt. Everyone got out safely, including all the family pets, however, the damage was done. Overnight, everyone who lived there, found themselves homeless.

Months later, in the fall of 2008, Levi would rent another apartment in Geneva, but in the interim, he tucked his tail between his legs and went down to the farm, asking if he could move back home for a while, just until he got back on his feet.

"Now, look where you're at!" Karl howled. "You have nothing! You know, when I was your age, I was in the Airforce. I wasn't screwing around!"

Karl thought Levi, at age 23, was too old to be running back to mommy and daddy, but he went along with whatever Cindy said, and she agreed to let Levi move in, under one condition: he would have to turn over his entire paycheck and he'd let *her* budget his money while he was under her roof.

"This is it, Levi," Cindy told him. "I'll help you with your bills and I'll help you learn how to budget, but if you're going to live here, you're going to have to follow our rules. You can't just do whatever you want."

"Okay, I agree with that."

"You're not going to be able to come in and out of here in the middle of the night. That's not how it's going to go."

"Okay. I understand."

"And you don't have to pay rent, but you'll have to do chores," she told him. "You'll have to help your dad cut the hay for the horses and clean out the stalls, and your dad will probably want you to mow the lawn too, and I don't want to hear any complaints."

"I can do that."

In the end, the arrangement with Levi turned out to be a good thing. Cindy was strict with his money, she had always been a penny-pincher, and she managed to help Levi save enough so that he could start over again. And as for the relationship between Levi and his father, the two of them had become very buddy-buddy for the first time in his life.

On their days off, the two of them would spend hours down at the barn, and Levi was slowly opening up. Levi felt comfortable with Karl, and was confiding about things he shouldn't have...

For starters, Levi admitted that he wasn't current with his child support payments. He knew Cassie was calling him a "dead-beat dad," and was trying her best to turn their daughters against him. He confided that he had deep concerns about the future, saying he didn't trust Cassie as a role model, that he worried about her being a bad influence on the girls. More than anything, Levi told his dad, he was concerned that Cassie would cut him out completely.

After a lifetime of distance, Karl sympathized with Levi, and it felt like they were developing a *real* relationship.

"Something had been missing our whole lives," Karl would later say, "but now he was a totally different person. We had a friendship, which we never had before. Levi just totally changed. He changed with Cindy, he changed with me, and I mean, he'd come to the house and he'd be all smiles. He was happy and laughing a lot and he'd finally put the past behind him, losing his mother and all that stuff."

Karl could see that Levi was living a new life.

It was like he'd been reborn.

## THIRTY-NINE

One of the best perks at Guardian Glass was their medical insurance program, which, according to Karl, was quite extensive. He claimed that once a year, Guardian paid everyone *overtime* to sit down with medical experts, including dietitians and physical therapists, to help them meet their health goals.

"They did everything to make you healthier," Karl recalled. "If you needed to quit smoking, they'd help you with that. If you needed to work out, they'd get you a trainer."

"They'd bring in different chefs," Karl claimed, "they'd get you meal plans and whatever, because the healthier you are, the cheaper the medical insurance is for them."

And it wasn't just medical insurance that the company handled. Guardian Glass also helped employees with their retirement plans and life insurance, setting up appointments for employees to meet with an approved list of financial advisors.

"After we did the health care thing," Karl later said, "we set up an appointment with a retirement insurance guy."

"And I talked to him about my own investments," Karl continued, "because I decided to have mine changed from a Roth IRA to an annuity. The insurance guy told us it was a better investment and we talked about it. Levi wanted to switch to an annuity, and he wanted life insurance and stuff like that."

Karl had convinced his son that life insurance was important. With it, Levi could prove to the court that he was serious about taking care of his girls, that he was concerned about their future should something ever happen to him.

# FORTY

It was a bitter cold day in November, right before Thanksgiving, when Karl and Levi met in Seneca Falls to take care of some banking business. The two of them walked into Five Star Bank shortly after 9AM. They needed to get something notarized and were in and out of there quickly. Levi had promised to work on his dad's old truck that morning and said he'd get to the farm within the hour.

"I offered him a few bucks to come out and help me out with the truck," Karl later explained. "We were going to change the transmission lines and the brake lines because it was leaking oil, and he wanted to come out anyway because his truck wasn't working right. It was freezing up."

Karl told Levi that he and Cindy had a funeral to attend that afternoon and asked that he get to the farm no later than 10:30. Cindy's Aunt Alice had passed away and the funeral service was being held in Penn Yan, about a forty-minute drive from Romulus.

Levi was usually punctual, but he was running late that morning, and when 10:30 came and went, Karl was getting antsy. Karl still needed to get showered and changed and the clock was ticking. Thankfully, Levi got there 15 minutes later, so Karl had time to go out to the garage to show him what needed to be done. Cindy wasn't thrilled that Karl pushed everything to the last minute, but Karl was a quick-change artist. He told Cindy to wait for him in the car and within a matter of minutes, he appeared in the driveway wearing a crisp white shirt and a sports jacket. He had pre-heated the car so Cindy wouldn't be cold, and then just as he opened the driver's side door, Karl realized he needed to let Levi know that they were leaving.

He'd only be a minute.

When they finally got going, the car ride was smooth and Cindy relaxed because they were making good time. But halfway to Penn Yan, Karl discovered a stain on his shirt and insisted on making a quick stop at the Walmart Supercenter in Geneva. Cindy was annoyed, she tried to talk him out of it, but Karl had already turned the car in that direction. He couldn't go to a funeral with a black grease stain on his shirt.

Once again, Karl was aggravating her. He never made things easy. But as promised, within minutes, he emerged from Walmart with a smile on his face, having changed clothes in the store. Karl threw his old shirt on the back seat and quickly put the car in gear, and they arrived at Weldon's Funeral Home just in time.

Cindy's sister, Bev, was waiting for her in the foyer and she scurried them to the seats that she'd reserved. The funeral service for their Aunt Alice was so incredibly touching that almost everyone in the room got teary eyed. But afterward, the mood lightened when people went to the "celebration of life" ceremony which was held at the Moose Lodge.

Karl knew Cindy's aunt, she was a sweet little old lady who'd always been nice to him, and he'd been very respectful at the funeral home. But once the Celebration of Life got underway, Karl went into his jester-mode, making sarcastic comments about the other guests, picking on people's weight, picking on people's outfits, making everyone at his table feel uncomfortable.

Karl liked to poke fun, especially when it was inappropriate.

He also made self-deprecating remarks, saying anything to get a chuckle.

"We sat at the same table and talked for about a half hour," Bev recalled. "I know he told a few jokes and we all laughed. I don't remember exactly what was said, but I know Karl was his same old self. That's just how he was. He liked being the center of attention."

Karl was lingering at the Moose Lodge. After cake and coffee, he continued his chat with Bev and her husband, Doug, which wasn't unusual because Karl loved to hear himself talk. To say that he was a blabber mouth would be an understatement.

But Cindy didn't want to stay any longer than necessary. She was emotionally drained and was annoyed that Karl was jabbering when all she wanted to do was get back home.

They arrived back at the farm around 4PM and were both surprised to see Levi's truck still parked out front. Karl couldn't imagine why Levi would still be there. He should have been gone hours before.

Cindy went into the house to let the dogs out who were barking like crazy, and Karl went out to the garage to see what Levi was up to. Within minutes, Karl appeared at the kitchen window, banging on the glass and screaming like a madman, telling Cindy to call 911. She couldn't understand what else he was saying, it was unintelligible, but Cindy saw the look of terror in his eyes.

"Seneca County 911 Center, what's the location of your emergency?"

"I live at 855 Yale Farm Road and we need an ambulance…"

"Okay. Can you tell me what's going on?"

"The truck fell on my stepson!"

By then, Cindy had taken the house phone with her and she was headed to the garage.

"The truck fell on your stepson?"

"Yes. And we just got home. We've been gone since noon and OH MY GOD! He's pinned under the truck!"

"He's already stiff," Karl told her. "He's been under there for a while."

"When I first saw Levi, I touched his leg and it was so cold," Cindy would later say. "But I couldn't let myself think he was dead. I just couldn't believe it."

While Cindy was still on the line with 911, one of their neighbors arrived. It was Mike Passalacqua, a friend of the family who was also a firefighter. Mike heard the 911 call come in over his scanner and was running toward the garage.

When Karl saw his neighbor, he began screaming Levi's name at the top of his lungs. Mike could see there was no use in trying CPR and he reached out to hug Karl, but before he had the chance, Karl dropped to the ground and was rolling around on the dirt floor.

"Oh my GOD! His fucking chest is crushed!" Karl was howling. "He's not breathing!"

The emergency team responded quickly, and Cindy watched in disbelief as the EMTs carefully moved Levi onto a stretcher, intubating him before lifting him into the ambulance. Levi's pupils were dilated, his face was a strange color of blue, but the EMTs weren't ready to give up on him.

Karl's sister-in-law, Jackie, arrived on the scene just after the ambulance pulled out of the driveway and when she heard what happened, she offered to drive them to the hospital. Jackie was a nurse, she was trained to have grace under pressure, but this was *her* nephew. This was the boy she'd watched grow up. Jackie was aware of Levi's painful divorce, she'd witnessed her nephew's depression, but she knew that Levi was getting his life back on track...

Levi had been taken from them in the most horrible way.

And none of them could believe it.

The drive to the hospital was surreal. It was like a horror movie.

Levi Holger Karlsen was pronounced dead-on-arrival at the Geneva General Hospital. Doctors ruled that he'd suffered a "massive chest and abdominal trauma" as the result of an accident. The 23-year-old male, the son of Karl H. Karlsen and Christina Alexander, the father of two precious girls, was gone forever.

The coroner, Dr. Jason Feinberg, would later certify that Levi's death was caused by "a truck falling off a jack." Ultimately, Seneca County law enforcement deduced that the accident occurred because the jack Levi used wasn't built to hold up a farm truck. The jack was too flimsy, it was too narrow, to hold up a 3,000-pound vehicle. By trusting it, Levi made a fatal mistake.

## FORTY-ONE

Levi's chest was crushed, it was literally caved in. When the medics removed his shirt, his upper torso looked like it had been hollowed out. It was ghastly.

"Once we got to the hospital everything was a blur to me," Cindy would later say, "I know they put us in a special waiting room that's meant for families who have lost a loved one. I know I called Terri and told her what happened so she could be with Cassie and the girls when they found out."

Cindy also made a frantic call to Bev, who was shaken up by the news, telling her sister she would get to the hospital as fast as she could. Then there was Mike, who was on his way to the ER and was bringing Alex with him.

It took some time for the hospital staff to prepare Levi's body for viewing. They had to remove the tube from his chest before Karl and Cindy would be allowed to see him, and Cindy was holding her breath as she walked into the room.

"It was hard for me to see Levi like that," Cindy would later say. "I touched his arm and kissed his cheek and said my good-bye to him. Then I had to go back to another room to wait for Alex. I knew the news would rock his world."

"When Alex got there, he asked if Levi was alright and I told him no. Both of us were crying and I took him aside where I could console him privately. Levi's death annihilated him."

Karl sat in the room with Levi for over an hour, taking a short break to go see Alex. While in the waiting room, Karl had tears in his eyes when he saw three of his brothers had come to console him. He managed to give them a weak smile and then in a flash, he disappeared.

He needed to get back to Levi.

"I just stood there looking at him and a million things ran through my head," Karl would later say. "I guess I was reliving his life from the time that he was a baby. I remembered when he had mumps and he didn't complain a bit. I just stood there rubbing my fingers through his hair. I was holding his hand and talking to him."

Karl never came back to the waiting room. He was so distraught that finally, Cindy went back to the room where Levi's body was. She was worried about Karl. It was unhealthy for him to stay with Levi's corpse for that long. She could see his eyes were red from crying, and as she approached him, Karl held up a small plastic envelope, dangling it in front of her.

"You don't want to know where *one of these* came from," he told her.

And he was right.

Cindy didn't want to know.

It contained Levi's private piercings, hidden from view.

"I immediately realized that he meant Levi's penis," Cindy later said, "and I thought, no, I didn't need to hear that."

Cindy got out of there, it was just too much for her, but one of the nurses stopped her and explained that they were running out of time. Apparently, Levi had checked off the box on his driver's license stating that he wanted to donate his organs, something Cindy nor Karl knew anything about.

"You're going to have to leave the room any minute," she told Karl, "because they're waiting to remove the corneas from Levi's eyes."

"Who's waiting? What are you talking about?"

"Levi signed up to be an organ doner, and they just told me that they need to put his eyes on ice, and they can't wait much longer."

"They want to take *his eyes* out?"

"They said they have the paperwork ready."

"But they can't do that!"

"Karl, it's what Levi wanted. And they're not taking the whole eye. They're just taking the corneas."

Karl grimaced at her, then looked toward his son for the last time, unable to say goodbye. When he finally got out toward the waiting room, he was too busy to talk with anyone, not his brothers, not even Alex. He didn't even look to see who was still in there because he had calls to make.

The first person he needed to call was Erin, he'd asked Cindy to let him do that, and he'd already let too much time slip by. At the time, Erin was stationed in Georgia, she was still in the Air Force, and of course the news of her brother's death came as a total shock. Erin's voice quivered when she asked her father how it happened. She was horrified to hear the details, and had to stop him from saying anything more, telling him she'd book the first flight she could get.

Karl also would give the news to Kati, reaching her in downstate New York. Kati was now a Park Police Officer working at Harriman State Park, and when she first picked up the phone, she didn't quite believe her ears. Her father didn't sugar-coat it, he didn't waste his breath. Karl told her that Levi was dead, that there was a terrible accident, and said she should get home right away.

At first Kati refused to believe it. She was hoping it was some kind of joke, but she too, would be heading home, to attend her brother's funeral.

The only other person left to call was Colette, but Erin had relieved Karl of that duty, sending an S.O.S text to her aunt in California. Colette immediately responded, worried that something happened to one of Erin's kids, and when she heard that it was Levi, that it was her nephew who died, Colette could hardly speak.

Levi was so young. It seemed impossible that he was gone. Colette couldn't wrap her brain around it. When Erin told her about the truck crushing him, Colette couldn't bear it. It felt like the walls were caving in, like all hell was breaking loose, and she hung up quickly, letting Erin know that she'd make arrangements for Art and Arlene to fly out with her as soon as possible. However, it was only Arlene who made the trip with Colette.

Art just couldn't handle it.

When he'd heard about the accident, something inside him churned.

Art couldn't stand the thought.

It was happening all over again.

## FORTY-TWO

Most people are familiar with the phrase "the Midas touch."

In modern times, the phrase is meant as a compliment. It refers to people who have the uncanny ability to make something from nothing, who can turn whatever they touch into gold. But the Greek myth from which this phrase stems has a dark irony within it.

As the story goes, King Midas was a man who had everything he could wish for. He ruled his kingdom from an opulent palace where he lived with his beautiful daughter, Marigold, but the King wanted more. Midas was obsessed with money, so much so, that he spent most his time counting gold coins, sometimes covering his body with gold.

There came a day when King Midas did a good deed for the Greek God Dionysus, and for his kindness, the God granted him one wish. "I wish everything I touch turns to gold," Midas told Dionysus, and when he woke up the next day, he was elated to find that when he touched the table next to his bedside, it instantly turned to gold. In a frenzy, Midas went running through his palace and touched all his possessions inside, then went outside, touching everything in his gardens as well, overjoyed that everything, indeed, became solid gold.

However, King Midas would soon discover that this blessing was a curse. When he went to eat a grape, it also turned to gold, as did his bread and water. When he came upon his daughter, he found her crying in her rose garden. Marigold was unhappy with the golden roses, which had lost their fragrance and beautiful colors. Without thinking, King Midas went to comfort Marigold, and when he hugged her, his beloved daughter turned into a golden statue.

And King Midas could not change it.

He could not turn her back.

With fear in his heart, the King prayed to the God Dionysus, promising to let go of his greed, promising to be grateful and generous. For having repented, Dionysus reversed the King's wish, and his precious daughter came back to life...

* * *

Of course we assume that every parent who's lost a child would give anything to bring them back, but curiously, Karl never once mentioned that he wished Levi was still alive. Karl cared much more about Levi's keepsakes. There was Levi's favorite baseball cap, which he gave to Alex. There was Levi's cherished guitar, which he ceremoniously handed to Alex as well.

When Karl found a book of Levi's original poetry hidden in the closet of his old bedroom, he brought it to Cindy with tears in his eyes. He told Cindy that he wanted Kati to have the book of poetry. He hoped that Levi's poetry would help heal Kati's heart, that it would make her feel close to him and be a comfort to her. And Cindy was happy that Karl found the small leather-bound book.

Losing Levi brought out a different side of Karl. He was absolutely devastated. Karl had everyone feeling sorry for him and he loved the attention. More than anything, Karl loved being fawned over. Without a doubt, Karl played the role of the grief-stricken father magnificently. His pain seemed real...

As the family prepared for Levi's funeral, there were countless streaming tears. They were all heartbroken, everyone in the family was shattered. It was a heavy, heavy, time for Karl and Cindy, and it was even heavier for Erin, Kati, and Alex, who could not understand why their brother had been taken from them.

Not one of them could imagine that anything was amiss. The idea that their father had an agenda, was a thought that never crossed their minds. At least, not then.

But Karl knew. And he was elated.

For him, Levi's death was a means to an end.

Very soon, Levi would become solid gold.

# FORTY-THREE

## <u>LAST WILL AND TESTAMENT</u>

---

I, Levi Karlsen, leave Karl Karlsen as power of attorney and executive of my will. I leave all assets to Karl Karlsen to distribute as he wishes to my daughters Elletra and Ivy Karlsen.

My wishes are not to remain on any life support and that my organs are to be donated. I would like to be cremated and my ashes to be buried as my parents see fit.

---

**Levi Karlsen**

Signed and stamped by Notary Public Michael Scaglione
State of New York, County of Seneca, on November 20, 2008

# FORTY-FOUR

The night Levi died, Karl spent over two hours on the phone with the organ donor folks, keeping Alex and Cindy waiting. Cindy did her best to console Alex on her own, and she was headed for a crash. She needed Karl to be her safety net, she needed Karl to console her, but the man didn't have it in him.

"Karl should have been right there beside me," Cindy would later say. "It shouldn't have mattered that I was Levi's stepmother, I was still his *mother*. But the only person Karl was concerned about was himself."

"He was actually annoyed that I was consoling Alex," Cindy recalled, "because he thought all my attention should be on him."

Karl wanted to be the point person for the funeral. He let Cindy handle the church arrangements but he was in control of everything else. The first item of business was to call Guardian Glass because the company had a $15,000 life insurance policy on each of their employees and Karl needed the cash to pay for the flowers, the minister, and whatever else, calling the director of the Covert Funeral home in Ovid to set up the calling hours for Levi's wake.

The other thing Karl needed was a suitable urn for Levi's ashes, but he'd lost the nerve to do that. He'd asked Cindy to look through a cremation catalogue, watching her page through images of urns, boxes, and caskets, which made him feel queasy. Karl was happy to let Cindy take care of that, and she'd chosen a simple wooden box with a metal plaque that had Levi's name engraved on it. Cindy had talked to Karl about writing an epitaph, but he couldn't come up with an appropriate phrase to memorialize his son.

Karl couldn't find the words...

Cindy would later place Levi's ashes on the mantle in the living room where all of them could see it, and Alex was happy about that, as was Karl. Levi's ashes were to be split evenly, half to be buried in the Mount Green Cemetery in Romulus (where the Karlsen family had plots) and the other half to be given to Christina's family to take back to California where they would lay Levi to rest next to his mother.

Cindy also ordered five cremation necklaces from the catalogue which she would later give to her remaining three children, and to Elletra and Ivy as well. Cindy thought she was doing a good thing. She felt the kids would want to have a part of Levi with them, always, but when she told Karl about it, he got angry.

"What the heck was *Cremation jewelry*?"

He'd never heard of such a thing.

*What was she thinking?*

On the day of Levi's wake, the Covert Funeral Home was jam packed, it was standing room only. Levi died so young, and the way he died was so tragic, it touched the whole community. Half the town showed up, and as expected, the entire Karlsen family was there, but as for Christina's side of the family, only two people were in attendance, Colette and Grandma Arlene.

Cindy was hurt that Art decided to stay home, as was Karl. They knew Levi had a good relationship with Grandpa Art. Levi had gone to visit his grandfather more than once throughout the years, so the fact that Art chose not to attend... didn't make any sense.

But Cindy was too caught up in the moment to give any more thought to Art. She was overwhelmed by the amount of people who crowded into the funeral parlor, and between greeting Levi's saddened friends and greeting everyone in the family from both sides, she had her hands full.

Everyone was in shock.

It happened so quickly, so unexpectedly.

Cindy became emotional when three of her co-workers from Connie's Diner came through, and she broke down in tears when she saw her sister, Bev.

Sitting next to Cindy was a shrine she'd put up on a table in the vestibule. It was filled with photos that marked Levi's milestones as a kid, that marked Levi's happiest days as a man, all of which stood in the shadow of a large photo of Levi smiling proudly, with his arms wrapped around Elletra and Ivy. And the shrine was nice, but it didn't really do much for Karl. Levi's tragic death had been reported in the Finger Lakes Times, which was more important to Karl because it meant there would be a slew of callers. He liked the idea of it being a big affair.

There were many callers who Cindy didn't know, and at one point, a well-dressed gentleman introduced himself to her as Levi's financial planner, shaking Cindy's hands profusely. Cindy had no idea that Levi had a financial planner, she thought she heard him wrong. But he was just one in a sea of strangers who Cindy met for the first time that day, and she didn't have time to ask questions.

There were dozens of callers who introduced themselves as Levi's elementary school classmates, as Levi's friends from his soccer team, as his friends from *Bible* camp, all of whom were now young adults. Levi's friends related their fond childhood memories and said that, beneath his shyness, Levi was kind-hearted and generous.

It was amazing, how many lives Levi touched...

Cindy thought about Levi's generous gift to science, she hadn't anticipated that, and she thought it was a heroic act on Levi's part. She later learned that the corneas of Levi's eyes were transplanted into a 14-year-old girl who was partially blind. She and Karl received a letter from the girl, thanking Levi for giving her the miracle of sight.

It was a letter that Karl proudly read aloud to Alex...

And then later threw away...

## FORTY-FIVE

A private funeral for Levi Karlsen was held at the Presbyterian Church In Geneva the following day, where there was an ongoing drama between Cindy and Cassie. Cassie's mother had purchased a flower arrangement from the girls with a sash across it that said, "Beloved father," but the additional arrangement that Cassie wanted to purchase, one that would say "Loving Husband," was something neither Karl nor Cindy would permit.

Levi had been at war with Cassie until his dying breath.

But still, Cassie felt slighted. What they were doing, she felt, was wrong.

And that decision caused an uncomfortable rift at the church.

Luckily Elletra and Ivy, at ages 3 and 5, didn't fully grasp what was going on, exactly. In fact, the girls weren't entirely sure why they were there. They knew their daddy was gone, they saw the photo of him near the altar, but the tears that Elletra and Ivy shed came more from seeing their mom and other adults cry. They could not fully grasp the gravity of the situation.

After the minister read a few passages from scripture, Uncle Mike went to the podium to speak about Levi's love for his daughters, saying that he was a kind soul who tried his best to treat others as he would want to be treated. Mike acknowledged that Levi had matured and had become a responsible adult. He also touched on some of Levi's quirks, particularly his addiction to Mountain Dew soda and his ever-present baseball cap that Cindy often threatened to wash, which got a quick laugh.

But for the most part, everyone in the family was sobbing.

It was appalling, the way Levi died.

No one deserved that.

Certainly not Levi.

## FORTY-SIX

Erin had become close to Colette over the years, very close. As a child, whenever Erin got reprimanded, she called her aunt to cry and complain about it. And most times, after she got off the phone with Colette, she'd come back at Cindy with a smart mouth.

"You're not my mother!"

"You can't tell me what to do!"

By the time Erin turned sixteen, things had gotten so tense between Erin and her stepmother that Cindy felt compelled to send an email to Colette, asking her, in a round-about way, to stop bad-mouthing.

"Every time you talk to Erin, she gets disrespectful," Cindy wrote. "You think you're helping her, but you're making it worse."

Erin idolized Colette, so much so, that she couldn't wait to join the

Air Force so she could follow in her aunt's footsteps. At some point in time, when the two of them were stationed in California, their bond solidified and Erin began to reveal bits and pieces of her memories of the fire. With Colette's prodding, new details came into focus. There were many things she'd repressed that began to fill in pieces of the puzzle.

But Cindy was never privy to any of that. Cindy knew Colette and Erin were always buddy-buddy and she attributed that, in part, to their similar personality traits. Both were strong-willed people and fiercely independent. Erin also had the habit of pushing people to the limit, and in that regard, she took after her father. Like Karl, Erin could suck all the life out of the room. Everything was the end of the world, and the death of her brother brought her to DEFCON 1.

As fate would have it, Levi died right before Thanksgiving which held up the date of his funeral. The calling hours at the funeral home shifted to Black Friday, and since Colette and her mother had arrived in Rochester on Thanksgiving Eve, Cindy was expecting them to come to the house on Thanksgiving, but Colette begged off. And that was understandable.

If it hadn't been for one of Cindy's friends, who brought over a fully cooked turkey, the family probably wouldn't have had a sit-down dinner. Of course everyone at the table was sullen. Erin and Kati could barely choke down their food, and Alex couldn't eat at all.

However, by that Saturday, just after Levi's funeral service, Cindy was prepared to host visitors. Colette and Arlene, along with family members on Cindy's side, all came to the house for an early lunch. Platters of cold cuts had been sent over, people had dropped off home-baked pies and other sweets, so they had a decent meal. And after coffee was served, Cindy felt relieved to have gotten through the worst of it. All of them were.

The kitchen table was too small for everyone to fit at, so people took their sandwich plates into the living room, joining Karl to reminisce about Levi. The only people who stayed with Cindy in the kitchen were Colette and Arlene, which was good, because Cindy wanted to have one-on-one time with them before they flew back home.

Cindy really didn't know either of them.

As they chatted, she found Arlene to be somewhat flighty. The woman didn't have much to say about her grandson at all. She never once mentioned his tragic accident. Instead, Arlene dwelled on the minister and how lovely his church service was, which to her, was the thing that counted most.

Colette, on the other hand, was much more outgoing. She was telling funny stories about Levi, she was telling Cindy about Murphys, and she had a lot to say about the summer when Levi, along with Erin and Kati, had come out for a two-week visit. It was so many years ago, but it seemed like yesterday.

"Why don't you come out and see me in California?" Colette asked Cindy before she said her goodbyes.

"We can make a girl's trip of it," Colette said. "We'll go to San Francisco and I can show you around. And I think it'll be good for you."

"I've always wanted to go out there," Cindy told her, "because the kids have raved about it for years."

"We'll plan it," Colette said, giving Cindy a slight hug.

"Sounds good!"

But that trip never materialized.

In fact, the two women never spoke again. Not a single word.

Christina Alexander's beautiful smile lit up a room. (Image: facebook)

Christina Alexander and first husband Allan Teets on their wedding day. (Courtesy of Allan Teets)

Christina finds love again with her new boyfriend, Karl. (People's Exhibit)

Karl happily holds Christina's baby bump. (Courtesy of Cindy Best).

AIC Karl Karlsen is the "Unit Missile Maintenance Team Chief" at the Grand Forks Air Force Base in North Dakota. (Courtesy of Cindy Best)

**I. RATEE IDENTIFICATION DATA**

| 1. NAME (Last, First, Middle Initial) | | 2. SSAN | 3. CURRENT GRADE |
|---|---|---|---|
| KARLSEN KARL H. | | FR101-46-0748 | A1C |
| 4. DAFSC | 5. DUTY TITLE OR TITLE OF ADDITIONAL DUTY | | |
| 44350G | Unit Missile Maintenance Team Member | | |

**II. TYPE OF REPORT** (Check appropriate block in Part A.) (Complete Part B as required.)

| A | ☐ SUPPLEMENTAL SHEET (Complete Part B, Items 1 and 2 only.) | ☒ LETTER OF EVALUATION (Complete Part B, Items 1 thru 4.) | ☐ AF ADVISOR REVIEW (Complete Part B, Items 1 and 2 only.) |
|---|---|---|---|

| | 1. FROM | 2. THRU | 3. |
|---|---|---|---|
| B | 18 December 83 | 28 March 84 | REPORT IS ☒ MANDATORY  ☐ OPTIONAL |

| | 4. REASON FOR REPORT | ☒ CRO 60 OR MORE DAYS SUPERVISION | IMPORTANT ADDITIONAL DUTY |
|---|---|---|---|
| | | CRO LESS THAN 60 DAYS SUPERVISION | PIPELINE STUDENT |
| | | TDY 60 OR MORE DAYS SUPERVISION | GEOGRAPHIC SEPARATION |
| | | TDY LESS THAN 60 DAYS SUPERVISION | OTHER - EXPLAIN IN SECTION III |

**III. COMMENTS** FACTS AND SPECIFIC ACHIEVEMENTS: A1C Karlsen has performed his duties as Assistant Team Chief and topside technician in an outstanding manner. A1C Karlsen's supervisory and mechanical abilities, have on numerous occasions prevented missile maintenance delays. He demonstrated these valuable qualities during a Reentry System (R/S) removal/replacement on Launch Facility G-18. The hydraulic pipe pusher unit used for launcher closure opening and closing failed, causing a maintenance delay. Through A1C Karlsen's superior systems knowledge, he identified and corrected the problem in minimum time by changing components and correcting a pressure leak on the failed unit. This allowed an on-time convoy departure back to the Strategic Missile Support Base. His driving ability of the Payload Transporter Container (PTC) during R/S convoy movements is also highly commendable. A1C Karlsen's rear PTC brakes caught fire, posing a hazard to personnel and equipment resources. He quickly stopped the convoy and extinguished the fire before any loss of resources could occur. He then continued without trailer brakes to a safe haven at Launch Control Facility F-00, where he and his team members crossloaded the reentry system into a serviceable PTC, a task never before accomplished under field conditions. A1C Karlsen's maintenance performances were a key factor in his being chosen to participate in an operational test launch at Vandenburg AFB during April 1984. STRENGTHS: A1C Karlsen's strengths are his mature "can do" attitude, his vast systems knowledge, and mechanical ability. OTHER COMMENTS: A1C Karlsen is an outstanding airman, capable of accepting all responsibilities assigned to him. He is definitely a valuable asset to the United States Air Force. Promote now!

**IV. EVALUATOR IDENTIFICATION DATA**

| 1. NAME, GRADE, BRANCH OF SERVICE, ORGANIZATION, COMMAND, LOCATION | 2. DUTY TITLE | 3. DATE |
|---|---|---|
| DANIEL R. GOSSEN, SSgt, USAF 321 Orgl Msl Maint Sq (SAC) Grand Forks AFB, ND | Unit Missile Maintenance Team Chief | 28 March 84 |
| | 4. SSAN | 5. SIGNATURE |
| | FR471-80-8322 | Daniel R. Gossen |

AF FORM 77   PREVIOUS EDITION WILL BE USED          SUPPLEMENTAL EVALUATION SHEET
AUG 82                                              ☆U.S. G.P.O. 1982-522-051/3291

PEOPLE'S EXHIBIT 60A

In 1983, The USAF commends Karlsen for having "extinguished a fire" when enroute to a nuclear missile Launch Control Facility. (People's Exhibit)

From left to right: Levi, Christina, Kati, Erin, and Karl enjoy a picnic in the beauty of Calaveras County, circa 1988. (Courtesy of Cindy Best)

Left to right: Cousin Blade, Levi, Kati, and Erin celebrate Easter together. In the backdrop, Levi's window is marked, as is the front door, and the living room of their house in Murphys. (People's Exhibit)

Left to right: Erin, Levi, and Kati first met Cindy just before
Thanksgiving in November of 1992. (Courtesy of Cindy Best)

Colette (right) visits with Cindy during her visit to Romulus in
1993. (Courtesy of Cindy Best)

Karl (pulls the reins) while participating in a horse pulling competition, circa 1993. (Courtesy of Cindy Best)

Newlyweds Karl and Cindy Karlsen are married on August 21, 1993. (Courtesy of Cindy Best)

Karl and Cindy's wedding reception was held at the Varick Fire Station where he once worked as a volunteer. (Courtesy of Cindy Best)

Cindy, deep in thought on her wedding day. (Courtesy of Cindy Best)

Left to right: Levi, Karl, Kati, Cindy, and Erin dress in matching outfits for the wedding ceremony. (Courtesy of Cindy Best)

Levi takes cover from the rain, circa 1993. (Courtesy of Cindy Best)

Cindy Best's glamour shot, circa 1993. (Courtesy of Cindy Best)

Levi's elementary school photo, circa 1994. (Courtesy of Cindy Best)

Left to right: Kati, Levi, and Erin (holding Alex) circa 1995. (Courtesy of Cindy Best)

Left to Right: Kati, Alex, Karl, Erin, Cindy, and Levi pose for a family photo, circa 1998. (Courtesy of Cindy Best)

Karl appears to be the All-American dad, circa 2001. (Courtesy of Cindy Best)

Karl plays kickball at a Karlsen family picnic, circa 2001. (Courtesy of Cindy Best

Left to right: Karl, Kati, and Alex have fun at a Guardian Glass employee event, circa 2001. (Courtesy of Cindy Best)

The Karlsen family strikes a pose in front of their Christmas tree, circa 2002. By then, Levi had moved out of the house. (Courtesy of Cindy Best)

Karl and Cindy took the family to Disney World, circa 2001. (Courtesy of Cindy Best)

Alex and Kati pose with The White Rabbit at Disney World, circa 2001. (Courtesy of Cindy Best)

Erin was a cheerleader at Romulus High School. (Courtesy of Cindy Best)

Erin joins the Air Force in 2002. (Courtesy of Cindy Best)

Karl, the "Knight in Shining Armor," poses with his beloved horse, Ginger, circa 2002. (Courtesy of Cindy Best)

Karl with Ginger just weeks before the fatal barn fire, circa 2002. (Courtesy of Cindy Best)

What remains of the barn after the fatal barn fire in November 2002. (Courtesy of Cindy Best)

Firefighters discover remnants of Karl's prized Belgian horses in the aftermath of the fire.  (Courtesy of Cindy Best)

## FORTY-SEVEN

In the days after Levi's funeral, Karl had become increasingly irrational. On the outside, he could keep it together, but inside, he was barely holding on. The neighbors and family who came in and out of his house, the endless flow of visitors, were phantoms who disappeared as quickly as they showed up. Karl had no time for them.

His mood swings went from depression to anger. One minute, Karl would tell people that the accident was nobody's fault, then the next, he would blame himself, getting angry about asking Levi to fix the farm truck in the first place. As for Cindy, she would forever regret that she and Levi had left off on a sour note. Every time Cindy thought about that, she would burst into tears. It was in that particularly emotional time, in the days immediately following the funeral, that Karl came into the house one day with a stack of opened mail in his hand.

"Look what I just got!" he told Cindy, handing over an envelope from Tony Crisci at New York Life.

"What is it?"

"Just read it... It says Levi has an insurance policy for $300,000. I just called over there because I thought it was a mistake, but it's not. Can you believe it?"

Cindy was surprised that Levi had taken out life insurance. She never knew him to be a planner. To herself, she questioned the large amount of the policy, but then Karl jumped in, telling her the amount wasn't that unusual.

"You know when you think about it, it's not that much money. Cause I mean, anything less than $300,000 wouldn't be enough for a family to live on. Not in the long run."

"How did Levi meet this guy? Do you know?"

"From what he just told me, it was at Guardian Glass. He said Levi set up an appointment to go into his office a few months ago."

And with that, Karl snatched the letter from Cindy's hands. He was going to take a quick ride to Tony Crisci's office to straighten this out.

"Will the girls get that money?" Cindy wanted to know. "Is it going to be put in a trust?"

"That's what I'm gonna find out..."

It was a few hours later that Karl returned with a look of shock on his face, reporting that *he'd* been named the sole beneficiary.

"What about the girls? You mean they aren't named?"

"No, it's just my name on there. The guy explained that Levi didn't want to name Elletra and Ivy as beneficiaries because Cassie would become the custodian of the money, and he didn't want her to have any access to it."

"But why was Levi getting insurance? Did this guy say why?"

"He said Levi wanted it so he could look good to the court."

It was a short time later, no more than two weeks after Levi's funeral, that Karl approached Cindy with another letter from New York Life, this time explaining that Levi had taken out an *accident rider* on his insurance policy in the amount of $400,000, bringing the total amount of his insurance to $700,000.

"Are you serious?"

"Look, it says it right here," Karl told her, pointing to the dollar amount.

"Holy cow! That's *a lot* of money!"

"I know. But what happened was, Levi added that rider as a backup plan. Pretty much everybody at Guardian adds a rider in case of an accident, cause it's only a few extra dollars a month."

"You know I've got one on myself too, cause it can be real dangerous working with heavy glass. You never know what could happen..."

After Karl had stopped talking, he paused for a moment, waiting to see what Cindy would say. She watched him gazing out the window, looking out at the garage with a solemn expression, and they were both thinking the same thing.

They would always be reminded of the horror Levi suffered. It was staring at them in the face every day.

"It should have been *me* under that truck," Karl suddenly blurted. "It should have been me!"

"Don't say that, Karl."

"I'm better off taking a bottle of pills and choking it down with vodka..."

"Stop talking like that. It's not your fault!"

"You know," Karl told her, "we can't let Cassie find out about this money."

"No?"

"For sure she'd be fighting me. It would be a nightmare."

"I guess you're right."

"I don't want *anybody* in the family to know," Karl told her.

And Cindy shook her head in agreement.

"It's nobody's business," he insisted. "It'll just cause more problems for us."

## FORTY-EIGHT

In the weeks leading up to Christmas, Karl felt slighted.

Visitors were no longer coming to the house.

He'd been brushed aside.

"People are forgetting Levi," Karl told Cindy. "It's like no one cares about him anymore. He's dead and gone and no one is saying a word about it."

"It's not that anyone has forgotten Levi," she assured him, "but the world can't come to a stop. Of course we all miss him, and everyone is still upset about what happened, but at the same time, life has to go on."

"And as far as I can tell, nobody's even gone to visit Levi's grave!"

"You know that's not true, Karl. I just took the girls down there last week and we brought Levi a Christmas wreath. We even took a picture of it."

But Karl didn't want to see the photo.

He was furious, reminding Cindy that no one in his family had gone to see Levi's grave, not even *his parents*. So yet again, his family was disrespecting him. Their blatant lack of concern was a total slap in the face.

"For months and months after Levi died, Karl would come crying to me about Levi," Cindy would later say. "Sometimes he would get so angry about it, I finally had to tell him that the reason people didn't want to keep talking about Levi was because they didn't want to make us feel sadder than we already were."

But Karl didn't get it.

"People are back to their routines," Cindy told him. "Everyone's getting ready for the holidays. It's a busy time of year. You can't expect..."

"Yes, I can expect!" Karl cut her off. "I can expect that my parents would go down there and put some flowers on his grave. But they don't care. Junior cares more about his horses than Levi and it's just wrong!"

But Cindy too, had to move on. She was busy working double

shifts so she could afford the right Christmas presents for everyone, and when Christmas came, she made sure a gift was under the tree for Levi. It was a token gift, a bottle of Mountain Dew and some of Levi's favorite chocolates.

But it was the thought that counted.

Cindy wanted to make it feel like Levi was still with them.

## FORTY-NINE

It was just after New Year's Day, on January 6, 2009, that Karl received a letter from New York Life headquarters that made his head spin. "As you know, since your son died shortly before completing his application for insurance," the letter said, "we are conducting our customary inquiries to further consider your claim."

New York Life was hedging.

Karl immediately called Tony Crisci who explained that the company had a legal right to deny the claim.

"It's true. We have no obligation to honor the policy," Crisci told him.

"You said the policy was active!"

"I'm sure we're going to honor it after the investigation is done."

"An investigation? Are you kidding me? There's nothing to investigate!"

Thankfully, the investigation that New York Life conducted was cursory, and within six months of that call, the insurance company processed the claim, sending Karl a check for $707,000.

The insurance agent would later brag to colleagues that it was a win-win situation because Karlsen had reinvested the money with New York Life. In a company newsletter, Crisci touted his client as "a caring and prudent grandfather," who reinvested the insurance money as "a gift of love" to his granddaughters.

"Two young girls will grow up with the knowledge that their father loved them," Crisci wrote, "that their father wanted to provide for the future."

The insurance agent was proud that they were able to help Karlsen secure "a father's legacy."

"There could have been a myriad of issues for the company to find excuses in honoring this claim," Crisci wrote, "but New York Life chose to do the right thing."

It was on July 22, 2009, when Cindy and Karl sat in Tony Crisci's office to sign off on a list of complicated documents. Cindy trusted the insurance agent, so much so, that he'd convinced her to take $5,000 from her own savings account to invest in an annuity in her name only. He'd convinced her that not only would she earn a high interest rate, she would get the benefit of a lump sum payment when the annuity account matured.

"I didn't need the money," Karl would later claim. "Why would I need the money from Levi when the farm is paid off, when everything is almost paid for? I've got my own insurance. I've got a good job. I've got a great retirement plan. And we're taking vacations, we're living the good life."

The amount Karl invested with New York Life was just shy of $607,000, but Karl made sure that, with so much paperwork flying back and forth, Cindy would be too confused to catch the $100,000 discrepancy. No doubt, the paperwork they signed that day was baffling. It included rollovers of funds into fixed payment annuities, deferred payment annuities, and lifetime annuities, all of which seemed like a bunch of gobbledygook to Cindy.

According to New York Life insurance records, Karl and Cindy invested that money into eight separate accounts.

1. Annuity – Elletra - $70,000
2. Annuity – Ivy - $300,000
3. Annuity – Karl & Cindy $100,000
4. Annuity – Karl - $66,318.29
5. Whole Life – Elletra - $2,669.20
6. Whole Life – Ivy - $2,672.47
7. Annuity – 10 year Fixed – Elletra - $30,000
8. Annuity – 10 year Fixed – Ivy - $30,000

According to the insurance agent...
The money couldn't be touched...
But apparently, there was a loophole...

As Cindy hastily co-signed the paperwork, she had no idea that the annuities could easily be surrendered with penalties. And Cindy certainly didn't realize that among the stack of paperwork she was signing, there were two additional life insurance policies. One on five-year-old Elletra, and one on three-year-old Ivy, each in the amount of $300,000.

"I was making *investments* for the girls," Karl would later claim. "They could borrow from it, they could invest it, they could do whatever they wanted... And if one girl died, the money went to the other."

## FIFTY

It wasn't until the spring of 2010, approximately two years after Levi's death, that Cindy began to ask herself serious questions, horrifying questions, about what happened that day. There were certain details that gnawed at her. That last-minute stop they made in Geneva so Karl could change his shirt now seemed suspect, it wasn't like him to be so persnickety. And the *country music* that was playing on the radio that day, didn't make sense either.

She knew Levi couldn't stand country music, and the more she thought about it, the more confused she got.

Was the radio playing when they left?

She couldn't remember.

Could Karl have done something?

Cindy told herself she was crazy to think that.

Still, she had questions about Levi's life insurance policy, questions she'd tried to suppress that kept getting louder. When she snooped through Karl's paperwork and discovered an article entitled *A Father's Legacy*, it was time for answers.

"It says here that *you* brought Levi in to see the agent at New York Life," Cindy showed him, pointing at the headline. "Is that true?"

"No, it wasn't me. It was Levi who found Tony Crisci."

"So why does the article say it was *you*?"

"The only thing I can think of is that I went with him to Tony's office," Karl told her, "because Levi wasn't sure about what he was doing."

"How come you never told me that you went with him?"

"It wasn't like it was some big secret. I mean, he asked me to go with him last minute, so I went."

"Well, the other thing that it says here," Cindy showed Karl, pointing to a passage in the article, is that Levi died before he was able to take the medical exam. Did you know that?"

"I'm not sure," Karl muttered. "All I remember is that Levi kept blowing it off. He didn't want to go to the doctor. I wound up making an appointment for a nurse to come to our house, but Levi didn't show up."

"What would have happened if Levi took the medical exam and didn't pass it? He might have failed it because he had those throat issues and he was a big smoker."

"Just because he smoked cigarettes, that wouldn't have been a reason for him to fail," Karl assured her. "Those insurance medical exams are almost a formality. Everyone passes them."

Cindy nodded her head, as if she agreed with Karl, and ended the conversation there. But Cindy later checked. And while it was true that smoking cigarettes was not typically a cause to be denied life insurance, she knew Levi's rare throat condition would have sent up red flags.

Levi suffered with a condition called achalasia, which made his throat close up and made it difficult for him to swallow. The condition was serious enough to require two in-hospital procedures where a balloon was put down Levi's throat to inflate his esophagus. At one point, Levi had a serious case of pneumonia and his throat condition was thought to be an underlying cause. Cindy was sure Levi's medical records would reflect that.

Cindy's mind was racing. She started off wondering about Levi, and then began to re-think other mishaps that Karl had been through. There was the accidental death of their dog, Mattie, who got caught under Karl's tractor wheels. Cindy recalled Karl bringing Mattie's stiff body to her, blaming her for letting the dog out while he was working the farm. There was also the mysterious death of Alex's favorite dog, Banjo, who was an older dog having health problems. Karl had claimed that Banjo followed him into the garage one day, and just laid down and died.

And there were other questionable things that happened on the farm, like the time three of their peacocks went missing. Cindy recalled asking Karl about it, asking him to check the entire property, and he came back to report that he'd found them dead. He said the peacocks most likely died from natural causes, explaining there was no way to tell because they had already been picked apart by vultures.

Everything was swirling around in her head, and Cindy couldn't stop backtracking. She thought about Karl's strange behavior with Levi at the hospital. It was creepy, the way he'd attached himself to Levi's corpse. She recalled his hysteria when the nursing staff came in and said they needed to get to Levi's eyes while the corneas were still viable. When Karl heard that, he started wailing. Cindy had to help the nurses *physically* pull him away from Levi's body.

None of it made sense.

Yet all of it made sense.

Cindy couldn't help thinking about the California house fire, wondering if Karl deliberately left Christina there to die. And then there was the barn fire, which killed their beloved Ginger. She recalled that Karl seemed somewhat blasé about it, and she couldn't understand why he seemed so aloof. It was like Ginger didn't mean anything to him at all.

Little by little, the pieces of the puzzle were coming together.

And Cindy couldn't handle it.

The next thing she knew, she started drinking again, big time.

## FIFTY-ONE

At first it was a glass of wine here and there, just to calm her nerves, and then it was vodka. After the big deal Karl made about her DUI years before, Cindy found it surprising that Karl didn't get angry when he found out about it. In fact, he was bringing home pint-sized bottles of liquor for her, encouraging her to drink.

Because of his chronic back problem, Karl established the status of being "permanently disabled" and was now working at the farm 24/7. Still, he continued to work with his horses and was able to manage his chores on the farm. Karl had already gone through back surgery and Cindy thought he was better, but Karl would come in after a day's work complaining about back pain, blaming his surgeon for being inept.

But Karl thrived on the melodrama, and his chronic pain seemed to be an excuse to take handfuls of Vicodin, and garner sympathy from his kids. Whenever Alex was around, he laid it on thick, convincing his son that he needed another surgery. He began to sleep on the couch, wincing and struggling after dinner.

At the time, Cindy felt Karl was faking it.

She had no intention of catering to him.

Cindy had her own issues. Her eyesight wasn't good anymore, she was having trouble driving. When she finally went to see a specialist, Cindy discovered that her eyelids were sagging. She was told that the only way to correct that was with surgery, and she was referred to a plastic surgeon in Rochester.

When she came home with that news, Karl felt sorry for her.

And for some odd reason, he decided to go with her to the appointment.

While there, the surgeon confirmed that the eyelid surgery was necessary, assuring her that the procedure would be fully covered by insurance. However, the plastic surgeon tried to up-sell her. Since she was going to be put under anesthesia, since she would already be under the knife, the surgeon thought Cindy should consider having her whole face done. The facelift would only cost an additional $8,000, which, the surgeon insisted, was a bargain.

And Cindy said she'd think about it.

On the drive home when she and Karl talked it over, he seemed to be all for it. Cindy thought she was too young for a facelift, but by the time she got home, she looked at her face with new scrutiny. Cindy was still in her forties, she'd never focused on her age before, but now she'd become self-conscious. The surgeon had pointed out the droopy skin around her jawline and the jowls she had, which he promised he could easily get rid of.

In the days that followed, Karl kept bugging her to have the facelift, telling Cindy it would build up her confidence. Karl kept saying that it would be silly for her not to have both procedures at the same time, and as for where the money would come from, he suggested they borrow $8,000 from the annuity accounts. They would not be touching the principle, he claimed, they would only be borrowing from the interest that had accrued.

Karl insisted they could pay it back quickly.

Borrowing from interest gained, wasn't such a big deal.

As it turned out, Cindy's surgery was a great success. Not only did she get her peripheral vision back, she looked ten years younger. Karl was thrilled about it and he complimented her to the hilt. He was showering her with affection for the first time in a long time and he was back to his old self. He was suddenly out of pain and was joking around, poking fun at himself.

With a new lease on life, Cindy squelched her sinister thoughts. Karl now had high hopes for the future and Karl was seeking out new business opportunities. He would eventually tell Cindy that he'd seen a promising advertisement in an agricultural flyer, that a "food broker" in New York City was looking for duck farmers, and he wanted to try his hand at it.

Initially, Cindy thought it was a kooky idea. Karl had zero experience in that area and she could just see ducks running all over the farm, leaving their droppings all over the place. But then again, she knew how Karl was. Once he got his mind set on something, he wouldn't let up.

After she'd recovered from the facelift, Karl badgered her. He was certain that it wouldn't cost much to get the duck business started, perhaps $15,000, at the most. All he needed was for her to co-sign for a loan from the annuity accounts and his business would make enough money to pay every cent back.

"I was leery of it because I thought this was just another one of Karl's hair-brained schemes," Cindy would later say. "When I agreed to sign for the loan, I told him it would only be that *one* time. I told him I didn't want any part of it."

By the spring of 2011, Karl's duck business began to thrive and by early June of that year, Karl was able to expand the business, ordering ducklings by the hundreds every month. When Karl went to Cindy, asking her to help him with the books, she reluctantly agreed to handle that end of the business, becoming his partner in "C&K Farms."

Karl's business was a success after all. He'd secured a sweet deal with an Amish family to handle the processing of the meat, and the food broker, Robert Rosenthal, was sending C&K Farms regular checks. The swanky restaurants in Manhattan couldn't get enough of Karl's succulent duck breasts, and later that summer, Karl decided to expand the business further.

By August, Karl was importing thousands of ducklings, not hundreds, and the demand was growing steadily. Every few weeks, Karl would make the hour-plus trip to the Rochester airport where he'd pick up his precious Duclair ducklings. He'd then move the duck-lings to his make-shift incubators, using his old grain silos that had been sitting empty for years.

Karl had always seen himself as an entrepreneur, but his rush for expansion came at a price. It wasn't long before the business started losing money, and when Cindy pressed Karl about it, he blamed the crunch in cash flow on the food broker.

The broker was not paying him his fair due. The guy was demanding more and more duck meat but the payments to C&K Farms were smaller. Karl promised Cindy he would straighten things out, and not long after that conversation, C&K Farms regained a posi-tive cash flow resumed. Karl's duck business was booming, Cindy thought. But that profit wasn't real. Cindy would later discover that

Karl had taken out a $12,000 line of credit against their house to make the business look flush.

But Karl ran through that money.

Out of desperation, he went back to Cindy, telling her he needed to borrow some money from the annuities. Because she'd been handling the books, Cindy already knew the business was in trouble. She'd been getting regular calls from their feed supplier, demanding back payments.

Karl finally admitted that he'd made a mistake. He'd gotten too big too quickly, and he needed her to co-sign for a $15,000 loan, just to tide him over.

Cindy balked.

But she couldn't say no.

Her decision to get that facelift, had come back to bite her.

# FIFTY-TWO

Alex was turning sixteen that summer and rather than having a party, he wanted to take a trip to see his sister, Erin, who'd been inviting him to visit her in California for over a year. Alex had a tight relationship with Kati, who was easy to visit in downstate New York, but with Erin, it was a whole different story. Erin's position in the Air Force had her moving from state to state. She'd moved from California to Hawaii and back again, and up until then, Alex was too young to fly on his own.

As a birthday gift, Karl and Cindy paid for Alex's round-trip ticket to San Francisco, where Erin would meet him and take him to stay with her at the military base in Monterey. The trip was an eye opener for Alex, not only because it was his first time seeing the grandeur of the Pacific Coast, but because for the first time in his life, he was seeing Erin in a completely different light.

Now that her brother was almost an adult, Erin felt it was time to get a few things off her chest. First she talked about simple things. She was so sorry not to have been there for him when he was growing up. She wanted him to know that she loved him and explained that she'd kept her distance from the family because she'd had too many run-ins with their father.

"One day he's gonna turn on you for no reason," she warned him, "because he's got a split personality and he can be sadistic. The day will come when you're going to see it."

"What do you mean, sadistic?"

"Why do you think I left and joined the Air Force? I had to get out of there because he threatened to kill me, and it was more than once."

"You're full of it!"

"No, I'm not. He told me that all the time, and you know why?"

"Why?"

"Because *I'm* the one who saw him beat on Levi," Erin confided. "He used Levi as *a whipping post* and the only reason I never told anyone was because of his threats."

"Stop saying that. You're making it up!"

"Look, this is something I would never lie about."

"All you do is exaggerate! You lie about everything. You always did!

"You don't know how many bad things happened after my mother died," Erin told him. "One time, he picked me up by my neck and slammed me up against the wall. He was holding me up there and he was choking me. I couldn't breathe, and he wouldn't let me down until I said "uncle.'"

"He was *choking you?*"

"Yes, and he didn't only do it to me, he did it to Levi more than once. I saw it!"

"I don't believe you," Alex said flatly.

"I'm telling you, you need to know the truth about dad and Levi," Erin said in a whisper. "Dad has always *hated him.*"

"He didn't hate Levi. I don't believe you."

"You were too little," she told him. "But right after we moved to the farm, I caught him hitting Levi with a broomstick. And he had this *weird grin* on his face, like it gave him satisfaction."

By then, Erin was all worked up. Her face was turning red and she was practically hyperventilating.

"*I'm the one* who saw all the bruises," she shrieked. Because Levi would come to my room and show me!"

"You're a liar!"

Alex knew Erin was an exaggerator, she liked to cry wolf, but now she'd gone too far. He wanted her to stop, he didn't want to hear it anymore, but Erin kept pressing the issue. She was angry at the world.

Erin didn't mince words. She needed Alex to know why she wanted nothing to do with her parents, and made her brother promise not to go home and repeat anything. When she dropped Alex off at the airport, she gave Alex a bear hug, saying that she hoped he'd come back to visit soon... But after his plane took off and the skyline of San Francisco dissolved into the heavens, he knew he'd never go back there.

On the long flight to Rochester, Alex kept thinking about Erin's accusations.

She had rattled off so many things, telling him that Levi had been treated so badly, Child Protective Services came to the house to investigate. But Alex didn't have the faintest recollection of that.

It was typical for Erin to re-write history.

And her version of things was always over the top.

## FIFTY-THREE

It was a sweltering day in late August when Karl got a call from a producer with the *Canadian Food Network* who was calling on behalf of a show called *"Pitchin' In."* Apparently, this woman had gotten Karl's number from his meat broker, Robert Rosenthal, who held him in high regard.

At first Karl thought it was a prank. The woman was fast-talking. But when she asked for photos of the farm and started mentioning possible shoot dates, Karl was elated. Apparently C&K Farms had been chosen over thirty other duck farms, and a shoot date was scheduled for the Friday before Labor Day.

Karl was giddy about it.

This was his big break and magically, his shoulder and back pain had disappeared. Karl hired his Amish workers to help him get the farm ready, asking them to clean out the duck silos, asking them to put in a new fence to create a large open field around them. By having a wide fence around the silos, it looked like the ducks had free range. It was perfect for farm-to-table sales.

Cindy was excited about it too. They didn't have much time to prepare, but she managed to spruce up the place, pruning overgrown bushes and planting bright yellow mums all around the house. She was caught up in the moment and was happy for Karl, who'd worked so hard to get the business running. She hoped his big dreams would come true. She was proud of him for once, and told herself that Karl was a good man.

He wasn't capable of murder.

It was a figment of her imagination.

When the crew from The Canadian Food Network arrived, the show's host, Lynn Miller, asked Cindy to appear on camera as well. Cindy wasn't thrilled about it, she was camera-shy, but she did so with a smile. Alex was also on camera, helping his mother serve a three-course meal comprised entirely of duck specialties.

As the cameras rolled, Lynn Miller couldn't praise Karl enough. She was full of compliments, telling her audience that Karl was "giving his ducks the best life possible." The host emphasized how crucial it was for these ducks to have free range, and how important it was that they were being raised without hormones or steroids.

"Consumers are getting the best duck meat you could possibly get your hands on," the TV host said. And Karl, mugging for the camera, bragged that he was flying in 3,000 Duclair ducklings a month, an impressive number for a small start-up business.

He beamed with pride when the TV host asked him about his "love for his ducks" and touted the "extra special care" with which he handled his ducklings, having dug out two ponds on the property so they could frolic and play freely.

"Everything they eat is as natural as you can get it," Karl bragged. "I let them run wild on the farm. And at night, I play music for them and I keep the lights on, because the more relaxed the bird is, the better the meat is."

Karl's ego blew up when *The Finger Lakes Times* ran an article about the TV shoot entitled, "Romulus Farm Just Ducky!" It featured a prominent photo of him holding a precious yellow duckling, which was perched on his thumb. The new reporter quoted the producer who praised Karl to the hilt, which was exactly what he needed.

"We chose Karl," the producer said, "not only because he has a great product, but because he's a great guy."

"The way Karl describes his ducks, the way he cares about his ducks, it's like he really does care about what's going on here, the producer said, describing Karl as someone who considered the ducklings "his kids."

With the show about to air, Karl was expecting a big boom in business.

"From here on, the sky's the limit!" he told Cindy, "we're about to strike gold!"

But after all the media hoopla was over, Cindy began to realize that Karl had become so completely obsessed with his ducks, he'd forgotten about Alex, about *her*, and about everything and everyone around him. The producer was right, Cindy thought, because Karl did treat his ducks like his children. They were all he cared about, all he talked about. It was obnoxious.

He showered them with love and attention...

Right up to the moment that he sent them off to be slaughtered...

# FIFTY-FOUR

Cindy had become a master at maneuvering Karl, but she'd had enough of his gloating. Living under the same roof with him, was more than difficult. The more he obsessed on his ducks, the more she began to question his character and it wasn't long before her suspicions about what happened to Levi began to haunt her again. Karl was prancing around with his chest puffed up, he was using Levi's money without paying any of it back.

Cindy couldn't stop thinking about Karl getting his hands on Levi's money. He'd waited for over a year to touch it, but now, he was treating it like his personal piggy bank. Karl was spending it with reckless abandon, asking her to sign for additional "loans" from the annuity accounts...always claiming the business was on the verge of success.

She didn't want to think it, but she couldn't help thinking that Karl had planned to get Levi's money, that he had no intention of paying the money back. He didn't care about his granddaughters, she realized, not one bit. In fact, he never bothered to buy the girls a Christmas or birthday present. He never spent a penny to buy them clothes or toys or anything at all.

He left the girls' money alone, just long enough to fool her.

Up until then, Cindy had kept it to herself, but her dark thoughts were festering. They were taking a toll on her. She needed to tell *someone*, she needed someone to confide in, and with trepidation, she called her sister Bev.

Cindy started off the conversation abruptly, telling Bev that she didn't trust Karl anymore. He was hiding things from her, she told her sister. She'd been looking for paperwork, trying to sort out the annuity accounts, Cindy explained, and she thought Karl might have figured that out.

"I caught Karl throwing paperwork in the burn pile out back," she told Bev," and ever since then I can't sleep. I keep running through things in my mind, and I'm starting to think something awful happened."

"Something awful? What's going on?"

"I'm starting to think Karl *did something* to Levi."

"What do you mean? I'm not following you."

"He did something to Levi the day of Aunt Alice's funeral."

"That's ridiculous!"

"I'm telling you, I think he did something before we left. I think Levi had been dead for hours because when I went out and touched him, he was ice cold."

"Of course he'd be cold. It had to be freezing in that garage," Bev quipped.

"Look, I've been afraid to tell anyone, but I think Karl *killed* Levi... and I think he did it... for the insurance money."

"Are you *crazy*? You can't be serious!"

"Karl keeps asking me to take money out of the accounts and I don't think it's legal."

"What accounts? Your joint banking accounts?"

"No. It's from the annuity accounts I told you about. That's why I'm trying to find that paperwork. He keeps asking to take money out of those accounts and I already signed for $15,000, and now he's asking me to sign for another $15,000..." Cindy's voice trailed off.

"He's taking money that belongs to Elletra and Ivy?"

"Yes. And he keeps promising to pay it all back, but lately, he's been acting like the money is *his*. I'm seeing new tractors show up on the farm and other equipment, and when I ask him about it, he lies."

Cindy was at her wit's end.

She wasn't sure she could stay in the marriage anymore.

She confided to her sister that she'd started drinking again, just to calm her nerves. Cindy had gotten so worked up, she was audibly crying, and she told Bev that she was thinking of hiring a private eye.

"There's no telling what he might do if he found out," Cindy said in a whisper. "I mean, who knows? I think he could *kill Alex*, just to get back at me."

"That's crazy talk!"

"I'm telling you, Bev, I'm scared for my life...   Just promise me, please, that if anything ever happens to me, promise me you'll get Alex away from Karl."

Bev assured Cindy that she'd always be there for Alex, but after they hung up, she chuckled to herself. Later that day, when her husband got home from work, Bev announced that Cindy was struggling with alcohol again. She was worried that her sister was slipping back down the rabbit hole.

That's what Bev took away from the conversation.

She thought Cindy was losing it.

## FIFTY-FIVE

When Cindy went to meet with private investigator, Steve Brown, she was shaking like a leaf. It wasn't until the fall of 2011 that she got the nerve to hire someone. She'd made the decision to hire someone who was located outside of Seneca County, worried that if she used anyone in her area, the word could get back to Karl. Still, Cindy felt she was taking a chance, but after making the 45-minute drive to his office in Newark, New York, she'd mustered up the courage to go through with it. Cindy was desperate to find someone she could trust, because at that point, she trusted no one, not even herself.

"When she came into the office, she was quite frail," Steve Brown recalled. "She reiterated her concerns about confidentiality numerous times, and it was obvious that she was nervous."

At first, Cindy hesitated. It seemed she didn't know where to start. She told the PI that her husband "may have committed some horrible acts," and with the PI's coaxing, she unraveled her list of suspicions, starting with the barn fire that killed three of her family's horses in 2002, almost a decade before.

Cindy then told Steve about the house fire out in California, explaining all the circumstances surrounding it, explaining that her husband saved his three kids, but could not save his first wife, Christina. She then brought up the "accidental" death of her stepson, Levi, telling the PI that she suspected that her husband had something to do with it.

She gave Steve a quick rundown of the events that took place on November 20, 2008, confiding that after Levi's death, her husband collected $700,000 from an insurance policy that her stepson had taken out with New York Life.

"Karl told me that Levi named him as the sole beneficiary because he didn't want his ex-wife to get the money," she told Steve.

"And was he married at the time?"

"Well, that's just it. Levi was recently divorced and he hated his ex-wife," Cindy told him, "so I thought it made sense. But now I'm questioning it because Levi didn't leave anything to his children. He has two little girls and that seems weird to me."

"So he named his father as the only beneficiary?"

"Yes. And my husband was supposed to keep that money safeguarded for our granddaughters until they became legal adults," Cindy told Steve, "but I don't think he's planning to turn any of that money over to them."

"How old did you say Levi was?"

"He was only 23, and I don't know why a kid that age would need that much life insurance," Cindy said. "And I'm not sure how he could have afforded it without getting help."

"That does seem odd."

"My stepson had no savings, nothing in the bank that I know of, and that's why I think he couldn't have done this on his own."

"Let me see if I can find out how many premiums were paid to New York Life and try to find out who paid for them."

"You think you can find that out?"

"Let's start there and then we can work our way back."

At that point, Cindy reached into her tote bag and pulled out a thick manilla envelope marked "New York Life Annuity Accounts" which she handed over to Steve, telling him that she couldn't make sense of it. Karl had made all these investments with the insurance money, and she had co-signed her name on everything, but there was no way for her to make sense of it.

There were layers of numbers implicating rollovers of cash.

And Karl had told her the accounts were secure...

But he'd been using the cash to start his own business.

"Cindy didn't know what they actually said," Steve later recalled, "because she'd been told a couple different stories from Karl as to what these investments were. There were inconsistencies. The documents were written in such a way that it would be difficult for anyone to understand."

Two days after she hired Steve, Cindy got a call from him. Steve needed to see her in person, which made her very nervous, and she immediately called in sick at work, ditching her afternoon shift so she could get to Steve's office right away.

Once there, Steve assured her that whatever they talked about was strictly confidential. Then he handed back the large manila envelope and with raised eyebrows, he told her that he was concerned about what the documents said.

"In this paperwork you gave me," he told Cindy. "From what it looks like, these annuity accounts come with significant death benefits."

"Death benefits? What does that mean?'

"From what I saw there, you could be worth well over a *million dollars* to your husband... if something were to happen to you."

"A *million* dollars? How can that be? I never signed anything like that!"

"Well I can't say I'm positive, because it's not worded exactly that way."

"Worded *what way*? How is it worded?"

"Well, it's tricky," Steve told her. "And I'm afraid there's more. I found two life insurance policies in there, written on Elletra and Ivy Karlsen, and you are named as the sole beneficiary on both of them."

Cindy didn't believe him.

It had to be a mistake.

So Steve had her pull out the documents...

And had Cindy read it for herself.

"I don't mean to scare you, I really don't," Steve told her. "I think you're safe as long as you play it cool. Because let's face it, if your husband was planning to do something to you -- it would have already happened."

But Cindy wasn't so sure.

She now had that seed planted in her head.

And she was petrified...

# FIFTY-SIX

In the days to follow, Cindy had only one other person to confide in, and that was Bev. But Cindy didn't want to take chances talking on the phone. She knew Karl was good at sneaking up on her. Instead, Cindy created a new email address and sent Bev a message, telling her sister it was the best way for them to communicate.

**Sent from Cindy Karlsen**
**Saturday October 1, 2011** at 11:50 AM
I told the PI that Karl was not acting nervous at the Moose Lodge. Did you think he looked nervous? I also told him about the fire in California and that insurance was involved but I forgot to tell him about Karl making the kids go outside and watch the Christmas tree burn. I always thought that was odd.

* * *

**Reply from Bev Bergstresser**
**October 1, 2011** at 4:53 PM
I worry about you writing all these emails and leaving them on your laptop. Just be careful. I know Karl doesn't use the computer but it still scares me. Maybe you should go through whatever papers you can while he's not home? I think you should make copies and keep them in a safe place. Actually, if you want, I can come help you go through stuff.

* * *

**Sent from Cindy Karlsen**

**Monday October 3, 2011** at 8:04 AM

I got up this morning about 6:30 and I realized I didn't explain everything to the PI about the barn fire. What makes me suspicious is that the night of the fire, Karl got up and went downstairs. He came back a few minutes later and I asked him where he went and he said he went to the bathroom. I figured he was lying because he usually goes downstairs to sneak ice cream. Then after he came back to bed it was only a few minutes later that he went to the window and said something like "OMG, the barn is on fire." It didn't cross my mind at the time but I realize I need to tell the PI about that."

\* \* \*

**Reply from Bev Bergstresser**

**Monday October 3, 2011** at 10:27 AM

You never told me about him going downstairs that night. Are you sure he was in the kitchen eating ice cream? Can you find the insurance policy that Karl took out on the barn? How much money did he get for that? Do you know? *Is there any way you can ask Karl to take a lie detector test?*

\* \* \*

**Sent from Cindy Karlsen**

**Tuesday October 4, 2011** at 8:21 AM

I wasn't going to tell you this but last night, I told Karl that I wanted a divorce. I said I wasn't happy and I haven't been happy for a long time and I told him I couldn't live this way any longer. I was drinking and I told him that I wanted to get Alex raised so that I could commit suicide. But believe me I am NOT suicidal. I could NEVER EVER do that to Alex. That was the drinking talking.

* * *

**Reply from Bev Bergstresser**
**Tuesday October 4, 2011** at 10:54 AM
Just make sure you delete these emails because you can't let Karl know you suspect him of anything. I have been reading up on sociopaths to see how they think and I do see some of the traits in Karl. If you get a chance, you should Google it and read some articles. Maybe it can help with some of your questions.

Cindy Googled "sociopath" with trepidation. She was blown over when she discovered that the tell-tale signs described Karl, almost exactly:

- Constantly lying and manipulating
- Not respecting the feelings of others
- Difficulty recognizing emotion
- Grandiose sense of self
- Overstepping boundaries
- No regard for negative consequences.

* * *

Cindy still didn't want to believe it.
But she knew Karl was guilty.

## FIFTY-SEVEN

It was a few weeks after she hired Steve that Cindy called him in a panic. She was worried that Karl was running out of money. She was worried that his business was going under. She was worried that he was making plans.

"I went to go make copies of the documents from New York Life and the manila envelope was missing," she told Steve.

"Are you sure you put it back in the same place?"

"Karl knows I looked through it. I can feel it."

"Don't jump to conclusions just yet. Just hang in there, I'm waiting to hear from my contact in Sacramento and then I'll be flying out there."

Cindy believed in him. He assured her that police reports were considered "public records" in the State of California, telling her he'd filed a request to see them. But thus far, Steve had come up empty handed and Cindy was freaking out.

"I started sleeping with a pair of scissors under my bed," she told him, "I can't take this much longer. I can't sleep. I can't eat. I'm losing my mind!"

"Look, Cindy, you're not thinking straight. Karl's not going to do anything to you where he could get caught. You're safer being in the house. You're safer there than anywhere else."

But Cindy wouldn't have it. She believed that if Karl needed money, he would create another "accident." She had been shut out of the C&K Farms business accounts and she needed Steve to get to them. Obviously, Karl was not required to disclose financial information to anyone (other than her) and she needed Steve to come up with a plan. She needed Steve to find out what Karl was hiding.

"I'm trying to figure out how you can get close to Karl," Cindy told him, "because Karl loves to talk."

"You think he would open up to a stranger?"

"If he thought you could help him with his business, I think he would."

The two of them kicked some ideas around and Steve, who was a jack of all trades, suggested that he could pose as a marketing consultant. Steve knew exactly how to play that part, he told Cindy. All he needed was for her to set up a "marketing consultation" and he would take it from there.

"I told Karl that I found someone on Google who could help expand the business," Cindy later explained. "I told him we needed someone who was good at marketing and I mentioned Steve Brown. One thing I knew was that Karl hated going on the internet, so I knew he wouldn't bother to Google it. And just like I thought, Karl didn't ask me one question about Steve's credentials."

Karl wasn't a fact-finder.

He acted on impulse.

He wanted Cindy to set up a meeting ASAP.

And he was already counting his money.

A few days after they devised the plan, Steve showed up at the Karlsen's doorstep to talk about marketing for the duck business, offering a free consultation. Cindy greeted Steve with a firm handshake, she was happy to meet him, and then she turned and introduced Steve to Karl.

"Steve says he can double our business," Cindy told Karl. "I know we both like that idea!"

And thankfully, Steve came prepared.

When the three of them sat down at the kitchen table, Steve laid out pamphlets that described USDA marketing strategies and alternative marketing ideas. He was full of information about how their duck business could gain traction. He wanted to start by placing a few strategic facebook ads and said it would only cost a few hundred dollars up front, promising that the return would be well worth it.

And just like that, the "marketing plan" was in motion.

"Karl talked a lot about himself and where he saw the duck business going," Steve later recalled. "He wanted to scale his business into a big conglomerate and said he wanted to build an FDA processing plant."

But Karl had not given any thought as to how an FDA plant would get funded. When Steve asked Karl if he had backers, Karl hemmed and hawed. He had no business sense whatsoever and after a while, Steve's questions were making him nervous.

"I realized I needed to get off that subject," Steve would later say. "I went back to the marketing element and talked about getting him more exposure and that got Karl's attention."

Steve came up with a game plan, telling Karl he wanted to shoot some short videos of him working with his ducks. He wanted to create a facebook page, create a website, and planned to post the videos online. There were so many ways to reach a wider consumer audience, Steve assured him, and Karl was salivating.

Karl wanted his face to be known.

By the end of October, with Cindy footing the bill all the while, Steve had become somewhat of a fixture at the farm. Cindy scraped up whatever she could to keep Steve on the case. Already, Steve had begun to gain Karl's confidence, and he genuinely liked Karl.

"This guy was the nicest guy in the world," Steve would later say. "Every interaction we had, just his eyes, his mannerisms, the way he talked with a smile, he was very charming."

But it didn't take long for Karl to show his ugly side. He was angry with Cindy, who he felt should be backing him financially. He confided that he and Cindy had co-mingled funds at New York Life, telling Steve that Cindy refused to co-sign for any loans against that money.

There were hundreds of thousands of dollars just sitting there.

But Cindy refused to release the cash.

She was standing in the way of his dream.

By November of 2011, Steve and Karl had become buddy-buddy. It was then that Karl asked Steve to consider investing in the duck business. The marketing was making a big difference, Karl claimed, the product was practically selling itself. There was so much demand that Karl was contemplating opening a USDA poultry facility.

"Karl was determined to process these ducks on a large scale," Steve later explained, "and when he started the process of looking at USDA plants, I wanted to find out what it entailed."

It didn't take much for Steve to convince Karl that he wanted to become his business partner and soon thereafter, Karl arranged for the two of them to take a tour of a USDA poultry plant in Pennsylvania.

Steve was all excited about it, he was really curious about what the business entailed.

However, once they got there, and the two men walked into the giant poultry plant, Steve thought he was going to pass out. The overpowering stench of animal carcasses was worse than the smell of rotting meat. The place reeked of the smell of manure, of the smell of blood, and Steve couldn't handle it.

As they worked their way past the slaughter rooms, Steve couldn't get over how nonchalant Karl was. If anything, Karl seemed to *enjoy* seeing how the birds were killed. Karl was mesmerized by the way the plant workers used an electric stun knife to knock each bird out, before slitting the throat.

"Looking back, you could tell he was in his element in that place,"

Steve later said. "And all I could think was, he loves killing things... and it wasn't just animals."

"So, when you kill the ducks at the farm, do you use an electric knife?" Steve wondered.

"No, I do it the old-fashioned way."

"What way is *that*?"

"Like this," Karl said, grabbing Steve in one big sweeping motion, tilting Steve's head back.

"This is how I normally do it," Karl told him, tightening his grip on Steve's neck, using his free hand to mimic the motion of slitting his throat.

"You just stick the knife through the neck," Karl said, "and you scramble the brain and then pump the blood out."

"We're talking *about ducks*, here, right?"

But Karl just stood there with a grin on his face.

"By the time we were finished touring the slaughterhouse, we both had a lot of blood on us," Steve would later confide. "And I told Karl that I needed to go to the men's room to wash some of it off, but once I got away from him, I started to feel chest pains..."

"We got to this plant and we're kind of walking through," Steve would later say, "and there was blood everywhere... And when I say everywhere, I'm not joking. There was blood on the floors, on the walls, on the ceilings. So you have this setting of death."

On their drive back to Romulus, Karl calculated that it would cost over a million dollars to open a USDA plant, which was undoable. However, he felt he could easily build a small poultry production plant, if only he could get Cindy to cooperate. When they made a pit stop at Denny's to grab a bite to eat, Karl told Steve that Cindy had become "too much of a problem." She was a roadblock that Karl needed to get out of his way.

While the two of them waited for their burgers and fries, Karl told Steve that the USDA plant manager gave him a heads-up about a new government program for small farmers. Apparently, the federal government was handing out money to poultry farmers who specialized in organic livestock, and all Karl needed was a little start-up money...

"If I start off with 50,000 birds a year," Karl said, "I can charge three dollars a bird for processing, so that's $150,000 a year. And that's just the beginning!"

"What kind of start-up money are we talking about?"

"Well, I've already got the farmland, so it really wouldn't be that much. I'm thinking, maybe $150,000."

"How do you get to that number?"

"Because if I'm selling thousands of birds, I'll need automated killing equipment. I'll need stunning knives and killing cones. And I'll also need chilling equipment to store the meat."

"I might be able to find somebody," Steve lied. "Let me think about it."

## FIFTY-EIGHT

"I had all these ducks running around the farm, thousands of 'em that I couldn't sell because they weren't big enough," Karl would later say. "And I had a friend who butchered the small ones for me and made sausage and bacon out of them, and then I went to a bunch of restaurants and handed out samples of duck sausage but no one wanted it."

"Then I came up with the idea of selling whole ducks in a can, or maybe in a jar," Karl explained. "So I went over to Cornell University to see what they thought, because this duck thing was hot and I heard they were raising big money. I talked to one guy who really liked the idea, but he never called me back."

Back at the farm, Cindy was up to her eyeballs in duck meat, there was a foul smell penetrating her house. When she discovered that Karl was throwing all of their frozen meat out of their freezer in the basement, that he was stuffing duck breasts and duck sausage into them and leaving the beef on the floor to rot, she'd had enough.

Cindy was ready to put an end to C&K Farms.

The charade had gone on too long.

It was just a few days after Steve made the trip with Karl to Pennsylvania that he called Cindy to give her a warning. Karl was actively looking for investors and his delusions of grandeur were falling short. There was no way Karl could open a USDA poultry plant, that was a pipe dream.

Steve didn't want to scare her, he really didn't, but Karl was acting very weird. It was obvious that he was losing more money every day, that he couldn't afford the feed, he couldn't afford to pay for the processing.

And there was no telling what he might do.

"I think you need to cash out some of those accounts," Steve told Cindy when he got her on the phone. "You should make up an excuse and tell Karl you've changed your mind about cashing them out."

"You think I should just close everything?"

"Yes. And I think you should keep your granddaughters away from him," Steve said. "Because you can't take any more chances."

Later that night, Cindy approached Karl with a proposal. She said she'd agree to co-sign and cash out the bulk of the annuity accounts, as long as they agreed to split the money fifty-fifty.

"This way you'll have plenty of cash for your ducks," she told him, "and I can invest my half in something else."

When Karl heard that, his eyes lit up. The first account he wanted to close was a $250,000 annuity account which, even after penalties, would net each of them a little over a hundred grand. As far as what Cindy planned to do with her half of that money, Karl didn't even ask. He didn't care.

Cindy had been hesitant to go through with it, she wasn't sure how to keep her half of the money safe, but Steve had advised her to invest in real estate, telling her that was the best bet. In fact, as luck would have it, Steve had a client who was looking to flip a nice little house in Newark, and he would arrange for her to see it right away.

"It's already got renters in it," Steve told her, "and if you keep it as a rental property, you'll get a nice income."

"But Karl will find a way to get his hands on that. I know he will."

"He can't get it if you put the house under a different name. You can name Alex as a co-owner of the house. And then you can open a new bank account with both of your names on it. That would make it very hard for him to get to it."

"But what if I've got to get that money in a hurry?" Cindy asked. "I don't know what's going to happen. I've got to have that money available just in case."

"Here's what we can do," Steve suggested, "I can get my client to sell it to you now, and if need be, I'll ask him to buy it back from you."

"What? I don't understand. Why would the seller do that?"

"Well, he'd be buying it back at a slightly lower price, so you would lose some of your money... but it would be worth it just to have peace of mind."

"You really think your client would agree to that?"

"Sure," Steve told her, "people do it all the time."

* * *

It wasn't until the day of the closing, after all the paperwork on the house in Newark was drawn up, that Cindy discovered something odd. It turned out that this cute little house she'd agreed to buy for cash, the one Steve said his "client" owned, actually belonged to *Steve.*

At first, when Cindy saw "Steve Brown" listed as the seller of the property, she thought it was a mistake. But Steve explained it away. He told her he'd shown her one of his rental properties because the client he'd told her about had backed out of the deal.

Of course, Cindy was irked.

She felt shafted.

But Steve leveled with her, explaining that he was the only one who could 100% guarantee a full cash buyback if necessary. Cindy didn't like it. This last minute switch was unnerving. She was tempted not to sign anything, but she was already sold on the idea, so she went through with the deal.

STATEMENT OF PURCHASE
Purchasers: Cindy Karlsen
Attorney: Nesbitt & Williams
Sellers: Steve Brown and Katie Brown
Attorney: Greg Powers, Esq.
Premises: 126 Trout Run, Newark, New York
Closing Date: December 19, 2011
Purchase Price $106,000.00
County Tax $1,067.99 yearly
School Tax $1,072.52 yearly
Village Tax $1,272.14 yearly

---

Total Funds Needed to Close $106, 178.75

Cindy had made the right choice, Steve assured her.

As long as she kept it rented out, she would have a monthly income flow.

It was a no-brainer.

## FIFTY-NINE

Even before she had any suspicions, Cindy often thought about leaving him, but the last thing she wanted was a second divorce. For years, she talked herself into staying the course. It was better not to give up, it was better for the kids.

But now she had to break free.

Cindy was done.

It was on January 15, 2012, that she told Karl she wanted a trial separation and Karl seemed to be absolutely devastated. He started hyperventilating, almost gagging, and he went over to the kitchen sink, hanging over it and rocking back and forth. It sounded like he was about to vomit but instead he managed to calm himself. Cindy watched him turn on the faucet and splash a handful of water on his face, and when he turned back around to face her, he'd irritated his eyes enough to make it look like he was crying.

Cindy told him she just needed a break.

They were arguing too much.

And Karl had to agree.

The two of them were fighting all the time, they were no longer a loving couple, and after he dried his eyes, patting his face with a napkin, Karl reluctantly agreed that a temporary separation would be good for both of them. Cindy knew it would impact Alex, and as expected, the teenager was adamant that he wasn't going anywhere. Alex wasn't going to leave home. He wasn't going to let his mother pull him away from his friends. No way.

Cindy told Karl it was temporary. She just needed some time to think. She realized it would be a bad choice to uproot Alex, so she found a rental house just five miles away from the farm, and Karl seemed to have no issue with that. In fact, he encouraged her to take whatever furniture she wanted, he encouraged her to take pots, pans, and whatever else she wanted from the kitchen, helping her pack more than half of their household goods.

Karl had promised to help her move. He was also letting her use his pickup, but when moving day came, he slipped on ice and had to put his arm in a sling. He'd re-injured his right shoulder.

Thankfully Cindy was able to hire a neighbor who helped her load Karl's truck, and Karl stood there watching the process, offering to help with his good arm, which somehow, he managed to do. He wanted Cindy to know that he loved her and was willing to let her go, hoping the separation would make their marriage stronger.

So everything was civilized between them early on.

But it didn't take long for the separation to turn ugly.

Karl did everything he could to drive a wedge between Alex and Cindy. He spoiled the kid rotten, letting his friends (and sometimes his girlfriend) sleep over. And the more time Alex spent with his dad, the more resentful he became of his mother.

Alex was angry about the separation. He couldn't understand why his mother had become so aloof. She wasn't herself anymore. His mother had become hateful. Alex had never seen this side of her before, but now that they lived on their own, he realized his mom's drinking was a problem.

His mother was becoming more incoherent and irrational by the day.

She was a hot mess.

At first, Alex decided to keep it secret, but when his mother's drinking snowballed, he called Kati to talk about it and then went to see his father. Alex couldn't stand living with her, and he was isolated because he was too embarrassed to let anyone see his mother staggering around the house. His mother would get drunk every night. She was slurring her words. She was repeating the same complaints all the time, like she was a broken record.

Karl was more than happy to rescue his son from an unhealthy situation. He wanted Alex to move back in with him, but Alex decided to split his time. He felt guilty about leaving his mom all alone.

Whenever Alex visited, Karl would harp on Cindy's drinking, telling Alex she could no longer be trusted. Karl promised Alex that one day, they would live like a normal family again, but not until his mother straightened out her life.

"Until she gets professional help," Karl told his son, "I won't take her back."

"Karl wanted to smear me," Cindy would later say. "He actually went to my church to tell my pastor that I had a drinking problem, which was a total violation of my privacy. And not long after that, I found out that he had the nerve to go to Connie's Diner when I wasn't on shift so he could blab about my "severe drinking problem" to my co-workers. He was actively trying to get me fired so I wouldn't be able to support myself."

To win Alex over, Karl continued to use Cindy's alcoholism as a weapon, claiming her drinking had gone undetected for years. Cindy had been a closet drinker all along, he insisted. She'd hidden it by stashing liquor bottles throughout the house, but Alex wasn't sure he believed it. However, there came a day when Karl yelled for Alex to come upstairs to see something, and there was the proof. Floating in the toilet tank was a half empty pint of vodka.

"Why would I hide alcohol in the toilet tank of my own house?" Cindy would later point out. "And if I did want to hide vodka, which I didn't, I would have put it in the back of the freezer, not in a toilet tank where the vodka could be contaminated."

But seeing that half empty pint in the toilet tank convinced Alex that his father was right. He agreed that his mom needed help, otherwise things would only get worse. And just as Karl predicted, that's exactly what happened. Cindy was riding an emotional rollercoaster and she'd gotten sloppy. One minute she hated him, then the next minute she'd call Karl in the middle of the night, crying and telling him she'd made a mistake.

"Let's work this out," Cindy told him in one of her drunken phone calls. "It's not too late, Karl. Why don't you pick me up so we can go for a quick drink? We need to talk."

"Absolutely not!" Karl howled. "You're already drunk!"

"I just want to talk to you. I miss you."

"That's not happening tonight. You need to sleep it off."

But Cindy couldn't sleep it off. She felt sick to her stomach day and night, and the drinking wasn't helping. She would pass out on the couch and then wake up a few hours later with a lump in her throat.

"There was a night when Alex called and told me that his mom was threatening to kill herself," Karl confided.

"Alex said he couldn't stand to be around her for another day, so I told him to pack his shit," Karl recalled. "And then I get up there, and Alex has a big duffle bag packed up, and Cindy wakes up because the dog was barking, and she's like, all lovey-dovey to me."

She was a flake.

She didn't know what she wanted.

And Karl was sick of it.

## SIXTY

In a drunken moment, without thinking it through, Cindy called her cousin, Jackie Hymel, confiding her dark suspicions. She needed to talk to someone. She was still within Karl's reach. And that's all she could think about.

When Jackie answered the phone at her home in Lexington, Kentucky, Cindy was crying and gulping between sentences. She was rambling about Levi's death, telling her cousin about the large insurance policy that Karl had been named as sole beneficiary.

Cindy confided that most of the money from Levi's insurance policy had already been spent, telling Jackie that Karl never intended to save any of that money for his granddaughters. Cindy was drunk-talking, slurring her words, telling Jackie that she'd been tricked into signing "loans" from that money.

Jackie wasn't sure what the "loans" were for, but she agreed that it made no sense for Karl to have been named as the sole beneficiary. Levi had daughters, why would he do that?

Cindy tried to explain why the money was re-invested with New York Life. She told Jackie that she and Karl were named as the co-owners of these investment accounts, and Jackie was surprised to hear that. And when Cindy confided that the payout from New York Life was over $700,000, her cousin was flabbergasted. She agreed with Cindy that Levi wouldn't have taken out that amount of insurance on his own and was certain that Karl had a hand in it.

"I've been up every night thinking," Cindy said, "and I keep coming back to the insurance money Karl collected after Christina's death. I think he had something to do with that. I think she was planning to divorce him."

"What makes you think that?"

"When I was packing Alex's baby book and all his baby pictures, it just hit me. I think Chris was doing the same thing. I think she was hiding things out in the garage. I remember Karl telling me they had a hidden storage area in the garage."

Jackie was stunned. She thought Cindy was delusional.

"I always wondered how the kids' baby pictures survived," Cindy told her. "And there was other baby stuff that didn't burn up, which means someone had put all of that in the garage."

But to Jackie, that claim seemed far-fetched.

When Cindy confided that she'd hired a private investigator and had recently discovered that Karl had put a $1.2 million bounty on her head, Jackie thought it was nonsense. Jackie didn't believe Cindy, not at all. And her suspicions were confirmed when Cindy admitted that she and Karl had cashed out most of the insurance money. Cindy claimed that she cashed out the accounts because she needed to get the bounty off her head, but Jackie didn't buy it.

If it was real, if what Cindy said was true, then why hadn't she gone to the police to report this. Jackie felt that cashing out the investment accounts meant for Elletra and Ivy had to be a crime, but she kept up the pretense, acting like she felt sorry for Cindy, letting her cousin dig herself into a hole.

With her body fueled with alcohol, Cindy was insisting that Karl had killed Levi, and at first, Jackie ignored it. She thought Cindy was paranoid, she thought it was the liquor talking, but suddenly, Cindy was spilling new details about Levi's "accident." There was much more to it, Jackie found out.

There was a pattern here.

There were deadly accidents all throughout Karl's life.

And Cindy was convinced that he was capable of murder.

Of course Jackie swore she could keep a secret...

But she couldn't.

# SIXTY-ONE

Cindy sat stewing for another few weeks, calling Steve daily to see if he had any updates about Levi, about Christina, about anything at all, but Steve had hit dead ends. As a last-ditch effort, he asked her to reach out to someone in Christina's family, hoping Cindy could get someone who would talk.

Cindy knew it would have to be Colette, there was no relationship between her and Art, and she worried about how to approach it. She hadn't spoken to Colette in years, they'd stopped all communication, and Cindy didn't want to make it seem like she was pointing fingers.

As per Steve's advice, Cindy wrote an email to Colette claiming she'd been contacted by a private investigator from California. Cindy had agreed that would probably draw Colette out, but unfortunately, the ruse backfired.

---

**Sent from Cindy Karlsen**
**Saturday, February 4, 2012** at 8:44 AM:

Hey Colette, How are things going? I am sure Erin has told you by now that Karl and I have split up. I wanted to email you though because I got an odd phone call the other day and wanted to run it by you. It was from some investigator from Calaveras County that said he was investigating the fire. He was asking questions about Karl and Chris's relationship and I was wondering if anyone had contacted you on it? If not, what are your thoughts?

Also, I want you to know that Karl and I split up over his dishonesty with money. I don't like this new duck raising adventure he is on, so it's probably for the best. Anyway, I just wanted your thoughts and your honest opinion on what happened the day of the fire. Did Chris plan to leave Karl? I'm just wondering. Anything you say, will stay with me.

Cindy

---

\* \* \*

---

**Reply from Colette Bousson**

**Saturday , February 4, 2012** at 10:25 AM:

Hi Cindy, No phone calls here. Please provide me the name and number of the investigator and I will do some research on this end. As for anything you should know...without being offensive, I believe my family and I *alluded* to a few things early on in your marriage with Karl. We found you unreceptive to anything regarding my sister's death. It would now be irrelevant.

Sorry to hear about you and Karl. I had no idea you two were struggling. If Alex is staying with you, tell him Aunt Colette said Hi. Take Care...

---

\* \* \*

---

**Sent from Cindy Karlsen**

**Saturday, February 4,** at 2:17 PM:

I know your mom had said something about Karl in the beginning but it took me years with Karl to realize how deceptive he could be. I did not get the man's name. I wish I had thought to ask. He said he was a student who was looking at cold cases.

Please accept my apology for not being receptive. At the time, I had thought that you all were just grieving your loss and that is what I chalked it up to. I knew your mom blamed him but I thought it was just a mother's grief (understandably). I am not out looking for trouble with Karl but if there was an injustice done, then it needs to be made right. Maybe it is not too late.

I don't mean to bring up old stuff but if you could fill me in on your thoughts, I would appreciate it. It has me very worried. If you have information that I need to know for the safety of Alex, the girls and I, please let me know.

***

**Reply from Colette Bousson**
**Saturday, February 4, 2012** at 6:31 PM:

Do you find it odd that you were contacted about an incident you have no first-hand knowledge of? I believe the young student missed his mark if as he stated, he was working on a questionable case. Either he needs to go back to school to learn appropriate follow up, or he was lying.

Please call your phone company for the incoming number. Once you provide me this youngster's number, I will do the rest of the follow through. If you are ever called again, tell him to call me and to leave the rest of my family alone. If you are fishing... your fishing expedition with me is done. You know Karl better than I do. Make your best judgment call and leave me and my family out of whatever you are trying to do. Kati is a cop... you should ask her for guidance.

***

**Sent from Cindy Karlsen**
**Saturday, February 4, 2012** at 7:38 PM:

One of the reasons why I was hesitant about contacting you is because I was afraid that it would come off like I was just trying to hurt Karl and I would never do that to the kids. I cannot contact Kati or Erin on this because it would devastate them. Please do not go to them with this.

I am not fishing. I'm not sure what your anger is about. If you believe Karl is guilty, wouldn't you want justice? I am sorry that this has caused you anguish. I just didn't know where else to go with it and I had thought that you and I had a halfway decent relationship. I am sorry and I won't email you on it again.

---

If Colette suspected Karl of doing something nefarious, the woman sure didn't show it when she'd visited them back in 1993. But Colette had a different memory of what went down during that visit.

"I was clear that I believed Karl set the fire," Colette would later say. "I very clearly told Cindy that Karl set the fire that my sister died in, and she blew me off. And was pretty snotty to me."

But according to Cindy, that conversation never occurred. In fact, just the opposite was true, and Cindy had proof. All along, Cindy kept up with a Facebook page called "Justice for Christina" and she'd seen Colette's posts.

In one post, Colette wrote that "for the good of the children, we put our best face on things."

Cindy printed that out, along with a few other posts in which Colette indicated that she had deliberately stayed closed mouthed. "I had to set aside everything that could have been a roadblock for me," Colette posted. "Because I was absolutely going to make sure that the kids knew their mother."

Looking back on it, Cindy realized she'd been duped.

What Colette was claiming on Facebook was a lie.

It was outrageous.

Colette had never said anything concrete...

She had not said *one single word* to warn Cindy.

"I would have never married this guy and have a kid with him if I thought he was a killer," Cindy would say. "I now realize that they didn't care about me one bit. All they wanted was a babysitter for Karl's kids. That's all I was to them. They kept their mouths shut. They didn't care if they put me and my son in harm's way."

## SIXTY-TWO

About a week after her failed attempts with Colette, Cindy made a drunk phone call to Jackie to tell her about an ugly scene she'd had with Karl. Apparently, Cindy had gone to the farm to grab a few things from her closet, and when she first got there, Karl was standing in the hallway blocking her. He was angry about a mix-up between Five Star Bank and New York Life because one of the wire transfers hadn't gone through.

"I told Karl it was his problem, not mine, and I brushed past him to go upstairs." Cindy told her cousin. "But then, when I tried to come back down, Karl was waiting for me at the bottom of the staircase and he punched an *effing hole* in the wall. It scared the crap out of me!"

"Oh my God, Cindy. *Why in the world* are you still going over there?"

"Because Alex needs me to drive him back and forth."

"I wish I was there to help you," Jackie told her. "Because if I was there, Karl would never pull that shit around me!"

But Jackie couldn't help.

She was hundreds of miles away.

After they hung up, Cindy drank vodka until everything went black.

Jackie didn't want Cindy to know how truly worried she was, how scared she was for her. In an effort to find some answers on her own, Jackie placed a call to the New York Life headquarters in Manhattan and identified herself as "a close relative" of Cindy Karlsen. She wanted to speak to a fraud investigator and said she had some new information pertaining to Levi Karlsen's fatal "accident."

Within 24 hours, Jackie got a call from Richard Matarante, an investigator with New York Life, and she proceeded to tell him that she had reason to believe her relative, Levi Karlsen, had been murdered. Jackie claimed to have inside information, asserting that the "freak accident" which caused Levi's death occurred just weeks after Levi had taken out the life insurance policy and she wanted the fraud investigator to check the records.

Jackie wanted to know if Karl Karlsen was there when Levi signed the policy, claiming that Karl had been a suspect in another insurance fraud scam which involved the accidental death of his first wife...

Within a few hours, the fraud investigator called Jackie to report that it was *Karl* who paid the initial insurance payment, *not Levi*, informing her that he would be opening an investigation into the matter.

In Matarante's opinion, Levi's death did not appear to be an accident. Apparently, there had been questions about the payout back in 2008. The fraud investigator thought a criminal investigation should be opened immediately and urged her to call the police.

It was about a week later, in late February of 2012, that Jackie got up the nerve to call the Seneca County Sheriff's office, leaving a cryptic message for Lt. John Cleere. But unfortunately, it took a few days for John Cleere to respond to the tipster and by that time, Jackie had changed her mind. She didn't want to get involved. It was all conjecture really, and she erased his voice message.

Jackie didn't want to borrow trouble.

She'd become afraid for her own safety.

But John Cleere didn't let the opportunity pass. He left a second voicemail explaining that as a tipster, Jackie Hymel could remain anonymous, and within minutes, Jackie called him back. Her conscience had been bothering her, she told the criminal investigator, reporting that her cousin, Cindy Karlsen, was 99% sure that her husband, Karl, had gotten away with murder.

She explained that she'd learned about this through Cindy, who called her when she got drunk enough, spilling the disturbing details that surrounded Levi's death. Beyond that, Jackie was making other allegations, telling Cleere about Levi's death, about the mysterious barn fire, about the "accidental" death of Karlsen's first wife, Christina, way back in 1991. But the woman was spewing information faster than Cleere could write, so he decided to stop her. He asked if she would be willing to write everything down in an email and promised to keep it strictly confidential.

**Sent from Jackie Hymel**
**Thursday March 28, 2012** at 10:56 AM:


Lieutenant Cleere, I will try and break down the reasons that I called you regarding the death of Levi Karlsen in 2009. This information is based on conversations that I've had with Cindy and everything that her and I talked about is pretty much in this email. I am extremely busy at work and have limited time to put this together. I hope this will help you.

- My cousin, Cindy Karlsen, has told me that she feels her husband, Karl, set up Levi's death for the insurance money.
- Karl collected $700,000 in life insurance on Levi's death and has spent close to every cent of the policy.
- <u>Karl never mentioned to Cindy that he was the one who had taken Levi to get the life insurance policy.</u> Karl also failed to tell her that he was the one who made the initial payment on the insurance policy.
- Karl and Cindy had a duck business going and Karl was having trouble paying the bills.
- The day of Levi's death, Levi showed up the morning to work on a farm truck that wound up crushing him.
- I feel there was a reason why Levi died *the day before* he was supposed to take his insurance physical.
- Karl and Cindy had a barn fire which killed one of their horses and Karl collected on a large insurance policy from this barn fire.
- Christine Alexander Karlsen, Levi's biological mother, died in a house fire in Murphys, California, and Karl collected on an insurance policy after her death as well.

**Let me know if you need anything else.**
**Sincerely, Jackie Hymel**

But Jackie had yet to report the whole story. She had other suspicions that she needed to report. Just three days after her initial email, Jackie wrote Cleere again, insinuating that her cousin might have dirty hands as well.

---

**Sent from Jackie Hymel**
**March 31, 2012** at 9:14 AM:

Hey John,

There are a few other things that you might need to know. I actually hesitated to say anything because I didn't want to get Cindy in trouble but as I thought more about it, I decided I better not be holding stuff back because of that. I know for a fact that Cindy took $100K from Levi's insurance money and put it on a fake business in Alex's name. I also know she spent $150K to buy a house in Romulus.

I think you should talk to Cindy and also check into the position Levi held at the glass factory. Did anyone ever get hurt on the machine he worked on? *Has there ever been any deaths in that factory?* Karl claims the reason he got Levi to get the insurance was that "it was so dangerous" there. Was it really?

I'm at work and short on time, but if I think of anything else, I will let you know. I do have conversations between Cindy and myself discussing her being afraid to leave Karl and her beliefs that he killed Levi which I can forward to you.

**Talk to you later,**
**Sincerely, Jackie Hymel**

---

# SIXTY-THREE

In the meantime, Cindy received a smug email from Kati who was blaming her for breaking up the family. In it, Kati chastised her step-mother, assuming it was Cindy's drunken behavior that caused the separation, and Cindy needed to defend herself.

---

**Sent from Cindy Karlsen**
**Friday March 9, 2012** at 8:34 PM:

Hi Kati,

I have put a lot of thought into what I want to say to you. First, let me apologize for my drinking. I know it looks bad and don't get me wrong, it is... and I have signed up for a group in Rochester in addition to the counseling I have already been receiving. I know you guys think that I need a 28-day program but right now my current counselor does not feel that it would be a good time for me to go away for that long.

There is much more going on with your dad that I can't get into but my main concern is that he is not taking his meds right. I know it sounds like I am calling the kettle black with my drinking, but Alex has told me that there would be times on the Thruway that he would see his dad drifting off into another lane with his eyes half closed. I don't ever want to keep Alex from him. He loves his dad and it would just be wrong. But I have legitimate concerns and if anything ever happened to Alex, I could never forgive myself.

Kati, please don't take this the wrong way. I am not going to lie to you and I am not trying to hurt your dad, but I did tell Cassie that I didn't think your dad should have the girls on his own. Not the way he is with his meds. I told her just for now, until he got his meds straight.

You know I love you just as much as if I had given birth to you. I am so proud of all that you've accomplished. I also know that you are very close with your dad but try to put your emotions aside and look at it from a police officer point of view. He is putting other people in danger and maybe there is something you can do to help him. It would only benefit his future no matter what path it takes.

Like I said, there is much more that I'm not going to get into, rightfully so. And just so you know, one of the counseling programs I'm trying to get into also includes family sessions that I thought we could all attend. I'm sorry if an email seems impersonal but I am much better at expressing myself through writing.

Ok, Love you... Mom

* * *

**Sent from Kati Karlsen**
**Sunday March 11. 2012** at 7:36 PM:

Mom,

The biggest issue I have with your email is that once again, you are trying to downplay the fact that you have a problem. When we got into an argument in December you even said that "you didn't realize that your drinking was affecting the family." Despite the fact that you've had multiple relapses since 2009, they seem to be getting more frequent... I'm glad you're finally acknowledging that you have been drinking, and that you need help.

Now, to get to the rest of the email, I have a major issue with you telling Cassie that you don't trust dad with the girls because he can't be trusted with driving. This is the pot calling the kettle black. Who is to say that you will not drive drunk with the girls in your car, because we both know you have drove drunk with Alex in the car.

I hope this new thing in Rochester helps you and makes a difference, particularly with Alex. Unfortunately, this has gone on so long, it is going to take time now to correct any issues that have arose because of it... Kati

---

Obviously Cindy knew there were bigger problems, serious problems, things that she couldn't talk about, not then. She knew Alex and Kati were angry that she'd moved out of the house, that they blamed her for letting their dad's life fall apart, and she couldn't say a word about it. For the time being, she had to be the bad guy.

When Alex came home one day and informed her that his dad would have to go through another shoulder surgery, she could see that Alex felt bad for him, but Cindy wasn't sympathetic. For months, Karl had carried on about being in pain so he'd have an excuse to numb himself with OxyContin. And at the same time, he was able to garner sympathy from Alex and Kati.

It was a perfect ploy.

## SIXTY-FOUR

Karl loved using Cindy's drinking as a weapon. He was happy about her binge drinking. It served a purpose.

Not long after their separation, Karl put a bug in Alex's ear, questioning Cindy's driving skills, telling him that he didn't trust her to drive Elletra and Ivy anymore. Cindy had stopped bringing their granddaughters to visit the farm and when he finally questioned Alex about it, his son couldn't lie.

"Mom thinks you're taking too many pills," Alex told him. "She says you don't take your pills right."

"I'm following doctor's orders!" Karl snapped. "She knows damn well that I'm scheduled for another shoulder surgery and now she's blaming me for being in pain? You've got to be kidding me!"

Alex felt his father was right and he felt sorry for him. Elletra and Ivy were being used as pawns, Karl was convinced, and he made sure Alex knew it. He became obsessed about seeing his granddaughters and had a few nasty blow-outs with Cindy over the phone, but then she stopped taking his calls.

Karl called her incessantly, leaving angry messages about her being manipulative. And when Cindy didn't respond, he started sending her emails telling her that Alex was disgusted with her, that he was disgusted with her, and Cassie would be disgusted too. Karl was threatening to expose her. He was certain that Cassie would cut her off. He continued to badger her until Cindy reached her boiling point.

---

**Sent from Cindy Karlsen**
   **Wednesday, March 7, 2012** at 7:29 PM:

Go ahead and tell Cassie I am a drunk. See what the kids think of you then. I don't know exactly what you told Kati but someday, Kati will see the truth. You call me a drunk but you are a drug addict. I know you drive when you are drugged up. I've seen you fall asleep at the wheel. Do you think that because you are prescribed pills that you're legal? You are not.

I'm done messing around. You think you can call me and order me around and yell and scream and I am supposed to just take it. Well, not anymore.

I am DONE playing these stupid little games you like to play. You may have Kati fooled (because she chooses to believe daddy) but that's about it. Why don't you tell the truth about your drug addiction and stop living in denial? You know, it isn't too late. You can do the right thing by your kids and your grandkids and I would have the utmost respect for you...

Start doing the right thing or I am going to go through with a divorce.

---

∗ ∗ ∗

---

**Sent from Karl Karlsen**
**Thursday March 8, 2012** at 7:53 AM:

I did not tell lies to Kati. She wants to know why you've made it so I will never get the girls again. Why? Why? Why? I have been out of my pain pills for two weeks and I do care about my driving.

Let's put this behind us or we can do this forever. It's up to you. I just feel like you stuck a knife in my back to hurt me about my driving when you don't know all the facts. You did that and made it so I can't take the girls out places. Well, I guess I can't say anything else. Have you heard from Tony?

---

But Cindy didn't write back.

The fact was, Cindy hadn't heard from Tony Crisci for months. There were numerous times that she'd left messages for him, but Tony would call Karl rather than call her, and she started to wonder if they were colluding against her. Cindy was worried that Karl might be forging her name on documents, but she had no way to prove it. All she could do was wait.

But being in limbo made Cindy drink even more.

She was up against her demons, she was up against Satan.

And she couldn't see her way out.

## SIXTY-FIVE

Cindy played tough with Karl, but deep down, his nasty threat weighed heavily on her. Having Alex and Kati in the know about her drinking problem was one thing. But if Karl blabbed to Cassie, Cindy knew she'd pay the price. The girls would be off-limits, she would lose Elletra and Ivy, and her fear prompted her to take a good look in the mirror.

Cindy's face had gotten puffy and her skin was blotchy, it looked like she'd developed rosacea or some similar skin disease. Cindy truly didn't recognize the person who was staring back at her, she looked bloated and her eyes had lost their sparkle.

She was a shadow of her former self.

And there was no magic pill or elixir that would save her.

But she was ready to fight.

Cindy made a call to the detox center at Crouse Memorial Hospital in Syracuse, and was grateful to learn that they had an available bed. She'd been there once before, she knew the program, and she called Bev, asking her to drive her to Syracuse. Cindy needed Bev to get there ASAP, afraid that if too much time slipped by, she might change her mind.

Bev knew how serious Cindy's drinking problem had gotten. Just like Jackie, she'd gotten drunk calls from Cindy late at night, so Bev dropped everything and arrived at her sister's house in less than an hour. When no one answered the door, Bev was scared that her sister had "done something to herself." As she pulled out her duplicate copy of Cindy's key, Bev braced herself for what she was about to walk into.

Bev was incensed when she found her sister slumped down behind the couch on the living room floor, swigging from a broken bottle of vodka.

"You're going to cut your lip on that!" Bev told her. "Give it to me. Hand it over right now!"

But Cindy was drunk and belligerent. She wouldn't let go.

Bev finally got tired of arguing and let Cindy keep the broken vodka bottle, the rest of which Cindy managed to chug down on the ride to Syracuse, promising that it was her last hurrah. Once at the detox center, Bev helped Cindy walk to the front desk and stayed there until her sister was officially admitted. She told her sister to be brave and stick with it this time, but she knew alcoholism ran in their family. On the drive back to Penn Yan, Bev couldn't help thinking that she'd wasted her time. She knew her sister would be "good" while she was in there, but wondered how long it would take Cindy to revert back to her old ways.

While at Crouse Memorial, Cindy suffered through headaches, tremors, and nausea, but she made it through to the other side. The final stage of the program involved attending two days of group therapy sessions, something similar to AA meetings, where Cindy admitted that her drinking cost her the respect of her teenage son, and the respect of her daughter, Kati. She described her home life as a living hell, admitting that she'd recently left her husband, who had not stopped harassing her.

Within her group, there was a successful businessman, Dave, from Syracuse who admitted that he'd lost everything because of his drinking. His wife had left him, his business had gone down the tubes, he had to move out of his big suburban house and was reduced to living with his aunt.

When Cindy heard his story, she felt sorry for the guy, but she didn't take it to heart. Cindy had bigger problems and her mind was adrift during those final sessions. She still had to face Karl. She still had to pretend that everything was going to be fine.

Still, Dave was strikingly handsome and he had a big personality. He was the type of guy who filled the room with laughter, using mannerisms to exaggerate his self-deprecating humor, and people were drawn to him. But his charisma didn't seem to work on Cindy. Unlike everyone else in the room, Cindy seemed aloof.

At the end of their final group session, Dave asked Cindy for her number but she hesitated. Even though he was good looking, even though he was her type, Cindy didn't want to get anything started. She told Dave her life was complicated, that it would be better if they went their own ways, but Dave was persistent.

Dave promised they would be nothing more than friends.

He said he wanted to be "phone buddies."

But Cindy's perfect little figure and beautiful blue eyes, stayed with him. After a few failed attempts to set up a date, Dave finally convinced Cindy to join him at an AA meeting in Syracuse, after which he took her to a pizza place for a quick bite to eat.

Dave already knew Cindy's history. She'd told the group that she was going through a messy divorce, that her husband was making her life more difficult and doing whatever he could to undermine her. He wanted Cindy to know she could lean on him, that he'd be there for her if she needed anyone, but Cindy didn't seem that interested.

She wanted Dave to stay away, explaining that her husband was keeping tabs on her. She couldn't risk having a new man around. That would only give her husband another reason to bully her.

And Dave respected that, to a point. He didn't push Cindy to see him, instead they spent hours talking on the phone, but with every day that passed, Cindy became more enamored. Dave was a hunk, he was quick-witted, and she began driving to Syracuse regularly to join Dave at AA.

Dave made her feel comfortable.

Cindy didn't know why, but she felt she could let her guard down.

Within a matter of weeks, Cindy developed feelings for him that she'd never felt before. He was caring and sincere, the exact opposite of Karl, and Cindy felt she could trust him.

It didn't take long for Cindy to break down crying, telling Dave about the suspicious death of her stepson and the grave fears she lived with. At the time, Dave listened intently, he did his best to show sympathy, but he didn't believe Cindy's story. The notion that she could be married to a murderer seemed preposterous, yet Dave knew it would be a mistake to dismiss her.

Still, Dave was convinced that Cindy was imagining things, he hadn't yet heard the stories about the barn or about Christina. If anything, from the way Cindy described Karl, Dave's curiosity was piqued. He wanted to protect her from this so-called monster and he convinced Cindy to let him visit her. Dave wasn't afraid of any bully. He was a strong-willed Italian guy who had an attitude befitting a mafioso. Nothing scared him. Certainly not some punk who was threatening this beautiful flower.

Their first official date was a picnic on the shore of Canandaigua Lake, one of Cindy's favorite places in the world where she knew a spot that was untouched. It happened to be a gorgeous Spring day, with clear blue skies and white puffy clouds, and the two of them sat mesmerized by the sparkling crystal-blue water, laughing the afternoon away.

Cindy knew that if Karl ever found out about Dave, he would absolutely explode, but the chemistry between them was undeniable. Neither Dave nor Cindy could let it go.

## SIXTY-SIX

It was on April 6, 2012, that John Cleere placed a call to Steve Brown, telling him about his investigation into Levi Karlsen's death. Having been told by a "tipster" that Cindy Karlsen had hired the PI, Cleere was interested to learn what Steve Brown had discovered, if anything.

Brown said that Karlsen was volatile, telling the investigator that in his opinion, Cindy Karlsen was in danger. He described Karlsen as a desperate man who was "contemplating future acts of violence."

It was a touchy situation, Brown said, there was no proof that Karl had anything to do with Levi's death, however, Cindy kept a diary that held some promise.

"It seems Karl inadvertently revealed some incriminating factors about his wife's death in California," Brown said, "because I felt that her diary contained details that only the killer would know."

"Do you think she'll turn that over to me?"

"I'll ask her. I see no reason for her to hide it."

"Okay, good to know," Cleere told him, "but I don't want you to ask her just yet. I'm still working on a few leads."

Steve offered to help in any way. He said he'd dealt with Karl for over six months and had a good insight into his personality. He described Cindy's suspicions about Levi's fatal "accident" and gave a run-down regarding the $700,000 payout that Karlsen received, explaining that the money was reinvested with New York Life, however, Karl was systematically emptying out those investment accounts.

After he listened to the PI ramble on for fifteen minutes, Cleere asked the PI to write everything down and send it to him in an email and Steve followed up later that day.

The email started out with Steve describing the harrowing scene he'd witnessed at the USDA poultry plant in Pennsylvania, telling Cleere, "it was unnerving to see how much Karl really enjoyed the process of death. We were *literally ankle deep in blood* and death and he took pleasure in it. That is who you are dealing with."

The private eye had a lot of information to impart and had come to the conclusion that Karl Karlsen was a verifiable psychopath. Brown supported his belief by writing down a list of disturbing bullet points:

- Karl is addicted to pain medications and I have noticed him getting progressively worse. He has highs and lows, mostly lows. When he vents to me about Cindy there is a lot of anger.
- Karl has also expressed interest in causing harm to Robert Rosenthal (Stone Church Farm, Rifton NY). Karl used to sell ducks to him and the relationship went south. He claims Rosenthal owes him $33K and has said several times that he wants to go down there and "rip his throat out."
- Karl has a mix of long guns (shotguns and rifles) that he keeps loaded throughout the house and the barns. I believe he will use them, if cornered, so be careful if you are on the property.
- He has been stressing about money lately. He cashed out another policy from New York Life and received the check from that policy a few days ago. The amount was approximately $66K, and he split that with Cindy. He owes a supplier roughly $30K, so that money will be gone in a few days. He is looking to get money from somewhere.
- Cindy has filed for divorce and he offered to pay her off. I believe he offered her $125K, to be broken up over a payment plan but he told me it would be "a cold day in hell" before she gets any of it. I don't know what he is planning, but I have stressed to her the importance of not setting him off.
- I was not able to uncover any insurance policies for their son, Alex, but Cindy has concern that Alex could be a target.
- Most of Karl's siblings despise him, and would likely be a good resource for you.
- Karl claims he was abused as a kid, and has dropped hints that he has "done things" from an early age. You may want to go back and look into his entire life, the accidental deaths.

You should talk to his friends, neighbors, and people in the Amish community, etc.

- There may be a record of disciplinary actions from Karl's time in the Air Force in North Dakota. He talks a lot about driving nuclear missiles around North Dakota and Wyoming. He has often claimed that he was part of a team that handled nuclear weapons.

## SIXTY-SEVEN

John Cleere didn't expect Cindy to cooperate, but when he got her on the phone, the first thing she said was "thank God you called." He was careful not to alarm her, casually asking if she could come down to the station to answer a few questions about Levi's death, and Cindy arrived bright and early the next day, April 9, 2012, ready to talk.

In her sworn statement, given over an eight-hour period that day, Cindy provided a detailed history of Levi's strained relationship with his father. In particular, she focused on the heated argument that Levi had with his father not long after he turned seventeen, telling Cleere that she witnessed Levi accusing his father of murder.

"What, exactly, did Levi say?"

"He accused Karl of killing their mom."

"He used those words?"

"Yes. I remember Erin was standing right next to Levi, kind of giving him silent support, and Karl pulled Levi to the floor, accusing him of making up rumors."

"Did anything come of it?"

"Not really. It became more like a wrestling match, but it took me, Erin, and Kati, to pull the two of them apart."

Looking back, there had been warning signs since Levi's death in 2008, which Cindy had regrettably ignored. As John Cleere observed the petite woman shrink further down into her chair, he wondered why, after all these years, Cindy was just now coming forward. He wondered why he'd first heard about the suspicious death from *Cindy's distant cousin…*

That question nagged at him.

Cindy talked a lot about insurance policies. Regarding the policy on Levi, Cindy admitted that most of the insurance payout had been swallowed up over the course of two years. She wasn't quite sure, but she thought most of the annuity accounts had been cashed out.

When Cindy reached in her bag and pulled out the envelope that contained copies of the New York Life paperwork and handed them over to John Cleere, the criminal investigator thanked her and said he'd make a copy.

Cleere wasn't about to tell her that he already had those documents, that he'd studied them carefully and was aware that two New York Life accounts remained active: the life insurance policies taken out on Elletra and Ivy Karlsen.

Moreover, John Cleere questioned why it was *Cindy* Karlsen, not Karl, who had been named as the sole beneficiary on those policies. It seemed odd to him. Never did he think that Cindy was unaware of what she'd signed.

He suspected Cindy played a part in all of this.

But it was only a hunch.

## SIXTY-EIGHT

After she left the Sheriff's Office. Cindy was relieved. John Cleere had asked her to hold off on filing divorce papers, he wanted her to keep tabs on Karl until they found something concrete. He asked her to keep up the pretense that she wanted to save her marriage, and now that the police were involved, Cindy was more comfortable and felt she could keep that going.

Dave was in the picture now, he was spending more time in Romulus, and Karl had yet to find out about him. Dave still lived in Syracuse and Cindy only let him visit on weekends when Alex was at the farm with his dad. As an added precaution, Cindy had Dave park his car in her garage.

Having Dave around was helpful, but it didn't mean Cindy was out of danger. During the week, when Cindy sat alone in her house, her anxiety was reaching new heights. Cindy had to figure out something, she had to try to lure Karl, and if possible, get him to trust her enough to give her a partial confession. It was a longshot, but maybe she could draw him out.

Karl was desperate to get her back and Cindy knew just how to play him.

She needed to make her move.

---

**Sent from Cindy Karlsen**
**Friday April 13, 2012** at 5:57PM:
Karl, I wish things could somehow be different for us. I feel like I tried so hard to get you to see how sad and unhappy I was and I don't want to rehash everything, but I want you to know that I love you and always will. I only want you to be happy and I want the same for me. And I hope we can be on the same page when it comes to Alex.

I'm not trying to knock you but I need honesty. I think whatever you went through in your childhood marred you for life but I feel that whatever you went through, you can overcome! I miss you holding me. It hurts everyday...

* * *

**Sent from Karl Karlsen**
**Saturday, April 14, 2012** at 9:25PM:

I can ask you or beg you to work on us... I too wish things were different and believe me with help they can be. You have your demons and I have mine. I would love for you to let things lie until we get the shock of things out of our system. If you love someone, you don't give up but it's up to you.

## SIXTY-NINE

With any separation, the kids find themselves in the middle. And in Alex's case, with his sisters out of the house and Levi gone, the push and pull between his parents was tenfold. Both wanted him in their corner, and now that Cindy was no longer drinking, she felt she could win Alex over.

But she was wrong.

Karl had been sabotaging her all along, making sure Alex understood that his mother had a "problem" that would never go away. Every chance he got, Karl would remind Alex that the family would have stayed together, if only his mother could control herself.

Karl now had money again, and not only did he pour thousands of dollars into the duck business, throwing good money after bad, but in his bid to win Alex over, he bought the kid whatever he asked for. And this time, Karl went overboard.

First, he bought Alex a dirt bike. Then there were the two bloodhounds that Alex wanted. Karl bought those as well, keeping them at the farm would be more reason for Alex to stick around. But it didn't end there. Karl bought Alex flying lessons, guitar lessons, you name it. The list went on and on.

During one of his son's weekend visits, Karl took Alex on a surprise shopping spree and let him pick out a Bonzi RC speed boat, to the tune of $1,500. Karl then bought the identical speed boat for himself so the two of them could go racing in Seneca Lake. The 17-year-old kid was bought and paid for. It was all fun and games whenever Alex was with his dad.

But then one day Alex told him that his mom was seeing someone.

He was a guy named Dave.

And all at once, Karl had a new focus...

The good times were over.

## SEVENTY

Not long after he learned about Dave, Karl sent a threatening text to Cindy. But the text wasn't about Dave. Karl was letting Cindy know that he'd heard from Erin that she'd been snooping around in California, sticking her nose where it didn't belong.

---

**Sent from Karl Karlsen**

**Tuesday April 24,2012** at 4:29 PM:

I can't believe you would email Colette and tell her that an investigator was asking about my past. You are a lying bitch and you should be proud of yourself for only waiting weeks after you left me to jump in the sack with a drunk like yourself. I was proud of you for getting help but I guess it's all a lie. You only care about you. You stole money that doesn't belong to you and believe me I WILL DO WHATEVER IT TAKES to get it back. I'm so glad you left and now I know the real you is a money hungry thief who would take money from two little girls. Well believe me, everyone will know what you have done. And jumping in the sack with a drunk from rehab, you're a sad sick selfish person who only cares about her, not her son nor anyone else. Don't worry, I will send this to your lawyer who's trying to dig shit up. Don't ever come near me or my family. You're asking for trouble.

---

That same afternoon, Cindy and Dave packed three suitcases and then went to grab Alex. Cindy didn't know where they were headed, nor did she care. She was certain that Karl would retaliate and was adamant that they couldn't stay in one place for very long. She convinced Dave that for now, they needed to live on the run, otherwise Karl would find a way to hunt them down.

"It was a guy thing, I wanted to protect her," Dave would later say. "The whole time we were together Cindy was saying that her husband murdered two people, but I couldn't process it. And then she got that text and it started to get creepy. I was shocked when I read it because now I'm thinking this guy *really is* crazy, you know, this guy is nuts!"

With Cindy's Prius stuffed to the max, Dave began to wonder how this was going to work out. For starters, grabbing Alex from his girlfriend's house was going to be a problem because the kid knew absolutely nothing about the criminal investigation against his father. He was sure Alex would put up a fight. But Cindy wasn't worried about that. She sent Alex a text saying, "I'm coming to get you. And don't tell your father. I'll explain when I get there."

"When they pulled in the driveway and I walked out, I noticed the car was packed with all our belongings and our dogs were in there," Alex later recounted, "and I got in the car and we drove off, and that's when my mom told me that my dad was being investigated for Levi's death."

At that moment, Alex sat frozen.

He didn't want to say anything, but the words just came out.

"Mom, when I went to see Erin, she told me our father had something to do with Levi's death and we had a big fight about it."

"Erin *told you that?*"

"Yeah. And I told her she was crazy."

"Alex, this is *real*," Cindy said. "I'm going to call the sheriff's office and let you talk to one of the detectives."

Cindy immediately got John Cleere on the line and asked if she could put him on speaker. Her heart was pounding when she asked Cleere to explain what was going on and she braced herself for Alex's reaction.

After identifying himself as a lieutenant from the Seneca Falls Sheriff's Department, Cleere confirmed that he was investigating "some allegations" made against Alex's father, telling Alex that a criminal investigation was underway.

Cleere explained that because it was an ongoing investigation, he wasn't at liberty to say anything more. Before they signed off, Cleere asked Alex not to say anything to his father about their conversation, and of course Alex said he understood. But in reality, he didn't.

## SEVENTY-ONE

All through the conversation, Dave was looking at Alex's face in the rear-view mirror. It looked like he was on the verge of tears and Dave feared that Alex might try to do something stupid.

"It was chaos, and now it was *real* for me," Dave would later say. "After we took off, Cindy tells Alex about Karl and I wished we could just keep driving." But Dave knew they had to make a stop.

"She tells Alex we were going to leave their dog, Mattie, at the boarding kennel, and the kid starts hyperventilating," Dave recalled. "Mattie was a Sheltie, much bigger than their Pomeranian, and I knew there was no way we could keep both dogs, not while we were staying at motels. And when we got to the kennel Cindy opened the car door, and BAM, the poor dog took off. That dog knew she was getting dumped. It broke my heart."

It was Alex who ran after his beloved Sheltie, saving Mattie from running into the road. When he got back to the car, he was refusing to give Mattie up, but Alex was given no choice. Watching his mom gather Mattie and her favorite chew toys together made Alex start to cry.

When the three of them arrived in Syracuse and checked into the Comfort Inn, Alex was giving them the silent treatment. Soon after Dave brought their bags to the room, Alex announced that he was going down to the hotel gym to lift weights. But an hour later, when Cindy went down to check on him, her son was nowhere to be found.

She called Alex's cell phone but he didn't pick up. In a panic, she grabbed Dave and they drove through the nearby streets. With each passing minute, Cindy's panic got worse, and just when she was about to reach her breaking point, she spotted Alex hiding in the parking lot of a nearby McDonalds. He was bent over, holding his hands over his face.

"This kid is just getting on with his life and now there's no more school, there's no more girlfriend, there's no more friends around," Dave would later say. "My heart went out to him because everything, just everything in his life, was suddenly gone."

But there was no turning back.

Now that Alex knew the truth, his life would never be the same.

"We kept moving from hotel to hotel. There was no plan," Dave recalled. "It was crazy, and it was getting crazier by the day."

The following day, Cindy took Alex to the Sherriff's office in Waterloo to meet with John Cleere. When the two of them emerged about 45 minutes later, Alex's face was ghost white. Dave did whatever he could do to calm Alex down, telling him that everything was going to be okay, but Alex knew it was lip service. Nothing was going to be okay, ever again.

"It was tough," Dave would later say. "I'm a guy he's only known for two months and as much as I wanted to say, 'he's a murderer!' I know this is his father we're talking about. I could see that Alex was shaken up but at the same time, it was obvious that he didn't want to believe it, that he wasn't 100% sure."

"If your father has done this," Dave told Alex, "he's nothing but a coward."

"What do you mean by that?"

"If he's done this, if he let the truck fall on your brother and if he just left him there to die, he's a total coward."

Alex didn't want to think about it, but that was all he could think about.

The day Levi died was the worst day of his life.

And now it was sinking in.

"Mom, maybe I should have said something about this before," Alex told Cindy on the drive back to Syracuse, "because a lot of times when I was helping dad out at the farm, he would get mad if I wasn't working fast enough, and he used to hit me with a stick or with a shovel."

"What!" He was *hurting* you? Why didn't you tell me? I would have stopped him!"

"He said if I went running to mommy, I'd get hit worse."

"During that time on the run I was thinking a lot of irrational thoughts," Alex would later say. "I never knew if he was gonna find out where I was, or if he was gonna try to follow me. If he could kill one son, he could kill another, and I didn't know what he would do. I really didn't."

## SEVENTY-TWO

Later that night, Karl got a call from the distressed mother of Alex's girlfriend. She had become friendly with Karl and wanted to let him know that Cindy had whisked Alex away without an explanation. The woman said she was ready to call the police but Karl discouraged her, promising he'd get to the bottom of it.

When he tried to reach Alex his call went straight to voicemail. So he called Cindy, who was not picking up. Absolutely enraged, Karl sent her a barrage of text messages in which he threatened to report a kidnapping if he didn't hear from her ASAP. And the minute Cindy read that, she texted him right back.

---

**Karl:** Where are you? Please call me

**Cindy:** I had to get away for a while and I took Alex with me

**Karl:** Where's Alex? Call me

**Cindy:** Alex is going to be staying with me because this is too hard on him with the divorce and all the fighting. For now, I will only respond to texts. I won't answer any calls

**Karl:** Have Alex call me

**Cindy:** No. U have to go thru me. This is too hard for Alex to deal with

**Karl:** Does Alex know you won't let him call me?

**Cindy:** Yes. He's too upset to talk right now. He's really upset about the divorce and I think he's having a nervous breakdown

**Karl:** If I don't talk to him in 5 min I'm calling the cops

**Cindy:** Okay

**Karl:** Why are you keeping him from me? Where are you?

**Cindy:** I just need to let the dust settle

**Karl:** Have him call me or if not I will see you in court for keeping him from me

**Cindy:** Alex wanted to tell u he loves u. Pls leave him alone. He needs a break

**Karl:** Tell him to call or text me

**Cindy:** I'm keeping Alex's phone for now and you need to leave him out of this. I have been trying to work with you and keep it simple but every time we come up with an agreement u change your mind. You need to go thru my lawyer on everything PLEASE

**Karl:** I better hear from him soon!

---

But Karl didn't hear from Alex, not that night, not the next day, or the day after that. Alex was officially on the run with his mother and Dave. They were moving from one hotel to another and his mother tried to keep him in the loop, putting her phone on speaker whenever she checked in with John Cleere but unfortunately, he had no updates for her. None at all.

In the meantime, Karl was getting creative. He spent five days staking out The Norman Howard School in Rochester where Alex was a student. He was hoping to catch him, but there was no sign of the kid. On the sixth day Karl called the school to report Alex missing. He then placed a call to Child Protective Services, reporting Cindy for child abuse.

Soon thereafter a CPS official contacted the Seneca County Sherriff's Department, and John Cleere immediately contacted Cindy, telling her to bring Alex down to the station the following day. When she and Alex arrived, a woman from CPS was waiting for them. The social worker then took Alex aside, asking questions to make sure that he was physically okay. Alex had no signs of injury but his mother was guilty of neglect. Cindy was then informed that by law, she had to get Alex back in school immediately and if she didn't comply, she would be facing serious consequences.

From that point forward, Cindy and Dave had to split their time between two cities, staying in Rochester during the week so Cindy could drive Alex back and forth to school, then going back to Dave's turf in Syracuse on weekends where they had a bit more freedom. Whenever Cindy dropped Alex off at school, the situation was tense. She and Alex made an arrangement with the school to keep Karl from entering the building. However the constant juggling and the ever-present fear, was beginning to take its toll.

They were able to evade Karl until Alex's school year finished, but Cindy was hanging on by a thread. It was the end of June when she suggested that they take a road trip down to Greensboro, North Carolina, to spend a few days with her brother, Jamie, who'd been apprised of the situation.

Cindy felt that a change in pace would do them good, and they landed at Jamie's place just in time to celebrate the 4$^{th}$ of July. It was a much-needed holiday that helped lift Cindy's spirits. Being with her brother in Greensboro gave her a sense of peace and she wished she could hide there forever.

But Cindy didn't want to overstay her welcome, so from there they headed to Mt Sterling, Kentucky, where they visited her cousin Jackie. At the time, Cindy felt like her cousin was like a sister. They'd been taking walks regularly and had gotten closer than ever. Not only had Jackie become her sounding board, Jackie also helped her financially by managing to get Cindy employee rate at the Fairfield Inn. And that was great, because the rate applied to any Fairfield Inn, allowing Cindy to stay at any location of her choosing for just $39 a night.

Because Jackie's house was small, the three of them stayed at the Fairfield Inn located in Lexington. It was a beautiful area, complete with blue grass, gorgeous horses, and white post railings, but none of that helped matters. Cindy was more paranoid than ever, and she placed a tearful call to John Cleere telling him she could no longer stand to be in limbo. By then, the three of them had been on the run for almost two months and Cindy had enough.

She was tired of being a nomad.

"You know, Cindy, I think you should *just come home*," Cleere told her. "You're probably better off being back here because there's no telling when we'll be able to arrest him."

Hearing that from Cleere made Cindy's heart sink. All along, she'd been led to believe that Cleere was making progress, but instead, Cindy was back where she started. Like Steve Brown, Cleere was at a stand-still. And now, with Cleere suggesting that she return to Romulus, she would be within Karl's reach. It was a conundrum. Cindy couldn't let Alex be anywhere near his father, but she knew it was time to head back. They needed to be on solid ground.

On the drive back North, Cindy called Bev to ask for a favor. She needed her sister to keep Alex in Penn Yan for the remainder of the summer, and Bev was amenable to that. She thanked Bev profusely, Bev was a lifesaver, but that didn't help her or Dave, who spent evenings hiding in Cindy's bedroom with the lights turned off.

During the day, Cindy was out and about doing errands, she had no choice about that, and not long after she and Dave returned, she spotted Karl's pickup slowly driving by. And it happened more than once.

The situation had become untenable.

Cindy wanted her life back.

## SEVENTY-THREE

In late September, Karl showed up to The Norman Howard School looking very preppy in his khaki pants and pink button-down shirt. Even though the school had directions to keep Karl off the property, he'd managed to charm his way into the administration office where he convinced someone that his wife had made false accusations against him.

Prior to their ugly separation, Karl was often on campus and was revered by the staff there. He was an extremely concerned father who rarely missed a parent-teacher conference, who often volunteered to be a chaperone for class field trips. In fact, the year prior, Karl had accompanied Alex's class on a three-day excursion to Washington D.C.

That's how much the administration trusted him.

Karl assured them that *he* was the parent that Alex wanted to live with, asserting that *Cindy* posed a danger to their son. Cindy was taking Alex's life in her hands, he explained, because he knew for a fact that she had a habit of drinking and driving with Alex in the car.

Karl said it was imperative that he speak with Alex.

He was there to rescue his son.

And an assistant at the administration office obliged him.

However, when Alex was told that his father was there to see him and was summoned to the front office, Alex refused to go. It wasn't that his father had done anything bad to him, Alex explained, he just didn't want to get caught in the middle of his parents' divorce.

Alex's psychologist had advised him to stay out of it.

When the administrative assistant returned to the office without Alex, Karl asked to speak to the principal. He was adamant that Cindy had been brainwashing the kid and thought it was downright criminal.

But he was told that it was Alex who made that decision.

It was not their place to intervene.

When Cindy later picked Alex up from school and heard about Karl's thwarted visit, she became convinced that he would find his way to Alex one way or another. Karl was steaming mad that Alex was living with Cindy again. He was crazy with jealously because Dave was over there, and Cindy knew that.

She ultimately decided that the only way to remedy the situation was to call Karl and tell him that she and Dave had broken up, to tell him that she wanted to get back together again and would do whatever it took.

But Karl was still furious about the scene at Alex's high school. He'd been humiliated and he blamed Cindy entirely. Before they could think about reconciling, Karl wanted her to go down to the school and set the record straight. Cindy promised she would do that, telling him it was a big misunderstanding, and then she cozied up to him, trying to soften his heart.

"I want to be Mrs. Karlsen again," she told him. "I need to see you."

"I've always said it's up to you. I just don't know if that's what you really want."

"I'm not saying it's going to be right away, because there's still a lot of things that need to change..." her voice trailed off.

"I agree with that. Let's meet for coffee on Saturday and see how things go."

## SEVENTY-FOUR

When Dave heard about Cindy's plan to meet with Karl that weekend it made him nervous. He knew he had no right to stop her, but Dave wanted some reassurance that she could protect herself. At first Cindy told him she'd be fine, but on second thought, she came up with the idea of hiding a small tape recorder in her purse. She figured if Karl made any threats, she'd have evidence to bring to John Cleere.

The more she thought about it, Cindy came to believe she not only could catch Karl in a lie, she might be able to trip him up and get him to admit something about the insurance money and maybe even get him to talk about the barn fire.

It was on October 4th that Cindy and Karl sat down for coffee at McDonald's. She was there to talk about getting back together, but first, she needed Karl to admit that he'd been lying to her about the insurance money. In an attempt to get Cindy to feel sorry for him, he admitted that he'd gone through all the money he'd cashed out, confiding that his duck business was finished, that he'd been forced to kill more than eight thousand ducklings because he didn't have the money to feed them.

"What! Why didn't you sell them?"

"They weren't fat enough, no one would buy them."

"So you just killed them?"

"Yeah, and then I threw them in the burn pile."

Cindy heard Karl talking, but she began to zone out. The conversation made her feel sick. She hoped Karl was lying, that he was just saying this out of spite, but either way, she didn't want to listen anymore.

She needed to get out of there.

And fast.

She looked at her watch and said Alex was waiting for her to pick him up at his friend's house. She said she didn't have much time, and that was enough to put Karl into a rage. He started yelling at her, claiming she poisoned Alex and turned their son against him. Karl was tired of talking, he was through with her, and he got up and left in a huff.

A week later, Cindy asked Dave to drive her over to the farm, convincing him that they needed to survey the property to see if the ducks were really gone. Cindy really hoped that Karl was bluffing, but what she saw was sheer carnage.

"We drove out back to the big barn behind the house and I saw dead ducks all over," Cindy later said. "It was like a sea of dead ducks. There were ducks piled a foot high and the smell was so bad that I thought I would throw up."

Cindy didn't need to walk any further. She snapped a few pictures and jumped back in the car, asking Dave to head back down the driveway so she could take a peek at her house and quickly look inside the garage.

"This time, Dave got out of the car with me," Cindy would later say, "and what we saw in the garage was a sea of garbage. It looked like animals had ripped through it. There were food scraps all over the walls."

When she and Dave got over to the back deck, they found a mound of garbage thrown on top of nasty duck droppings. It looked like a waste site. However, just off the side of the deck were new "home improvements" that Cindy was shocked to see. Karl had put in a koi pond which he loaded with fish, and just to the left of that, he'd built a new patio, complete with an outdoor bar and a portico.

"I was stunned that Karl had put this stuff up," Cindy later said. "It was extremely disturbing because I knew he threw the money away, not caring one bit about those poor ducks."

Cindy took a few pictures of the back yard "additions" but after a few minutes, with Dave getting antsy, they took off. That turned out to be the right call because not long after, Karl pulled in the driveway.

"It was like the world was crashing around me and all of a sudden I'm losing my business," Karl would later explain. "I did kill a lot of the ducks, but I cut the breast meat out of the ones I could salvage to grind up for sausage. But the thing is, there were so many thousands of ducks. That's why I wound up having to kill 'em."

"I could hold 'em pretty easy because they weren't fearful," Karl continued, "cause I'm the guy who fed 'em all the time, so I'd put some feed down and then I'd stick one under my arm and cuddle it like a football. I'd just grab one, snap its neck and then grab the next one, and snap."

"I'm an animal lover, so I'd say a little prayer to myself cause I knew I had to do it... I had a wheelbarrow and I'd fill it up and take them and throw 'em in the fire, cause I didn't want other animals to get to 'em... It wasn't a big deal. I'd snap their neck and I'd hear a little eek and then it was over.

## SEVENTY-FIVE

After Karl walked out on Cindy that day, he immediately regretted it. He hated her for leaving him, but he couldn't blame her. He'd made mistakes. He'd gotten mean in the end.

"You know, you weigh the good against the bad and I think my temper was coming back and I was starting to get nasty," Karl later admitted. "I was pushing her away and yet I'm standing there expecting her to take it. And looking back at it now, it's like, hey you dumb ass, you blew it."

Like most people who want a second chance, Karl promised himself he'd do better next time. He was changing. He really was. He started to believe in God. He'd even started praying. And he needed Cindy to know that.

"Can you give me a little room to change?" he wrote in an email. "Don't close the door on us cause you know, I'm not the most religious person, but I've been going to church lately. And whenever I go there, I feel at ease. I know this sounds weird, but when I went into church the other day, I found the right pages in the book and started singing a hymn and it just felt right."

Karl claimed he was ready to confess his wrongdoings, telling Cindy he'd held "so many things in the vault." He said there were things he'd done in the past that tore him up, things he was afraid to tell her about, unless she could promise him complete confidence.

"I know we took oaths to be honest with each other and the sad part is that not being able to tell someone about your past is like having two lives, it's worse than hell," Karl wrote. "There are many things I'm ashamed of. There are things I did which scare me to death when I think about the afterlife. There are so many things from my past that have made me who I am, and there is no excuse for it, but I know I have to take ownership of it."

When Cindy wrote back, she said she agreed it would benefit everyone in the family if they could work things out. She wanted them to take it slow. She wanted all the pettiness to stop and told Karl if they both acted like adults, if they both truly trusted each other, they could make it work. Cindy hoped he was telling her the truth.

"If you truly have changed, and if there's more you want to tell me," Cindy wrote, "now would be the time to do it."

In early November they met for the second time, this time at a local diner called Jim & Georgia's. It was almost like the old days. The two of them sat in one of the back booths and looked deep into each other's eyes. Cindy talked about how good they were together, she wanted Karl to know she missed him, that their distance had made her appreciate him.

Karl was taking it in, he loved the compliments, and Cindy was studying his eyes, waiting for an opening. Karl had recently been in a car accident and he wanted sympathy. His car was totaled, he told her, claiming that he'd hit a tree when he swerved around a deer but Cindy knew it was the drugs. Karl seemed doped up.

"Alex told me it was bad. I guess you're going to buy another truck?"

"Yeah, but I haven't even had the chance to look."

"Oh really? Why not?"

"I'm waiting for the check from the insurance. Anything over $5,000 you have to wait for. I thought it would only take seven days but I've had to keep calling them for it."

"Bev and I are taking the girls out for their birthdays later today," Cindy said, skipping the subject. "I've been trying to see more of them but Cassie is making it hard."

"It is what it is," Karl said. "We know why Cassie has an attitude and it's not all my fault, you know what I mean?"

"Yeah. There's been a lot of bad blood."

"I mean, I'm not innocent, but you're not innocent either.," he told her. "But I'm not blaming you. I'm really not. I'm done with it because you know what?"

"What?"

"I can't change what happened from this moment back. This isn't just about you. It's about Levi. It's always been about Levi."

"What do you mean?"

"His life was a trainwreck and I blame myself for the way I handled things," Karl said. "The kid was never happy. The kid was always scrounging, asking for money."

"Yeah. He had a tough time of it."

"And you know, I went back there that day because I forgot to give him fifty bucks... and I've been thinking about this and I remember him going under the truck but he couldn't get quite underneath so I jacked up the truck, but the thing is, I didn't raise the blocks."

"You didn't raise it? I don't understand."

"He was trying to get underneath and he asked me to jack it up, and it was one of those old railroad jacks that dad used to have... It was really tall and I jacked it up as high as it would go, but I never put the fucking blocks underneath..." his voice trailed off.

"How come you never said anything about this before?"

"Because I was scared," Karl told her. "It sort of like, slipped. It fell over, and there's not a day that goes by that I don't..."

"What are you trying to say, Karl?"

'I don't want to say that I tried to cover it up, because it was an accident. I mean, come on. Two hours later he passes away. But it's the idea of what I did."

"But if it was an accident, why wouldn't you say something?"

"I mean, put yourself in my shoes... if I would have put the fucking blocks underneath maybe it would have stopped it. You know, maybe it would have... It's just when Levi died, everything unraveled."

"But, I mean, it was *an accident*, right?"

"That's what I'm saying."

"Okay. Then it wasn't your fault."

"It's just hard to get rid of everything I've been blaming myself for," Karl told her. "And the money helped me keep going... Not the money, but what we could do with it... You know what I'm saying? All of a sudden we're raising ducks, we're being noticed... and all of a sudden we're on a TV show and you just..."

At this point Cindy was holding her breath.

She was staring into his eyes, just waiting.

"So you know, in a way, I've lost two sons, because Alex won't talk to me now, and I don't know what else I can do. And I mean, it's sad."

"Karl, I've told you about Alex. Everything is just too much for him right now. He's confused. You just have to give him time."

"But why won't he even text me?"

"He has an old phone and the texting doesn't work on it," Cindy lied. "I need to get him a new phone."

"He can't text at all?"

"He's been bugging me for a phone for weeks," Cindy told him, taking a long pause. "You know, Karl, I feel like if I accept what you just said about Levi, we could go on. We could try to get back together. But my instinct tells me that you're not telling me everything."

"Cindy, you gotta look at it sensibly. We were gone for hours and there's nothing else I could have done. I mean, *why would I kill him?* And if I said I did it, which I didn't, why would you want to be with me?"

"I'm not saying it's going to be easy, we have to work at this," Cindy promised, "but what I'm saying is if you come clean, if you put everything out in the open, I'm not going to say anything to anybody."

"I told you what happened with Levi. I just never thought by jacking it up that this would have happened. I should have blocked… And I mean, look at the devastation that I caused us, his kids, his sisters, you, me, and the family… And I mean, look at Alex. He's still in counseling."

"Well, that's my number one issue, is to get Alex better. And then we can put one foot in front of the other to see if I can get beyond this."

"I'm not saying jump back in," Karl told her, "because this whole freaking thing is like a life changing thing, and I mean, you can go out and find somebody else."

"That's not what I want, Karl."

Cindy hated to rush off, she really did, but she had to meet Bev and she was already late. She told Karl she needed to have a few days to think about things, and said she'd like to have lunch again. She'd figure out what day would work and would call him.

When she pulled out of the parking lot, Cindy drove straight to John Cleere's office. She'd already called him with the news on the way there, and she couldn't wait for him to listen to the recording.

Cindy was anxious for an arrest, she knew she nabbed him, but after listening to the tape, Cleere burst her bubble.

"Unfortunately," he told her, "admitting to an accident is not enough."

"But he said it! He said he jacked the car up! He blamed himself!"

But Cleere needed Karl to admit intent.

Karl didn't confide his guilt.

He was claiming that the accident happened when he wasn't there.

## SEVENTY-SIX

It was when they met yet again, this time at Parker's Restaurant, a college hangout in Geneva, that Karl promised to tell Cindy the truth, the whole truth… and Cindy was ready to capture it on the recorder that was tucked in her bra.

Karl was wide-eyed, barely touching his burger and fries. He sat staring at Cindy like a kid who'd been caught with his hand in the cookie jar, and he started off by telling her what "a mean son-of-bitch" he was back when he served in the military, whispering "I'm gonna tell you stuff that we're not supposed to tell."

Among other things, Karl claimed he was in a special ops unit that was involved in undercover "hit and run" missions overseas. He said he had paperwork to prove it, claiming that he'd been sent to Kuwait to look for nukes, and while there, his team's mission was to hit certain targets, "top officials that Uncle Sam didn't like."

"So you had to kill people? Is that what you're telling me?"

"Any person that got in the way, you did what you had to do."

"Just tell me what you're trying to say," Cindy insisted, "I'm not going to say anything to anybody."

But Karl's brain was overloaded. He didn't want to tell her exactly what his special ops unit was called, he didn't recall how many people his unit killed, but when Cindy pressed the issue, Karl confided that he personally killed seven men. He told her it was hard on him, mentally, to live with that secret, that he could close his eyes and see it over and over again.

"It never leaves you," Karl said. "And I didn't want you to find out because I didn't want you to judge me. All I want right now is to start dating you again. I want to get your respect back."

"Well, if that was a military thing, that's between yourself and God," Cindy said, "but it scares me because I'm a believer."

"You weigh the pluses," Karl told her, "it's like it's either you or me, and you take charge."

Karl claimed the image of the Gulf was always fresh in his mind.

"It was hell, not being able to tell you," he said. "I've lived thirty years with my past tearing me up inside. But we took an oath and it was pounded into us that we had to live two lives, that we could never talk about it."

Cindy made a feeble attempt to placate him, telling Karl he should find a way to forgive himself for his past wrongs, but she was clearly annoyed. When she'd agreed to meet him in Geneva, it was under the condition that he'd be straight with her about Levi, and after sitting there for over an hour, she was tired of hearing the bullshit.

"I don't want you to beat around the bush, Karl... I don't want to get jerked around," she snapped. "If you want me to trust you, then you have to show me you're serious about this. Without you completely coming clean, there will be no us!"

"You can't get blood from a stone," he told her.

"This is your last chance, Karl," she paused. "Are you willing to admit to me that you did it?"

Karl looked stunned, but then his eyes welled up.

"If we get through this, you really think we could move forward?"

"Yes, because everything would be out in the open and we would be in the same boat. Neither one of us would have to talk about it ever again."

It took more cajoling, but somehow Cindy got Karl to trust her. She reminded him that she would always be his wife, that she'd vowed to love him in good times and bad. And she must have hit a nerve because all of a sudden, Karl spit it out. He said he'd jacked the vehicle up high and which made the truck wobble and then he just tipped the truck over.

"How would you be able to do that?"

"It's like when you tip over a wheelbarrow...

"And, I mean, I did it without thinking....

---

## SEVENTY-SEVEN

**Murphys' Law:** Anything that can go wrong *will* go wrong.

**Derivative of Murphy's Law:** Just when you think things can't get any worse, they will.

---

&#42; &#42; &#42;

There was an unexpected twist that occurred after Cindy's devastating lunch meeting with Karl at Parker's. She'd gotten him to confess, she'd heard the words come out of his mouth, but there was a problem.

When she arrived at the Seneca County Sheriff's Office with her recorder in hand, pressing 'play' so she and John Cleere could listen to it together, most of the sound was garbled. At first, Cleere assured her that they would be able to enhance the quality of the audio, that it shouldn't have been difficult.

But in the end, whatever incriminating statements Karl might have made at Parker's, were lost. The enhancement device allowed them to hear Karl talking about Levi's life insurance, it allowed them to hear Karl complaining about running out of money, but Karl's voice went down to a whisper when Cindy brought up Levi's "accident."

Cindy insisted that Karl admitted that he tipped the truck over on Levi. She listened to the garbled tape over and over, straining to pinpoint the exact moment when Karl said he'd tipped the truck over "like a wheelbarrow..." But the background noise in the restaurant, the clinking of silverware and dishes, was all she could hear.

The buzz at restaurant thwarted Cindy's valiant effort.

Karl had deliberately chosen a college hangout.

He suspected her, she now realized that.

## SEVENTY-EIGHT

"She was baiting me, and stupid me, I fell into it," Karl later said. "I don't know *why I would say the word* wheelbarrow. This is where I seriously put my foot in my mouth. I thought, maybe if I said whatever she wanted to hear, things would get better."

And in a way, Karl was right.

Eventually, things did get better. But not for him.

John Cleere had sent the audiotape to a lab, thinking Karl's voice could be deciphered, but that wasn't meant to be. His next move was to call Cindy into the station and ask if she'd be willing to wear a wire. He wanted her to re-create the conversation she'd had with Karl at Parker's.

It would be risky, they both knew that, but he assured Cindy that she'd be surrounded by undercover cops, that he had her back. Cindy waited a few days and then called Karl, asking him to meet her for lunch at Abigail's, a cozy restaurant in Waterloo.

She still loved him.

She was willing to work things out.

It was John Cleere who chose Abigail's because it had a full dining room that would allow plain clothes officers to find seats at an array of tables within earshot.

That was a brilliant move on Cleere's part because it provided a loophole around the rule of "marital privilege."

If Cindy was successful, if she was able to elicit a confession at Abagail's, a defense attorney would argue to keep it out of court by asserting marital privilege. However, the one exception to that rule was if the confession was made in a public setting where others could overhear it. So Cleere's undercover officers served two purposes. They gave peace of mind to Cindy and were also acting as witnesses.

On November 16, 2012, after police wired her up, three pairs of undercover detectives followed Cindy over to Abigail's an hour before the set meeting time. They remained in their unmarked vehicles until Karl pulled up and then waited ten minutes for the couple to get situated.

Cindy had been asked to find a table near the brick fireplace, which she did. But rather than feeling protected because undercover "customers" would be arriving, she felt added pressure.

Cindy was a bundle of nerves. She already knew Karl was suspicious because he'd mentioned something about "a booby trap" when they set the date. She'd been able to convince Karl he was the only man for her, that she didn't want to throw 18 years of marriage away. But now, watching Karl walk toward her with a slight grin on his face, Cindy felt like her heart was going to stop.

It was go time.

Cindy greeted Karl with a kiss on the cheek before he sat down. She'd chosen the best table in the place, situated directly in front of the electric- powered fireplace. The goosebumps on her arms were hidden by her sweater, the wire was tugging at her back, and she couldn't believe the situation she was in. But she was following a script.

And she was told to take her time.

Cindy sat through the lunch, letting Karl do most of the talking. As usual, he went into a dissertation about his latest health problems, opening up the conversation by telling her that his most recent shoulder surgery left him with an open wound, that he couldn't stop the yellow puss from oozing out of it.

That was Karl.

Always inappropriate.

Always making people squirm.

Karl seemed to enjoy making people feel uneasy, disgusted even, and Cindy let him go on. As he described his other physical problems, including a bleeding ulcer, Cindy pretended to care.

But she wasn't really listening.

She was waiting for coffee and dessert to be served.

"I don't have a lot of time today," she finally said, looking at her watch. "I was wondering if we could finish our story from the other day, cause it's still not making sense to me."

"Okay, I guess. But I already told you everything."

"Can you just tell me how things went that day? So I can just know in my head that..."

"I mean, I'm being honest with you," he said, cutting her off.

"Cause I think we're both at the point where we understand what happened."

"Well, I can't accept things just like that. I mean, I need to know you're *sorry* about it, right?"

"Every minute of every day."

"Okay Karl, and I believe that... But I still can't wrap my head around it."

"Alright. Let me say this. *Did I purposely do it?* Not at all."

"Can you just tell me what happened that day?"

"What I remember is, I jacked it up and it slipped."

"It slid? That's not what you told me the other day."

"Remember I told you I jacked it up? Well, while I was in there the truck slid back and BOOM! And I fuckin' shit my pants and just about panicked right there."

"That's not what you told me before, Karl."

"Yes it is."

"No Karl. I asked you if you pushed the truck and you said yes."

"I didn't push the truck! I said I had nothing to do with it. But I said I took advantage of the situation once it happened. That's exactly what I said to you."

"Karl, you told me that you didn't set it up that way, but when you were in there, you saw the opportunity."

"After it happened! Then I panicked and I saw the opportunity. That's exactly what I said!"

Cindy kept at it, trying to get Karl to repeat what was lost on the prior tape, but her continuous questions made Karl skittish. He wanted to know why she was backtracking and repeatedly asked her if she was setting up a trap.

"Do you have a tape recorder in your purse?"

"Why would you ask that?

Cool as a cucumber, Cindy handed her purse over and asked him if he wanted to go through it... but he stopped short.

"Okay, just hear me out," he told her. "It was never meant to be. It was never planned from day one."

"What do you mean, from day one?"

"You know, from the time we did the insurance stuff... But I mean, I don't ever think like that."

"The other day you told me how you felt after the fact... You said that Levi had so many problems in the past and you were reminding me about all the trouble he caused…"

"Right. It was almost sort of a relief," he admitted. "You could look at it like that. Cause you know, Levi's done things in life. He got married, he experienced kids. You know what I'm saying?"

"Yeah."

"And it's almost like I can justify…"

"Mmm Hmm."

"You know what I'm telling you? It's just, it wasn't me. The truck just fell over on him."

"Did it fall hard, or?"

"No."

"You had to bump it?"

"No, cause it's so wobbly cause the front is off the ground two feet…"

"It only fell two feet?"

"No. You take the whole front end of the car and pick it up in the air."

"Mmm Hmmm."

"It's like picking up a wheelbarrow, except do it the opposite. You pick up the wheelbarrow, except pick it up from the front. And rolling it forward and backwards is going to be hard, but moving it from right to left is simple. It just rolls."

Cindy wanted Karl to tell her what happened next, she wanted to know if Levi suffered, hoping her stepson died instantly. Karl promised her that Levi didn't suffer. He then confided that he often contemplated suicide. He said that being with Levi in the garage was like a "hallucinogen-type out-of-body experience."

In the end, Karl blamed his methadone addiction for what happened. He said he'd done research on the effects of that drug, telling her "it was almost like I was sitting back and watching myself."

"Any more coffee?" the waitress came over and asked.

But the coffee talk was over.

## SEVENTY-NINE

That time, Cindy nailed it.

John Cleere had enough to arrest him, but if he could get Karl down to the station if he could get Karl talking on videotape, that would build an air-tight case. It was just before Thanksgiving when Cindy got another call from John Cleere. She'd gone down to North Carolina to spend the holiday, so when he asked her to set up one last "rendezvous," she couldn't help him.

"No, no, it doesn't have to be with you there," Cleere told her. "It will be a fake rendezvous. I'll be there with my partner waiting for him in the parking lot. We want you to stay out of it."

"Are you going to arrest him?"

"Not yet. We want to see if we can get him down to the station to see if he'll talk on the record. Just call and ask him to meet you at the Golden Buck restaurant. It's in Ovid. I'm sure you know it."

Cindy called Karl on Thanksgiving Day to say that she missed him, that the holidays always made her melancholy. Of course, Karl was happy to hear that. He was happy to meet her for lunch the next day and held out hope that he'd won her over.

On November 23, 2012, Karl was met in the Golden Buck parking lot by John Cleere and investigator Tom Crowley. He'd been looking around for Cindy's car when the two officers got out of their unmarked vehicle and approached him.

"Are you Karl Karlsen?" Cleere asked.

"Yes I am."

"Do you know why we're here?"

"Yeah," Karl said. "You want to talk about my dead wife and my dead son."

* * *

"He was almost happy to get in our vehicle and go with us," Cleere later recalled. "I tried not to show it, but I was pretty stunned by Karl's response. It was wild. It was a hell of a thing for him to say."

When Cleere asked Karl if he'd be willing to take a ride down to the sheriff's office to answer a few questions, he didn't seem to be rattled. If anything, he seemed smug.

Cleere had chosen Investigator Tom Crowley to join him in the interrogation room and had New York State Investigator Jeff Arnold sitting in the observation room to listen and take notes. At 12:32 PM, Cleere pressed 'start' on a video recorder and Karlsen was read his rights. Initially, he agreed to talk to them without a lawyer, but soon thereafter, when Crowley confronted him with what they already knew, telling Karlsen they were aware of the confession he'd made to his wife, Karl hesitated for a minute, asking if he needed an attorney. Cleere gave him the opportunity to make a phone call, but for some reason Karl changed his mind.

He had nothing to hide and was happy to talk.

Cleere and Crowley had no idea that they were in for a marathon interrogation. Karl sat there talking to them for over *nine hours,* getting increasingly tangled up in his own lies, at first insisting that he didn't know his son was dead until he returned from a funeral at 4PM on the day in question.

---

CROWLEY: When you were telling the truth to your wife, you were being a good person, a good person like you are.

KARLSEN: *No, I did not kill my son.*

CROWLEY: No one said you killed your son. What we are saying is what we know to be true, that you pushed that car over on him.

KARLSEN: I did not.

CROWLEY: Well, here's the thing. You confessed to your wife.

KARLSEN: I lied to my wife. Did you have her wired? Be honest with me.

CROWLEY: Yes, we did. It's all recorded, and it's witnessed. You went with your conscience and you did the right thing.

KARLSEN: No, I didn't go with my conscience.

CROWLEY: All you are going to do is make yourself look like a monster because it's not only what you told your wife, there's scientific evidence.

KARLSEN: Well, I'm sorry. I did not push it over.

CROWLEY: You told your wife multiple times, that you did what you had to do. You took an opportunity to benefit your family.

KARLSEN: They call that murder.

CROWLEY: I never called it murder.

KARLSEN: Well, I do. You don't kill your son. You don't kill anybody for money.

CROWLEY: Who said anything about money?

---

Karl admitted that he made the first payment on Levi's insurance policy to help his son out. He continually called Cindy a liar and was angry that she set him up. He claimed his drug addiction played into everything he told her, claiming that he was on a mixture of drugs. He quickly rattled off the list: methadone, anti-depressants, Fentanyl patches, and Vicodin. He didn't know what he was saying at Abagail's, how could he? He was so doped up.

---

CROWLEY: I know what happened in the garage. You pushed that car on your son. Was it the medicine that caused you to not know what you were doing?

KARLSEN: With the medicine, you don't know shit. Whenever I walked, I had to have help. Back then, I didn't know what I was doing.

CROWLEY: Did the medicine cause you to push the truck? We know you told Cindy that you caused his death.

KARLSEN: I did not cause it to happen. I said I felt I caused it because it was my truck. Wouldn't you feel guilty if you asked your kid to help you and something like that happened?

---

Karl told the investigators that he loved Levi more than anything, that he offered his son a few dollars to work on his truck because Levi didn't have a job at the time. He explained that he was the sole beneficiary of his son's life insurance policy because Levi didn't trust his ex-wife and claimed he never knew there was an accidental death rider until after Levi died. As for where the money went, Karl said he and Cindy spent the money "to pay some bills," adding that he used part of the insurance money to pay for the funeral.

At that point, Cleere and Crowley exited the room with only Cleere re-entering to offer Karl a cup of water. Interrogation rooms are set up to make the suspect as uncomfortable as possible, to help break the suspect down, and as Cleere took his seat on a metal chair, he was ready to break him. He started from the top, asking Karl when he last saw his son alive, but Karl skipped over that.

"I got back home at 4PM and went in the garage and saw him," Karl told Cleere. "Levi was more under the side of the truck, so the wheelbarrow analogy I told Cindy was accurate."

Karl quickly moved away from the wheelbarrow analogy, shifting back to his drug issues. The guy had health problems, and Cleere let him ramble on, waiting to trip him up.

With Crowley and Arnold watching through a two-way mirror and taking notes, Cleere would switch off periodically, letting Arnold take the lead, and then Crowley. It was amazing, how much this guy loved to talk, and the three of them sat through the longest interrogation on record.

Karl did whatever he could to keep away from the topic of insurance money, telling the investigators about Levi and Cassie's custody battle, even bragging about his time spent in the Air Force handling nukes. He was ready to go on, he wanted to explain that he was part of the team that was trusted with top secret launch codes, and the investigators were tempted to ask follow-up questions about that, but they were done with Karlsen's Alice in Wonderland trip.

It was time to get down to business.

Enough was enough.

## EIGHTY

"We're aware that Levi's life insurance policy was taken out less than a month before he died," Crowley said, "was that also the case with your first wife?" But Karl didn't want to talk about that.

Instead, he told them about his unhappy second marriage, describing Cindy as a raging alcoholic, blaming Cindy for the demise of his duck business. Then without batting an eyelash, Karl made a slashing motion across his neck, telling Crowley that because his business went under, he wound up having to kill 8,000 ducks...

But Crowley wasn't taking the bait.

He walked out of the room and brought Cleere in for backup.

Cleere knew that Karl loved sympathy, he'd been coached by Cindy about that, so he went into a grandfatherly mode, saying it must have been tough being in so much pain, having to take so many drugs just to be able to walk upright. Cleere wondered if Karl was too "out of it" to realize that he pushed the truck on Levi. But Karl said he wasn't. He was drugged, but not that drugged.

"Let's stop the dancing," Crowley finally said. "We all know what happened." And then for whatever reason, Karl let his guard down. With his body swaying back and forth as if he was sitting in a rocking chair, Karl tearfully admitted that he knew Levi was dead before he left for the funeral. He said that when he'd gone out to the garage that morning to hand Levi fifty dollars, he saw him lying there, crushed under the truck.

"I just blanked," Karl said. "I knew Levi was dead because I reached down and touched his leg and *I knew*. His legs were blue."

With John Cleere trying to console him, telling him to let it all out, Karl yelled, "I freaked! I fucking freaked!"

Karl said that he didn't know what to do, so he ran to the house. He explained that he had to get ready for the funeral, so he took a shower, shaved, and got dressed. He said he turned on the TV because it didn't seem real to him. It wasn't registering with him that Levi was gone.

"I could never *ever* kill my son," he insisted.

John Cleere and his men had been able to pull a partial confession out of Karl, but in order to charge him with first degree murder, they needed Karl to admit intent.

---

**CLEERE:** I believe part of what you're saying, but I need you to fill in the blanks.

**KARLSEN:** I made the decision to walk out on my son and not get him out from under the truck.

**CLEERE:** Why?

**KARLSEN:** I panicked.

**CLEERE:** Why?

**KARLSEN:** I bawled my eyes out like a baby because I finally pulled him out and seen his face... I'll take the rap for walking out on my son, but I did not kill him! I did not!

---

For Cleere, that confession was sheer gold.

It ensured that Karlsen would be charged with second degree murder.

But Cleere was still hoping for platinum.

## EIGHTY-ONE

"You went away for *four* hours and came back and put on a big show," Cleere said, eyeballing Karl up and down. Cleere then turned on the Abigail's tape, letting Karl hear the beginning of the conversation after inviting Jeff Arnold into the room to follow along with the corresponding transcript.

Arnold had a gruff way about him, he didn't mince words, so when Karl claimed he was playing a game with Cindy, asserting that he was testing her, Arnold cut him off.

Jeff Arnold kept asking Karl why he *pretended* to find Levi, why he *pretended* that it was an accident when he knew the truth, but Karl stuck to his story, insisting that he wasn't there when it happened.

"I did not cause his death," Karl insisted. "I didn't kill him, okay? Let's get that straight. I *did not* kill him.

But Karl's body language, his jittery feet and anxious eyes, were giving him away. The man was squirming and he was asking for someone to get him his drugs. He said he was in too much pain to keep going, but remarkably, Karl kept on talking. He wanted to tell Arnold, in excruciating detail, about his many surgeries. Like a masochist, Karl seemed to enjoy describing his pain, focusing on the blood and puss that oozed from his surgery sites. It was disgusting.

"I've got wires that go from my brain to my spinal cord," Karl said, sinking down into his metal chair. "But like, right now, the batteries aren't working, so it's tough."

But it couldn't have been that tough, because it had been over eight hours by then and Karl held up, without so much as an aspirin. When Cleere took the reins again, Karl said he wanted to stand up and stretch, and it was then, once he was out of his seat, that Karl asked about calling an attorney. It was a blow, Cleere thought, it was over. But all of a sudden, Karl changed his mind.

He was willing to keep talking.

But with that threat now on the table...

It was time to ratchet things up a notch...

CLEERE: You know, no one will believe your story. You better start doing damage control, Karl.

KARLSEN: I did not do anything.

CLEERE: Why did you do it, Karl?

KARLSEN: I couldn't kill my kid. I loved him more than anything.

CLEERE: Think about helping yourself.

KARLSEN: I didn't do it! It was an accident!

CLEERE: Come on. You're *this close* man. Come on. I'll walk with you. I'll stand up for you. I'm going to stand up and say this wasn't premeditated, that it was something that just happened. Shit happens sometimes Karl. That's what I'll do for you.

KARLSEN: It was an accident...I opened the truck door...And when I did, it fucking fell.

**And there it was – they were another step closer to a full confession.**

"I asked him if it was a split-second thing," Cleere would later say, "and when he said he opened the truck door and the truck fell, he started crying to me, which I thought was his first real emotion."

# EIGHTY-TWO

John Cleere had successfully brought Karl one step closer to admitting to first degree murder, and he felt with a little more pressure, he could get there.

---

**CLEERE:** Karl, if it was an accident, why did you try to hide it?

**KARLSEN:** I was scared.

**CLEERE:** You're very very close Karl. Come on.

**KARLSEN:** (now crying): I didn't do it.

**CLEERE:** Karl, you can do it. Just get it off your chest.

**KARLSEN:** Listen, (still crying) I opened up the fucking door and I stepped in.

**CLEERE:** So you opened up the car door?

**KARLSEN:** I opened the truck door because I had to get inside to move the linkage from the fucking truck. And when I did, it tipped. It fucking fell over.

**CLEERE:** You're almost there my friend.

**KARLSEN::** (sobbing loudly) I don't give a shit how bad it looks. I got in the car because he couldn't get the linkages out. And it was because I stepped in the truck that it just fucking fell. It just fucking tipped and I was so fucking scared.

---

John Cleere applauded Karl for coming closer to the truth. He praised Karl for being a stand-up guy.

---

**CLEERE:** You said it fell when you opened the door. Now take the final step, Karl.

**KARLSEN:** There is no more to tell. I'll swear on anything. I stepped in the truck and the fucking thing fell. And I was fucking scared shitless.

**CLEERE:** I know you talked to Cindy about making hard decisions and sometimes you had to take people's lives when you were in the military.

**KARLSEN:** *Yeah, but this is your kid. And there's a difference.*

**CLEERE:** So you're saying you walked away and left him there.

**KARLSEN:** (squirming) I know. Yeah.

**CLEERE:** Come on Karl. Go the distance.

**KARLSEN:** That's it. I mean, I walked away. How could I do that? I don't know if it was the fucking drugs that made me not register. I didn't think it was real.

---

It was then that Jeff Arnold jumped in, asking Karl if he realized that Levi died from suffocation because his lung was collapsed, claiming that if the truck had been lifted off Levi immediately, *Levi would have lived.*

---

**ARNOLD:** So the truck fell on your son and instead of jacking it back up, you ran.

**KARLSEN:** I was scared as shit. I just blanked. I just got the hell out of there like a kid who threw a rock through a window and didn't want to get caught. And when I come home and I pulled him out, I seen his face and it was like – the switch turned back on. Like, this is my kid. What did I just do?

---

It was heading on nine hours, and Arnold thought there was more blood to get from that stone. The investigator outright accused Karlsen of murder, but Karl sat silent. Arnold then accused Karl of deliberately making Levi's death look like an accident, saying that he knew that Karl turned on the radio so no one could hear Levi's screams...

"I didn't give a shit about the money," Karl insisted. "I got kids, I got grandkids, and to sit here and say I killed my son, there's just no way. There's no way!"

By then it was after 9:00 PM, and the three investigators were exhausted. They'd done all they could and finally had come to the realization that Karlsen wasn't going to bear any more fruit. At that point, Cleere asked Karl to write down a summary of what he'd just told them, and at 9:43 PM, Karlsen wrote and signed the following statement:

---

*"On November 20th 2008 my son Levi was working on my truck to rewire the transmission line and brake line. The truck was jacked up and he and I worked on it. Then I had to go in and take a shower and when I came out my wife and I were going to a funeral. She got into the car and I went into the garage to give Levi some money for helping and he could not get the line unhooked so I got in the truck. I opened the passenger door and jumped in and laid on the front seat to move the four-wheel drive over. At that time the truck rocked over and fell on top of Levi and I got out of the truck after it fell and panicked and went to the funeral with my wife. After that we came back and I went to the garage and saw him there and I lifted the truck up and pulled him out. Once I saw him I went up to the house to tell my wife and*

*then went back and hand held him until help came. It was like I was not accepting what happened but when I saw his face, it came to being real."*

## EIGHTY-THREE

Before the ink dried, Karlsen was charged with second-degree murder and insurance fraud, then was handcuffed and led to a jail cell. His bail was set at $500,000 and because Karl couldn't come up with the money, he would spend over a year in jail awaiting his trial.

Just weeks after Karl was put behind bars, in between Christmas and New Year's Day, Erin flew to Rochester to pay a visit to her father. A strong-willed woman, Erin believed she could get him to fess up about the house fire and what he did to her mother. She later claimed that when she grilled him, her dad "smiled like a Cheshire cat."

"It's been over twenty years since her death," Karl told her. "What makes you think they're going to get me now?"

A few months later, toward the end of February, Cassie Hohn decided to visit her former father-in-law at the Seneca County Jail as well. Karl didn't ask her how she was holding up, he wasn't interested in the least. Instead, started off the conversation by bragging about his high-powered attorney, insisting he'd been framed. He told Cassie that he'd already spent $50,000 to retain the hotshot and claimed that he needed to raise another $500,000 "or else the attorney will walk."

Again, it was all about him. It was always about him.

After complaining relentlessly about the twisted justice system and ridiculously high amount of his bail, Karl finally got around to asking about his granddaughters. He wanted to know what they knew about the charges against him. He wanted to know what they thought of "Grandpa."

"The girls are having a hard time grasping what is going on," Cassie told him. "I'm having a hard enough time getting them to speak."

"Maybe if you brought the girls to see me in jail they would understand that Grandpa is still Grandpa."

To that, Cassie rolled her eyes.

"Maybe if they write to me while I'm here, maybe that would help them cope."

"Right now I'm just focusing on getting them through each day at a time," she told him, "but I will run it by their therapist."

"You know, my attorney is trying to get me reduced bail, and if not, I'm going to sell the farm and then go after Cindy legally."

Cassie gave him a quizzical look. She wasn't sure what he meant by that.

"Cindy took all the insurance money about two months before she left me," Karl told her. "She bought an expensive house in Newark that cost $117,000 and I don't know where the rest of the money went, but when I get out of here, I'm going to make sure she pays back the girl's scholarship fund!"

Karl ranted about Cindy being a greedy person, telling Cassie that Cindy couldn't spend the money fast enough, revealing that she'd spent thousands of dollars on an unnecessary facelift and had recently bought herself a new car. Cassie was furious when she heard that, vowing that she'd never let Cindy see the girls again.

"I'm gonna stick it to Cindy in civil court, Karl said, "because she had no right to use that money!"

"Did Levi have a will?"

"No."

"Did he have an account at Five Star Bank?"

"I'm not sure," Karl told her. "I would really like the girls to come visit me while I'm in here because they will always have a grandpa."

Karl wanted to establish "a tight relationship" with the girls as soon as he was released. He wanted Cassie to know that as soon as he got out of there, he was going to take her and the girls on a cruise so he could "show them a good time." Karl promised that he would buy each of his granddaughters a car when they turned 16 and vowed that he would find a way to pay for their college educations.

The girls would be taken care of. That was always the plan.

He wanted her to be sure of that, and Cassie nodded, giving him a smile.

She promised to come back and visit again real soon.

But Cassie never stepped foot in the jail again.

Cindy's cousin Jackie Hymel (left) was like a sister to Cindy for many years, circa 2012. (Courtesy of Bev Best)

Karl helps Alex get dressed for a family holiday gathering, circa 2002. (Courtesy of Cindy Best)

Kati holds her Sweet Sixteen birthday cake, circa 2002. (Courtesy of Cindy Best)

Karl washing pots and pans, circa 2003. (Courtesy of Cindy Best)

Levi takes baby Alex for a ride on his back, circa 1996. (Courtesy of Cindy Best)

Levi plays with his baby brother, Alex, circa 2004. (Courtesy of
Cindy Best)

"Grandpa Art" spins Alex around in the swimming pool while
visiting Romulus for the second time, circa 2004. (Courtesy of
Cindy Best)

Cassie and Levi beam with pride on their wedding day, circa 2003. (Courtesy of Cindy Best)

Left to right: Cindy, Kati, Karl, Alice, Junior, Erin, Art, his girlfriend, Mary and Alex attend Erin's high school graduation, circa 2002. (Courtesy of Cindy Best)

Left to right: Cindy, Karl, Alex, and Kati celebrate Kati's high school graduation, circa 2004. (Courtesy of Cindy Best)

Left to right: Cindy, Alex, Karl, and Kati pose for their church registry, circa 2004. (Courtesy of Cindy Best)

Karl looks over at and his first grandchild, Elletra Karlsen, circa 2004. (Courtesy of Cindy Best)

Karl deep in thought while on a camping trip, circa 2004.
(Courtesy of Cindy Best)

Left to right: Cindy, Alex, and Karl dress for dinner while on a
cruise to Mexico, circa 2004. (Courtesy Cindy Best)

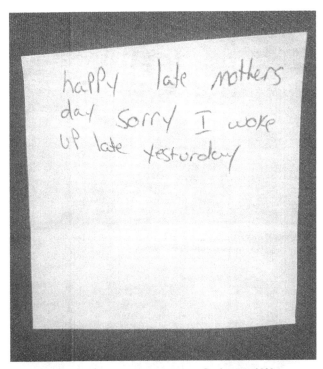

happy late mothers day sorry I woke up late yesterday

Levi wrote this Mother's Day post-it note to Cindy, circa 2008. (Courtesy of Cindy Best)

Cindy earns her red belt in Taekwondo. She would later hide nun chucks under her bed, sleeping with one eye open. (Courtesy of Cindy Best)

Karl was always a bulky guy and his presence could be unnerving. (Courtesy Cindy Best)

The family attends Kati's graduation from the New York State Park Police Academy, circa 2008. Left to right: Karl, Erin, Kati, Cindy, Alex, and Levi. (Courtesy of Cindy Best)

Levi acting goofy, circa 2006. (Courtesy of Cindy Best)

Elletra (left) and Ivy celebrate Ivy's 2nd birthday at Grandma
Cindy's house, circa 2007. (Courtesy of Cindy Best)

Page 1 of 1                                           CR#: _____

**Seneca County Sheriff's Department**
6150 Route 96
Romulus, New York 14541

### *Statement / Deposition*

Statement of: Karl H Karlsen          Date of Birth: 01/17/1960
Address: 885 Yale Farm Road, Romulus, N.Y
Phone #: 315-651-1157

On Nov 20th 2008 my son Levi was working on my truck to Remove Transmission Lines + Brake Line and the power steer pump the truck was jacked up and he and i worked on it then i had to go in to take a shower when i came out my wife and i were going to a funeral she got into the car and i went to the garage to give Levi money for helping and he could not get the Line un hook so i got in the truck opened passenger door Jumped in and Layed on front seat to move it when Drive Lever at that time the truck Rocked over and fell ontop of Levi and i got out of truck and then it fell and panicked. and went with my wife to the funeral after that we came back and went to the garage and saw him then, lifted truck off him and pulled him out once i saw him went to house to tell wife and then went Back and realized that it all really happened and held him till help came. It was like i was not accepting it happened but when i saw his face it all came to being real

Verification by subscription and notice under penal law section 210.45
It is a crime punishable as a Class A misdemeanor under the law of the State of New York, for a person, in and by a written instrument, to knowingly make a false statement, or to make a statement which such person does not believe to be true.
Affirmed under the penalty of perjury this 23 Day of November, 2012

Witness: _____          Signed: Karl Karlsen

Date: 11/23/2012                  Date: 11/23/12
2146 hrs.

Karl's hand-written confession, given to Lt. John Cleere on November 23, 2012.
(Courtesy of the Seneca County Sheriff's Department)

Karl Karlsen's mug shot after being charged with the murder of his son, Levi, taken November 23, 2012. (Courtesy of the Seneca County Sheriff's Office)

Karl was high on pain killers when he slammed his pickup truck into a tree, circa 2012. (Courtesy of Cindy Best)

Elletra's 1ST grade school photo, circa 2009. (Courtesy of Cindy Best)

Ivy's pre-k school photo, circa 2009. (Courtesy of Cindy Best)

992005927
NEW YORK LIFE
PO Box 6916
Cleveland, OH 44101-1916
www.newyorklife.com

*The Company You Keep®*

**New York Life Insurance Company**
**Annual Policy Summary**

Page 1 of 2

| Policyowner | Agent/Representative |
|---|---|

THIS IS NOT A BILL
>016663 3032395 0001 092154 102

MRS CINDY S KARLSEN
PO BOX 25351
FARMINGTON, NY 14425-0351

ANTHONY CRISCI MS
(315) 331-2627

DATE PREPARED: AUG 25, 2014

This annual summary highlights the financial activity for your policy during the period from Aug 27, 2013 to Aug 25, 2014. All values quoted in this statement are applicable on the date the statement was prepared. Your future values may be higher or lower based on a number of factors including premium payments. If you have any questions, please contact your New York Life agent listed above or one of our Customer Service Representatives at 1-800-695-9873.

| | | |
|---|---|---|
| Coverage | Insured: | ELLETRA C KARLSEN |
| | Policy Number: | 49 377 767 |
| | Policy Plan: | Term Extension Life Insurance |
| | Base Plan Death Benefit: | $274,728 |
| | Policy Date: | Aug 24, 2009 |
| | Premiums are Paid To: | Aug 24, 2013 |
| | Insurance Expiration Date: | Aug 25, 2078 |
| Life Insurance Death Benefit | Total Death Benefit on Aug 24, 2014: (See Page 2 for details.) | $274,728.00 |
| Policy Cash Value * | Net Cash Value on Aug 24, 2014: (See Page 2 for details.) | $11,494.62 |

This coverage results from the nonpayment of premium for the above policy. Pursuant to your policy's provisions, coverage is being continued as Extended Term Insurance, with no further premiums due. Please contact your agent or customer service representative with any questions.

The **NUMBER ONE** cause of problems in processing claims is inaccurate or invalid beneficiary designations - Call your Agent **TODAY** to review yours.

For policy information and online service, please visit us at ------> www.newyorklife.com/vsc

Please refer to the Definition of Terms and other information on the reverse side of page 2.
* Any gain in the policy may be subject to taxation if it lapses or is surrendered.

**IMPORTANT POLICYOWNER NOTICE:** You should consider requesting more detailed information about your policy to understand how it may perform in the future. You should not consider replacement of your policy or make changes in your coverage without requesting a current illustration. You may annually request, without charge, such an illustration by contacting your agent or broker at (315) 331-2627, sending a fax to your Service Center at 1-800-695-9873. If you do not receive a current illustration of your policy within 30 days from your request, you should contact your state insurance department.

The New York Life insurance policy written on Elletra C. Karlsen (Courtesy of Cindy Best)

992005927
NEW YORK LIFE
PO Box 6916
Cleveland, OH 44101-1916
www.newyorklife.com

The Company You Keep®

**New York Life Insurance Company**
**Annual Policy Summary**

Page 1 of 2

Policyowner

Agent/Representative

THIS IS NOT A BILL
>005927 3032395 0001 092154 107

MRS CINDY S KARLSEN
PO BOX 25351
FARMINGTON, NY 14425-0351

ANTHONY CRISCI MS
(315) 331-2627

DATE PREPARED: AUG 25, 2014

This annual summary highlights the financial activity for your policy during the period from **Aug 27, 2013** to **Aug 25, 2014.** All values quoted in this statement are applicable on the date the statement was prepared. Your future values may be higher or lower based on a number of factors including premium payments. If you have any questions, please contact your New York Life agent listed above or one of our Customer Service Representatives at 1-800-695-9873.

| Coverage | Insured: | IVY P KARLSEN |
|---|---|---|
| | Policy Number: | 49 377 835 |
| | Policy Plan: | Term Extension Life Insurance |
| | Base Plan Death Benefit: | $287,426 |
| | Policy Date: | Aug 24, 2009 |
| | Premiums are Paid To: | Aug 24, 2013 |
| | Insurance Expiration Date | Feb 2, 2080 |
| Life Insurance Death Benefit | Total Death Benefit on Aug 24, 2014: (See Page 2 for details.) | $287,426.00 |
| Policy Cash Value * | Net Cash Value on Aug 24, 2014: (See Page 2 for details.) | $10,996.92 |

This coverage results from the nonpayment of premium for the above policy. Pursuant to your policy's provisions, coverage is being continued as Extended Term Insurance, with no further premiums due. Please contact your agent or customer service representative with any questions.

The **NUMBER ONE** cause of problems in processing claims is inaccurate or invalid beneficiary designations - Call your Agent **TODAY** to review yours.

For policy information and online service, please visit us at ------> www.newyorklife.com/vsc

Please refer to the Definition of Terms and other information on the reverse side of page 2.
* Any gain in the policy may be subject to taxation if it lapses or is surrendered.

IMPORTANT POLICYOWNER NOTICE: You should consider requesting more detailed information about your policy to understand how it may perform in the future. You should not consider replacement of your policy or make changes in your coverage without requesting a current illustration. You may annually request, without charge, such an illustration by contacting your agent or broker at (315) 331-2627, sending a fax to your Service Center at 1-800-278-4117, writing to New York Life at PO Box 6916, Cleveland, OH 44101-1916, or by calling your Service Center at 1-800-695-9873. If you do not receive a current illustration of your policy within 30 days from your request, you should contact your state insurance department.

The New York Life Insurance Policy written on Ivy P. Karlsen. (Courtesy of Cindy Best)

Alex stands behind his nieces, Elletra and Ivy, after placing a Christmas wreath at Levi's gravesite, circa 2009. (Courtesy of Cindy Best)

Left to right: Ivy, Cindy, and Elletra, circa 2012. (Courtesy of Cindy Best)

Ivy, Dave, and Elletra, circa 2012. (Courtesy of Cindy Best)

Levi wearing his favorite baseball cap just months before his
death. (Courtesy Cindy Best)

A sea of duck feathers cover the ground after Karl killed thousands of ducklings. He claimed that it took him two months to kill 8,000 birds. (Courtesy of Cindy Best)

Allan Teets later pointed to the plastic coating over their window (far right) that he and Christina used to keep the cold out. On the back, Chris had written "Look at our icicles." (Courtesy of Allan Teets)

Karl was outraged when he saw Christina's glamour shot, calling her a whore.
(People's Exhibit)

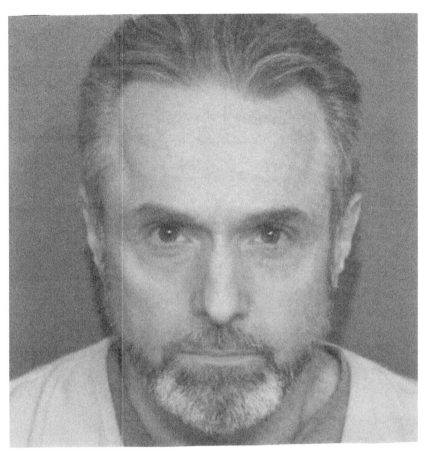

Karl Karlsen's mug shot, taken in September of 2014. (Courtesy of Calaveras County Sheriffs' Office)

## EIGHTY-FOUR

It was on November 29, 2012, that a Seneca County grand jury indicted Karl Karlsen on one count of second-degree murder and one count of insurance fraud. To his attorney, Lawrence Kasperek, Karl asserted that his confession to police was coerced. Karl felt sure that the charges wouldn't stick.

Karlsen's trial had been scheduled for late October of 2013 and already Levi Karlsen's horrifying death had become the focus of national media attention. By the time Karlsen's suppression hearing was held, May 27, 2013, true crime fanatics were closely tracking the case.

Karl's defense attorney, Lawrence Kaserek, argued that the statement Karl made at Abigail's should be thrown out, but the judge ruled that marital privilege didn't apply. The Abigail's tape would be allowed in, as would the nine-hour taped interrogation conducted at the Seneca County Sherriff's Office. Karlsen was facing an avalanche of headlines.

The public was mesmerized. They couldn't get enough.

The Karlsen case was becoming larger-than-life.

---

"WIFE'S FEAR LEADS TO NEW LOOK AT HUSBAND IN DEATHS..."

"HUSBAND ACCUSED OF MURDERING HIS SON..."

"SECOND WIFE WIRE-TAPPED HIM DURING RESTAURANT CONFESSIONAL..."

---

Once Karlsen's preliminary hearing formally began, on September 16, 2013, each lurid detail was revealed by the news media. The facts were shocking and people became obsessed with the case. It was hard to believe that a man would murder his own son for money. It was unthinkable, but there he was, Karl Karlsen, at age 52, wearing a bright orange jumpsuit and shackles, hobbling into the Seneca County Courthouse holding himself up with a walker.

It was a great prop.

On the other side of the courtroom was the star witness, Cindy Karlsen, who testified about the large insurance payouts from both Levi' and Christina's deaths. She explained that her suspicions came to a boiling point in the fall of 2012, telling the court that on November 16, 2012, she agreed to wear a wire. On that day, Cindy told the court, her husband admitted that he "took the opportunity" to let Levi die...

However, when it came to Cindy, the media wasn't kind. News reports indicated that Cindy's cooperation came only after she learned that her husband had taken an insurance policy out on *her*. At the prelim, Cindy told the court she would be worth $1.2 million to Karl if she died.

And after that admission, Cindy Karlsen was being accused of holding back, of coming forward only after finding out that she, herself, was a target... The news media and the folks on social media were all over it.

"Nobody in the media gave me any credit for what I did." Cindy would later say. "They made me look like I didn't care about anybody but myself. And they portrayed my cousin Jackie as the hero, which really hurt me."

When the Abigail's tape was played in court, people were aghast. You could hear a pin drop in that courtroom. Later, Seneca County DA Barry Porsch would tell reporters that the statements Karlsen made to his wife were "crucial to our case."

After that statement, a barrage of reporters tried to get "an exclusive" with Cindy, and before the pre-lim ended, she was being hounded by producers from Dateline and ABC's 20/20 – and it snowballed from there. Her life was no longer her own. She was in the middle of a media circus.

"NY MAN ON TRIAL FOR SON'S MURDER SAYS HE LEFT HIM
TO DIE..."

"CONFESSION ON NEVER-BEFORE-HEARD TAPE..."

After Cindy's testimony, the video-taped police interrogation was
played in court and people listened for nine hours with bated breath,
waiting to hear a confession.

"I opened the truck door because I had to get inside to move the
linkage for the f---ing truck," they heard and saw Karlsen say. "And
when I did, it tipped. And it just, whoosh, f---ing fell over."

After the pre-lim ended, with Karlsen's trial date looming, DA
Barry Porsch had offered Karlsen a plea deal which he categorically
turned down.

Karl would *never* plead guilty to something he didn't do.

He was innocent. He was framed.

But on November 6, 2013, the day Karlsen's criminal trial was
scheduled to begin...

The weasel decided to take a plea deal after all.

# EIGHTY-FIVE

When it came time for the sentencing, on December 16, 2013, almost a year has passed since Karlsen's arrest and the defendant would plead guilty, offering a carefully rehearsed confession.

---

THE COURT: On November 20<sup>th</sup> of 2008, were you at your residence here in Seneca County, New York?

MR. KARLSEN: Yes, Sir.

THE COURT: Were you in the garage on that property on the morning of that date with your son, Levi Karlsen?

MR. KARSEN: Yes, I was in the garage.

THE COURT: Was your son on his back underneath the front of the truck doing repair work on it?

MR. KARLSEN: Yes.

THE COURT: The truck was held up by a single jack near the center of it?

MR: KARLSEN: Yes, it was up on the front bumper.

THE COURT: Is it true that you knew the jack which held up the front of the truck was not stable?

MR. KARLSEN: Yes.

THE COURT: Is it true that you jumped in the cab of the truck knowing that Levi was under it?

MR: KARLSEN: Yes.

THE COURT: The truck did, in fact, fall on Levi as the result of your actions, correct?

MR. KARLSEN: Correct.

THE COURT: Is it also true that you realized that Levi was still alive?

MR. KARLSEN: Correct.

THE COURT: Is it correct that you made no attempt to lift the truck off him or summon any help?

MR. KARLSEN: Correct.

THE COURT: And do you acknowledge that Levi was unable to help himself when you left, and without help, he was highly likely to die?

MR. KARLSEN: Correct.

---

After pleading guilty, Karlsen was facing a sentence of 15 years to life. The sentencing date was set for December 16th and with the news spreading like wildfire, Erin decided to fly to New York to hold a press conference in front of the Seneca County Sheriff's Office. She stood at a podium, with her Uncle Mike at her side, where each of them took turns feeding answers to a hungry media throng.

"I can't speak for every member of my family," Mike told the crowd, "but I think a lot of us had our suspicions after Levi died. When Karl was arrested for it, I don't think any of us were terribly shocked."

"My stepmother is responsible for having stolen my niece's financial futures," Erin told reporters. "While my father is answering for what he's done, we're still not getting any answers from *her...*"

On the following day, Cindy granted her first media interview, speaking to a reporter at Syracuse.com. She was stunned that she was being maligned by her stepdaughter and other family members who completely ignored the role she played in solving the case.

"Not to pat myself on the back," Cindy told the reporter, "but if it wasn't for me, Karl would still be free."

Cindy had honestly anticipated that once the truth was out, her stepdaughters, her former daughter-in-law, and the rest of the Karlsen family would be grateful to her, but that wasn't the case. Not at all. They wanted her to account for the insurance money that was missing, and they were treating her like she was a criminal.

"Elletra wants to know why the money went to Karl and Cindy," Cassie told a reporter, pulling at people's heartstrings. "My daughter asked me why Grandma and Grandpa got new cars and went on vacations and why daddy didn't leave any money for them."

Cassie admitted that she'd become aware that Elletra and Ivy were the next targets for Karl, but she didn't want to credit Cindy. In fact, the only thing she seemed to care about, really, was the money.

"I'm happy that a killer is off the street, and that my children are safe," Cassie told a reporter. "But it doesn't give my kids their dad back, and it doesn't give them anything back that was stolen from them."

Cassie was horrified by the guilty plea. She couldn't fathom how a man could kill his own son. Knowing that her daughters would now grow up without a father, wasn't only painful, it was devastating. She told the reporter that she was doing everything possible to keep Levi's memory alive, that she and the girls put up a small Christmas tree every year, dedicated to "Daddy Levi."

Her remarks were heartbreaking.

At that time, Elletra (age 10) and Ivy (age 8) couldn't begin to comprehend the magnitude of their loss. The girls had been regularly visiting their father's grave for five years already. It had become a normal routine.

There's a photo of the girls posing in front of their father's tomb-stone, with their solemn Uncle Alex standing between them. The three of them had proudly placed a Christmas wreath on Levi's grave, and both Elletra and Ivy were smiling for the camera.

Being there made them happy.

It made the girls feel like their daddy was still around.

## EIGHTY-SIX

On December 16, 2013, in front of a packed courtroom at the Seneca County Courthouse, Karl Karlsen was caught smiling at his defense attorney. Karlsen thought his attorney planned to file an appeal immediately following the sentencing. He thought the whole thing was a joke.

But the joke was on him.

Plea deals do not allow for an appeal.

That's the whole point.

Inside the courtroom, only two people would stand up to give victim impact statements. It was Cassie Hohn first, who told the court that she was "overjoyed" that Karl was going to be sent to prison. Cassie stated that she was grateful to Cindy for helping to get her former father-in-law put behind bars and then read a short statement written by her daughters, which brought people to tears.

The second victim statement came from Colette Bousson, who had flown to New York to be present for the sentencing. With her cold blue eyes darting around the courtroom like daggers. Colette was spewing venom at Karl.

As she spoke, Colette's tone became increasingly enraged. Colette not only wanted Karl to pay for her nephew's murder, she wanted him to pay for her sister's death as well. However, she wasn't permitted to accuse Karl of her sister's murder because that case had just been re-opened. Nothing had been adjudicated and Colette couldn't jeopardize what police in California were working on. In the end, Colette accused Karl of leaving her sister in a burning house and told the court that he deserved to rot in jail forever.

The two victim impact statements came as a shock to Cindy that day. Barry Porsch had led her to believe that no one would be making statements at the sentencing, so Cindy sat there dumfounded, wondering why she hadn't been given the chance to speak. As she listened to Cassie and Colette, Cindy broke down in tears. She desperately wanted to confront Karl, but she was being robbed of that opportunity. She was being robbed of much-needed closure.

It would take years for Cindy to realize that the DA didn't want her up there because it could open the door to the issue of "marital privilege." Barry Porsh was rightly being cautious at the time. The DA knew if that door was somehow re-opened, it would give the defense more fodder for their appeal.

Ironically, Karl didn't even notice that Cindy was muted. In fact, he'd only glanced in her direction once. He'd seen her crying on Dave's shoulder, but that didn't seem to faze him. And as for the impact statements given by Cassie and Colette, Karl felt they were traitors. He was openly smug when Colette spoke, showing his disdain by giving her a smirk.

Colette was a lying bitch.

Nothing would come of her accusations, Karl felt sure of that.

And just before the sentence was imposed, as is protocol, the judge gave Karlsen a chance to speak. But the monster had absolutely nothing to say.

Karl was stone-cold silent.

For the crimes of Second-Degree Murder and Insurance Fraud, Seneca County Court Judge Dennis Bender handed down the maximum sentence of 15 years-to-life, telling Karlsen he was "not fully human."

"You belong in prison," the judge told Karlsen, "and I suggest you belong there until you die."

When it was over, the media throng outside the courtroom was thick. DA Barry Porsch gave a brief statement, describing Karlsen as a sociopath, telling reporters, "There was no remorse, no 'I'm sorry,' no apologies, nothing."

Porsch believed Karlsen would likely die in prison, and his sentiment was mirrored by everyone in the courtroom, except for Karl...

Karl was busy accusing his lawyer of being unethical.

Kasperek had tricked him into making a false confession.

Karl was planning to sue the lazy bum after the appeal was filed.

## EIGHTY-SEVEN

Karl had become a master puppeteer from behind bars, he knew how to work the system, he was smarter than anyone else, and he convinced fellow inmates that this was all a big mistake. To his daughter Kati, he characterized it as a cruel misunderstanding.

He had nothing to do with Levi's death.

He'd been lied to, he'd accepted a plea deal so he wouldn't have to put his family through a grueling trial. There was proof that he wasn't at home when Levi died, he told anyone who would listen.

Levi's death was caused by a freak accident and Kati believed him.

Kati had seen a copy of the Medical Examiner's report which recorded Levi's time of death at 3PM. Karl wanted Kati to share that information with Erin and Alex so they could see the truth for themselves. There was no way he could have done it. Levi died at the same time that he was leaving Penn Yan. And Kati was fully in her father's corner.

Kati was 100% convinced that Cindy's "new recollections" about Levi's death were lies. It was too coincidental, her father had convinced her, that all these years later, with their divorce looming, that Cindy had come to this new "realization." Cindy was a lying drunkard. She was a turncoat who had an agenda.

"It wasn't until we were getting a divorce that Cindy made all this stuff up about Levi," Karl would later say. "Why did she wait so long to accuse me? It's because she's looking for a bigger divorce settlement, that's why."

To add fuel to the fire, Karl let it be known that Alex was the only child Cindy ever really cared about. He was good at twisting the knife. He excelled at it, and said whatever he could to trash Cindy, constantly harping on the insurance money "she stole." He knew exactly how to raise their ire.

"It was bizarre to me that after Karl was arrested, Erin and Kati completely turned on me," Cindy would later say. "I tried talking with Erin the day of the arrest and I told her the whole story, but she didn't want to hear it. She and Kati were still focusing on the money, and I couldn't understand their thinking. It was almost like they were giving Karl a free pass."

But it wasn't only "talk" that Karl was using, he was also building a scheme. He'd teamed up with Kati and had given her a written power of attorney, asking her to keep an eye on the farm. Cindy was no longer living there, the place sat vacant, and Karl was worried that sooner or later, Cindy would try to clean him out.

"With me stuck in jail, I knew she'd try to steal whatever she could from the farm," Karl later said. "So I signed over the power of attorney to Kati because I wasn't going to let Cindy ruin me."

From the time he had first been arrested, there had been many incidents that caused bad blood between Cindy and her stepdaughters. The trouble began in December of 2012. It was a week before Christmas that Cindy stopped by to check on her house, discovering that the place had been robbed. She immediately called John Cleere to report the break-in, telling him there was no forced entry.

"I'm sure Kati has something to do with this!" she told him, "because whoever got in here, had a key."

"Well, I'm gonna stop you right there," Cleere said, "because I'm guessing nobody told you that Karl signed over a power of attorney to Kati."

"He gave her power of attorney? That's not possible!"

"Well, I've got a copy of it right here if you want to come take a look at it."

"But that's not legal!"

"Well, Karl signed over his rights to her," Cleere said. "So as far as we're concerned, Kati has every legal right to be there."

Cindy was confused and upset. She couldn't understand how it could be legal for an adult child to have unfettered access to a property that was being disputed in her divorce. She rambled on about her rights as a homeowner and because Cleere didn't want to be caught in the middle, he sent a deputy down to take a police report from her.

"The dining room furniture was missing, the bedroom furniture was gone, the flat screen TV was ripped off the wall," Cindy later said. "But what really devastated me was that *Levi's ashes* were missing."

In an absolute fury, Cindy sent her stepdaughter a scathing email, threatening to take legal action if the missing items weren't returned. She warned Kati that her divorce attorney had gotten a judge's order demanding that "no assets be removed from the house." She informed Kati that the order stipulated that "all the contents therein are subject to the divorce settlement."

But Kati never responded.

Kati felt she had the legal right to keep whatever items she wanted, including Levi's ashes...

And apparently, Karl thought so too, because he'd instructed Kati to remove all the valuables from the house, asking his daughter to sell off whatever big-ticket items she could, including his tractors, his expensive tools, and other farm equipment. Karl needed that money to pay for his defense.

"Cindy made a big deal about the whole situation with the ashes and I guess it should have been handled differently," Karl later recalled. "She could have just gone to Kati and asked if she could have a little of his ashes, but instead she tried to kick Kati off the farm and that just pissed her off."

"It was *my* house. It was where I raised my kids," Cindy later said. "It had been *years* since Kati or Erin had lived there, yet they thought *nothing* in the house belonged to me."

And it wasn't only Cindy who felt violated. It was Alex too. Alex wanted to hold onto every fragment of Levi that he could. He thought Levi's ashes should have been divided up equally between them.

But that didn't seem to matter to his sister.

Not one bit.

## EIGHTY-EIGHT

It was when Alex found out about Levi's missing ashes that he decided to tell his mother about another incident that had occurred between him and his sisters. For months, he'd been afraid to say anything because he knew it would cause more of a rift, but...

"I told my mom about what happened because I felt like Erin and Kati were ganging up on me," Alex confided. "It was right after the press conference and they invited me to lunch at Connie's Diner. And after we got there Erin said she knew I was stealing things from the house and said she would have me arrested if I didn't put the stuff back."

When Cindy heard that, her jaw dropped. It was bad enough that the girls hated her for no good reason, but to threaten Alex, their little brother who was an innocent victim, really got her blood boiling. She was done with Erin and done with Kati too. Neither of them cared about Alex, that was clear. And try as she did, neither of them were willing to listen to the truth about the insurance money either.

Cindy was outraged.

She fired off a missive to Erin via Facebook messenger.

And she let her have it.

---

*"Erin, I have offered the olive branch once again, to no avail. This time, I will say what I want to say and be done with the two of you. You say that Alex has your dad's traits but thankfully not the ones that you two inherited. At least Alex has a heart which is not true of you two. Obviously you inherited your dad's cruel and inhumane manner.*

*What you did to Alex when you came here to hold a press conference is unforgivable. Alex told me he tried to reach out to you but got no response and he was at the point of wanting to take his life over it.*

*I refuse to sit back any longer and just take it. You and all the other Karlsens deserve each other. I cannot wait until I no longer have to be associated with that name.*

*And Erin, if you figured it out when you were 12, if you're now saying you knew what your father did, then why would you let your children stay at the home of a murderer? Doesn't make sense to me. I know one thing, if I knew my dad killed my mother, I certainly would not let my children spend a minute in that house with him, but you let your kids stay here for two months after Levi died when you needed a babysitter.*

*And thank you Kati for reporting everything to your dad when we were hiding from him. FYI the farm is neither one of yours to decide what can be taken off there or not. You two complain about a few things that Alex took when you have taken everything else? I have pictures of everything that was on that farm and guess what? The judge signed orders a long time ago which gave me exclusive use of that property so you are breaking the law.*

*I might need to look into charges being filed against you. And Kati, how would that look for your career?*

*You two get on your high horses and want to go on TV and bash me? I put the two of you in the same category as your dad and I am certain Levi and Christina are totally ashamed of you two. What I do with the money for the girls is no longer your concern.*

*I will take care of it myself. I handed everything over to you that was yours and you will not get another thing. I do, however, want Levi's wooden ashes returned. I bought that and picked that urn myself and had the plate engraved, and whether you think I deserve it or not does not matter. You forgot that Alex was his brother too.*

*If it is not returned I will bring charges against you. You two look like ASSES, turning on the one person who had the guts to do something about it. What I went through is HELL for these past two years and I know you could care less about that but I am hereby putting you on notice.*

*If you step one foot on that farm I will have you arrested. Go visit your dad in jail and tell him I'm sure he will get what is coming to him in State Prison. They don't like murderers who kill their own children..."*

## EIGHTY-NINE

But Cindy's missive didn't faze anyone, least of all, Erin. In the wake of Karl's murder conviction, not one of the Karlsens, not Erin, not Kati, nor any of Karl's siblings...ever spoke to Cindy again.

Kati was the easiest for Karl to convince because she never believed that he was capable of murder, not for a second. For her own well-being, she leaned on defense mechanisms to block out that possibility.

It was actually Sigmund Freud, along with his daughter, Anna, who first came up with the term "defense mechanisms" which when they were both hypothesized was a way for the brain to mitigate mental pain. "The ego will employ an unconscious *distortion of events*," Freud wrote.

Defense mechanisms allow people to override the truth.

And these inner workings of the mind are so powerful...

Because they operate without a person being aware of it.

1. **Denial.** The failure to recognize the reality of a stressful or hurtful situation in order to protect oneself from overwhelming anxiety.
2. **Distortion.** The conscious or unconscious misrepresentation of facts which serves to disguise that which is unacceptable.
3. **Projection.** The process by which a person attributes their own characteristics or failures onto another person. This can be a way of avoiding responsibility and deflecting criticism away from oneself.
4. **Dissociation.** This involves a person feeling disconnected from a traumatic event by keeping threatening thoughts away from other parts of the psyche. It is used to protect the mind from mental trauma.
5. **Repression.** The unconscious process of blocking out painful experiences or memories to avoid thinking about them.
6. **Suppression.** Unlike repression, this involves the conscious effort to avoid certain thoughts and feelings to keep them out of consciousness.

7. **Isolation.** The act of creating a mental barrier around threatening thoughts, of compartmentalizing fearful thoughts in order to isolate them from other thoughts.

8. **Intellectualization.** Involves a person using reason and logic as a way of explaining or understanding a negative event. It allows a person to rationalize why a particular event occurred.

9. **Displacement.** The act of displacing a negative emotion and redirecting that negative emotion toward someone else. This occurs when someone refuses to recognize the person who created the negative emotion, and instead, finds *a more suitable person to blame.*

## NINETY

Even before Karl was sentenced, Colette Bousson was on the case. She'd never let the unsolved death of her sister go, and once a murder charge was brought against her former brother-in-law, Colette was hell-bent on getting action. As soon as the news reports came out, accusing Karl Karlsen of being the prime suspect in the murder of his son, Colette placed a call to the Seneca County Sheriff's Office, urging John Cleere to put pressure on the California investigators who had mishandled the case.

For years, Colette had contacted the Calaveras County DA, she'd kept them apprised of everything, including the 2002 barn fire after which Karl collected insurance money, but all she got was lip service.

"We'll look into it," Colette was constantly told.

But nothing ever happened.

But now, with Karl having taken a plea deal, Colette believed the Calaveras County DA would take a fresh look at the case, especially if New York law enforcement got in contact with someone there. When he got the call from her, John Cleere was headed to the FBI headquarters in Quantico for special training, so he turned the matter over to New York State Investigator Jeff Arnold.

Acting as the go-between, Jeff Arnold wrote up a 110-page report detailing the intricate web of lies and "accidental events" in Karl Karlsen's life. He sent that report to the Calaveras County DA, Barbara Yook (pronounced YOU-K) anticipating an immediate response.

Arnold's report was thorough. He began his report by notifying the Calaveras DA that Karl Karlsen had been a volunteer member of the Varick Fire Department in Romulus back in 1978, stating that he'd checked the Varick Fire Department records. What Arnold discovered was that Karlsen, as a teenage volunteer, had assisted in *at least seven fire scenes*. And coincidently, one of those fires, on March 1, 1978, had been started by a dryer.

Attached to Arnold's intricate report were documents that detailed a timeline of "accidents" involving fire. From Karlsen's "heroic act" while he was in the Airforce, to taped statements about his Dodge

Charger which burned up in 1986, Arnold had spelled it all out. He included depositions from various insurance investigators, statements from Christina's family members, and most significantly, an interview with Merle Lucken of State Farm Insurance who stated that Christina Karlsen had taken the medical exam which activated her life insurance policy *just three days* before the house fire.

The timing was too close.

It was more than a coincidence.

Jeff Arnold also presented an overview of Karl's relationship with his first wife, which, according to the various witnesses he'd interviewed, was on the rocks at the time of Christina's death. Specifically, Colette Bousson had described Karl as being emotionally and physically abusive toward her sister, stating that Karl and Christina's marriage was "pretty much over with" when the fire occurred.

In the sworn statement she gave to Jeff Arnold, Colette confided that Karl often humiliated her sister by calling her fat, using the word "chubby" to describe Chris in front of others. Colette mentioned that at the time of her death, Chris was the heaviest that she'd ever been, and Karl was very unhappy about that. Chris was dieting and had started jogging, but the weight wouldn't come off. By the fall of 1990, her sister was calling quite often and was talking about getting a divorce.

"Chris was afraid of Karl and was very concerned for her children," Colette explained in her deposition. "I encouraged her to leave Karl and told her she could stay with me and my husband but she had gone through a divorce earlier in her life and was scared of going through a second one."

Also attached to the report was the deposition of Donna Karlsen, Karl's sister-in-law, who viewed Karl as a man who hid his anger. In her opinion, Karl was a controlling husband who had difficulty holding down a job, and he took his frustration out on Chris. Donna recalled that while Chris and Karl lived in Romulus in the 1980's, Karl filed for bankruptcy, which caused serious trouble in their marriage.

"After the bankruptcy, their financial hardship led them to move to California," Donna stated, "but Karl didn't like it there."

However, just before the Murphys fire, Karl had called members of his family, making it known that he was anxious to move back to New York, claiming that Chris was fully on board with the move. However, in the fall of 1990, Chris sent a letter to her landlord and was happy to report that she and Karl would be moving out of the house and were planning to stay in Calaveras County.

"When we move out, we're planning to buy a house," Chris wrote, telling Jo Lucero that she and Karl had been looking at numerous properties in the area, that they'd also been talking to her father about buying a parcel of his land in Douglas Flat.

However, Douglas Flat, just like Murphys, had very little to offer. During the Gold Rush in the 1850's, Douglas Flat was a boomtown, as was Murphys, but all that was left were empty historical buildings. Murphys was a quaint little town, but Douglas Flat was barely a spot on the map. It didn't have a store or a streetlight.

But by far, the most telling thing in Arnold's report came from a damming statement made by Colette, who had a clear recollection of her last visit to her sister's house where they celebrated Christmas of 1990.  Colette stayed in the Murphys house from December 22 to December 24, during which time the bathroom window worked perfectly. It was not boarded up with plywood.

Colette's eyewitness account was a direct contradiction to Karl's version of the days leading up to the fire during his interrogation on November 23, 2012, and Arnold made sure that his report included the verbatim conversation he and Karl had on that date:

---

ARNOLD: When did you board up that window? A day before the fire? Or two days before?

KARLSEN: No, it was months before.

ARNOLD: You sure it was months?

KARLSEN: I know it was months.

ARNOLD: It wasn't days or weeks?

**KARLSEN:** No.

**ARNOLD:** When you say months, how many would you say beforehand was it?

**KARLSEN:** It's got to be a month or so, maybe a month and a half. You know that house was built back in the 1820's or 1830's. It was a goldminer's chow hall and it needed a lot of work.

**ARNOLD:** Gotcha.

**KARLSEN:** So the people who owned it basically paid me to work on fixing windows, fixing doors. I ripped out the floors, put new walls in, insulated it, and they didn't charge me rent.

---

Jeff Arnold's report also included sworn statements about the suspicious 2002 barn fire, which came from Karl's brothers, Kris and Mike Karlsen. Both brothers confirmed that Karl had removed all of the valuables from the barn just days before it went up in flames.

And last but not least, the report provided the Calaveras County DA with a sworn statement by Alex Karlsen in which he stated that his father had explained that the barn fire was caused by a spark in the radio that was out there.

Another radio story, and another fire.

It was all too much.

But there was more, much more, that Alex had to say, and Arnold included the sworn statement that Alexander Karlsen had handwritten and signed his name to.

---

### SWORN STATEMENT OF ALEXANDER KARLSEN

*"My name is Alex Karlsen. I am 16 years old. My parents, Karl and Cindy, are separated. Right now I am staying with my mother because I'm a little scared something will happen. I'm afraid that my dad might hurt me or my mom.*

*I think my father Karl is capable of murder. I think he killed his first wife and my brother Levi. I think if my dad finds out that he is being investigated for murder he will kill himself or he won't go down without a fight. I think that if there's a restraining order for my dad to stay away from us it won't do any good.*

*I remember that dad and Levi didn't get along. They fought a lot. The day Levi died I was at basketball practice at school and I remember my uncle brought me to the hospital. Dad told me that when he found Levi that Levi had a wrench in his hands.*

*My dad also told me some things about the fire in California where his first wife died. He said the dog knocked over the kerosene heater. There were also a few times when he denied knowing how it started.*

*Last Friday my dad admitted to me that he spent over a million dollars in the past year. My dad lies to me a lot, even about little things."*

## NINETY-ONE

It was on August 29, 2014, that Calaveras County DA Barbara Yook filed murder charges against Karl Karlsen in connection with the murder of his wife, Christina. More than *25 years* after Christina Alexander Karlsen died of smoke inhalation inside the bathroom of her burning home, her "accidental death" had been ruled a homicide and the case was turned over to Deputy District Attorney Jeff Stone.

For the murder charge to stick, law enforcement had to put the case under a microscope, so Calaveras District Attorney Investigator Mike Whitney, along with DDA Jeff Stone, flew to New York to interview Karlsen at the Clinton Correctional Facility, where a six-and-a-alf-hour video-taped interrogation took place. It was there that the two men pounced on Karlsen and were able to pull his lies apart. That damning interrogation tape would later be put into evidence.

The effort to bring this case to trial was gargantuan. Members of Calaveras law enforcement had to sort through a long list of witnesses, each of whom had to be reinterviewed and it was going to take time.

More time than anyone first imagined.

Up until then, members of Christina's family had lost all hope, especially Colette, who had become so disgusted with the "stall tactics" of the Calaveras County DA that, out of sheer desperation, she wrote formal letters to Senator Nancy Pelosi and Senator Dianne Feinstein asking them to intervene. But the matter was within the jurisdiction of the courts, the judicial branch, and neither Pelosi nor Feinstein could offer a comment, much less help.

It wasn't until March of 2016, almost two years after he was charged, that Karlsen was extradited to a jail cell in San Andreas, California. Finally, there might be justice for Christina. Colette, Art, Arlene, and other family members prayed that justice would come swiftly, but instead there were endless hearings, including numerous defense motions for dismissal.

A lengthy preliminary hearing was held in September of 2017, with Scott Gross representing Karlsen, fighting for his client every step of the way. All along, the defense attorney argued that there was not enough evidence to go to trial. Gross was under the impression (rightfully so) that all the records and physical evidence from the fire incident that occurred decades prior had been destroyed. Gross was adamant that the court throw the case out.

But as it happened, Carl Kent, the Fire Chief who investigated the scene with Bob Monson back in 1991, had taken the liberty of removing boxes of evidence from the storage locker to take with him when he retired in 1997.

At the preliminary hearing, DDA Jeff Stone put Carl Kent on the spot, questioning him about his role in the investigation, asking him why evidence had been released from the formal chain of custody. Kent explained that he removed two boxes of evidence when he retired from the CDF because back in the late 1990's, the standard for keeping evidence was seven years.

---

STONE: Do you recall if you ever gathered any physical evidence from the fire scene on January 8, 1991?

KENT: The only thing I can readily remember is an extension cord that had a drop light on it and it was totally consumed. And I know that I did take some samples from the hallway and put them in one-quart cans but I don't recall if it was that day.

STONE: Other than that, do you recall if you found anything else?

KENT: I searched the garbage can outside the residence looking for any other possible source of the ignition and I didn't find any wine bottles. I think that would have been significant if I had. I did find lobster tail shells that were near the top of the heap. I don't know how long they had been there.

STONE: Do you know what happened to that collection of materials?

**KENT:** I had an evidence locker here in San Andreas that was locked. Everything would have been deposited there.

---

When questioned once again about the chain of custody, Kent testified that he'd taken the boxes directly from the evidence locker to his basement, where they remained sealed until he was contacted by the Calaveras County Sheriff's Office in 2013.

In those two boxes were witness statements, tape recordings of interviews conducted with Karlsen, and a video tape of the fire scene.

---

**STONE:** Why had you kept these items?

**KENT:** I figured number one, the fire was very concerning to me that there was a death we did not have a conclusion on. And I knew that the children who were there at the fire scene would probably someday...

---

But Kent was not permitted to finish his statement. An objection was raised regarding improper speculation, and the judge sustained it, calling the Kent's opinion "irrelevant."

In the end, however, Judge Thomas Smith ruled that the chain of custody was satisfactory, therefore all of Kent's audio and video evidence from 1991, along with corresponding transcripts and the original witness statements, would be entered into trial.

The judge set Karlsen's trial date for February 20, 2018.

It was a huge blow for the defense.

"Carl Kent contradicted himself so many times," Karl would later assert. "He sat up there and lied. All the evidence he claims he collected, all of it was a lie. He said he first got to the house on January 8th, right? Well, by then, the whole house had been ripped down by a bulldozer!"

Karl scoffed at that assertion.

"And this guy said he saw a piece of plywood nailed to the bathroom window?" Karl said with a chuckle. "I know for a fact that board was taken off there on January 4$^{th}$ so how is that possible? He's a bold-faced liar!"

## NINETY-TWO

In preparation for the trial, Carl Kent's evidence wasn't the only thing that the Calaveras County DA's Office had at their disposal. The Calaveras County Sheriff's Office had located and interviewed over 75 relevant witnesses, 11 of whom provided them with substantial ammunition.

**ERIN DEROCHE:** Who had been whisked away before fire investigators could conduct an in-depth interview. DeRoche described the lack of effort by the defendant to rescue her mother from the fire. She also described, in great detail, the numerous incidents of domestic violence by the defendant against her and her brother.

**LYNN SANDERS:** A bartender at the Murphys Hotel who knew the defendant well. She told investigators that her father, Victor Lyons (now deceased) lived by himself in the house located next door to the Karlsens. She said Karlsen was "friendly" with her dad and was aware that he left town on weekends to participate in sporting events. Sanders stated that on the weekend of New Year's Eve 1990, her dad had gone to Sacramento to do a polar bear swim, later testifying that "Mr. Karlsen seemed pretty concerned about what my father was doing. He was overly concerned about my dad's whereabouts."

**DENNIS HERTZ:** The nephew of Nic and Jo Lucero, the owners of the house that had gone up in flames. Mr. Hertz told investigators that he was in the midst of preparing to move into the rental house and was waiting for the Karlsens to vacate the premises. Lucero's nephew would later testify that he'd "stopped by the residence the day before the fire" and did not see the bathroom window boarded up.

**MIKE KARLSEN:** The defendant's brother, who provided a receipt from the travel agency showing that on January 4, 1991, he'd bought four tickets for the defendant and his children to fly to New York the following day. This negated Karl's claim that he'd spent "thousands and thousands" to transport all of his family members to New York after Christina's death.

**ART ALEXANDER:** Christina's father and the defendant's employer. Art had kept all of his business' checking account records, including those from 1990 and 1991. He presented cancelled checks which proved that he paid Karlsen in full in December of 1990. He would testify that he'd given his son-in-law an early Christmas bonus around the same time that the defendant purchased the life insurance policy on his daughter.

**MERLE LUCKEN:** the original State Farm Insurance agent who was now deceased. In his original statement, given to Carl Kent in 1991, Lucken stated 'that he found it unusual for someone to walk into his office to inquire solely about life insurance. "That never happened before, not once in forty years," Lucken stated in his deposition. "Mr. Karlsen was there to buy insurance for his wife, not himself. We discussed it and I explained that he would have to bring his wife into my office in order to do that."

**MIKE WINN:** A volunteer fireman who'd been at the original scene, who was also familiar with the Karlsen family because they were regular customers at his ice-cream shop in Murphys, called The Peppermint Stick. Winn told investigators he'd had an awkward encounter with Karlsen approximately six months after the fire when the defendant had returned to Murphys unannounced. "He wanted me to help him get the fire report settled and said that without it, the life insurance wouldn't pay out," Winn would later testify. "Karlsen said that he and his kids were struggling, that he was concerned about the payout. He told me 'they think I did it.'"

**ALLEN TEETS:** Christina's first husband who met the defendant when the two of them served in the Air Force. He described the bitter cold nights they endured while in North Dakota where temperatures could get as low as 25 degrees below zero in the winter. He said Christina was very familiar with kerosene, that she often filled the barrels of kerosene to use for their heater. Teets did not believe that his former wife could mistake a barrel of kerosene for a barrel of water.

In his testimony, Alan Teets would also call into question the defendant's use of plywood to seal up the bathroom window, explaining that while living on the Air Force base, "it was common practice to use a clear heat-shrink plastic to seal up a window, never plywood." Teets would produce a photo of a window that he had been sealed with that specific plastic, on the back of which Christina had inscribed, "Look at our icicles!"

**HEATHER GOWEN-SMALL:** The State Farm fire claim representative who conducted a three-hour taped interview with Karlsen a few weeks after Christina's death. She recalled that Karlsen had an "angry outburst" during that interview, reading into the record what Karlsen said in his own words: "If I had been in it for the money, why not the kids?" I'd be a rich man! I'd have a half a million dollars. But here I am stuck with these kids. It's a bitch." Gowen-Small would testify that in 1991, she had recommended that Karlsen's claim be denied.

**MIKE WHITNEY:** The Calaveras District Attorney's Office Investigator. In 2013, Whitney had gone to the Karlsen's former address, located at 4060 Pennsylvania Gulch Road, and had photographed the exact location where the house once stood. While there, he discovered "a worn path" that went between the destroyed Karlsen residence and Victor Lyon's house. Whitney would tell the jury that the path between the two properties was "easy to walk through." He testified that at a brisk pace, it took him less than one minute to walk between one house to the other.

**JAN STARR:** Christina's first cousin who became a critical witness for the prosecution because she was able to authenticate the video footage that had been taken of the burned-out Karlsen house by one of her relatives. The prosecution would later present this videotape in its entirety, which showed, not only the fire scene, but also footage of the birthday party which Jan Starr held for her son. The birthday party was held on the same day that Jan Starr went to the fire scene, marking the date of the video as January 5, 1991.

In both the birthday party footage and the footage of the fire scene, Jan Starr was wearing the exact same clothes, a long jean skirt with a peach blouse. The defense wanted the video footage thrown out because in it, Starr had made incriminating comments. Ultimately, the judge ruled that the video could be shown in court, without sound.

In some ways, watching that footage without sound, as if it was a silent movie, made it more impactful. It was eerie to see Ms. Starr pulling away at the plywood that covered the bathroom window, making motions of distress and giving expressions of doubt. The jury would see a thick covering of black soot over the bathtub, the floor, and the sink, but the wall with the plywood over the window, for some reason, had not burned up at all.

The jury would also see Ms. Starr poking around Christina's medicine cabinet, pulling out Christina's cosmetics and toiletries that were completely unscathed. They watched as Starr pointed to the roll of toilet paper that was still in place, just under the bathroom window.

It was unnerving to see that single roll sitting in its holder.

The thin paper was not burned at all.

NINETY-THREE

However, with all that they had, the prosecution still had a problem. It turned out that Carl Kent, as much of a hero that he was – had inadvertently left behind a third box of evidence which held Kent's 2,000-page report as well as every photo of the fire scene. All of that had been discarded or destroyed, and enough evidence was missing, Scott Gross believed, that it would deprive his client of "due process of the law."

Once again, Scott Gross sought dismissal of the case, arguing that his client could not get a fair trial because "all proof of Mr. Karlsen's side of the story has been lost." Gross maintained that the missing box contained exculpatory evidence that would be "devastating" to the State's case. Without it, there was no way for the defense to conduct an independent investigation. There was no way for his experts to determine the origin of the fire. In his Motion to Dismiss, Gross attached a list of the missing evidence that was crucial for him to be able to defend the murder case.

### 911 CALL AND DISPATCH RECORDS
The 911 call made on January 1, 1991, along with other dispatch calls, would have proven that Karlsen had placed a distress call while Christina was trapped inside the residence, a call which Gross alleged was placed while Christina was still alive. The tape of that 911 could not be located.

### MISSING FIRE REPORTS
All that existed of the fire reports was one short report from one of the fire crews who responded to the scene that day. Other reports, such as debriefing reports and the reports of lead investigators, Bob Monson and Carl Kent, had been destroyed.

### PHOTOGRAPHS OF THE FIRE SCENE
There had been testimony at the preliminary hearing, during which State Farm's hired fire investigator, Ken Buske, said he had taken 142

photos of the fire scene. However, not one of those photos existed. "The information those photos contained are relevant to our case," Gross argued. "Without being able to review those photos, the defense is operating at a disadvantage."

## ITEMS FROM INSIDE THE RESIDENCE

Numerous items from the fire scene had been examined in February of 1991 by fire expert, Ken Buske, who had determined the origin of the fire. The list of physical evidence that had been discarded included:
The furnace.
The washer and dryer.
The water heater, an electric heater, and the kerosene heater.
A swatch of carpet taken from the hallway of the residence.
And the piece of plywood that covered the bathroom window.

## BANK RECORDS

Bank records of the defendant would prove that he wrote a check to his brother, Mike, to cover the flights for all family members to get from Sacramento to Syracuse. However, the National Bank Of Geneva only kept records for a 10-year period. Karlsen's bank records could not be retrieved.

## MEDICAL RECORDS

Scott Gross and his investigator, Dan Quinn, had gone to the Mark Twain Hospital in San Andreas to see if any medical records from 1991 were available. They weren't. Gross argued that the records would show that his client had been prescribed a large dose of Valium on the day of the fire, which Karlsen used in the days following the event.

"The prosecution contends that Mr. Karlsen 'acted strangely' immediately after the fire," Gross wrote, "and we believe it was the Valium causing him to have changed behavior. A complete review of the medical records would have gone a long way to prove Mr. Karlsen's side of the story."

And that wasn't all.

There were important material witnesses for the defense...

Who were no longer alive...

Deceased witness Jeanette Sprong had done an interview with Carl Kent and Bob Monson on January 24, 1991. A transcript of that interview revealed that Christina Karlsen had called Jeanette on New Year's Day and during that call, Christina said that the dog and cat had just knocked over a container of kerosene. She had called Jeanette to ask how to absorb a kerosene spill.

Also deceased was Florence Virginia Kahn who had invited the Karlsen family to her home to celebrate New Year's Eve. Ms. Kahn was a close friend of the Karlsens and had never witnessed discord between the couple. On December 31, 1990, Ms. Kahn watched the family interact together without incident. There was no trouble in the marriage.

In addition, two neighbors of Mr. Karlsen, Lillie Spiva and Joyce Ingram, were the persons who Karlsen had run to for help on January 1,1991. Ms. Ingram was the person who made the 911 call. And immediately after that, Ms. Ingram and Ms. Spiva followed Mr. Karlsen to the fire scene and witnessed him direct the fire personnel to his residence.

Both women saw flames coming out of the boy's bedroom and offered to take the children away from the scene. Both witnessed Mr. Karlsen break down in tears that day and saw him crying uncontrollably.

## NINETY-FOUR

Karl wanted a speedy trial. He was ready to take the stand in his own defense and was pushing to get the trial date moved up and often said he wished to represent himself. Karl hated attorneys. He didn't trust them. For years now, Karl had put his faith in Scott Gross. The man had represented Karlsen from the day he was first arraigned, back in 2016.

However, Scott Gross kept moving the goal posts.

The clock was ticking and nothing was moving forward.

There seemed to be continuance after continuance.

At one point, Gross requested a change of venue, but that was denied. At another point, the Judge vacated Karlsen's February 2018 trial date, allowing Gross to have an expert conduct a "mental evaluation" of his client, who Gross had come to believe was *mentally unable to stand trial.*

But Karl knew he wasn't insane. He thought his attorney was insane and was annoyed by the suggestion that he be evaluated. Karl passed the mental evaluation with no problem, and he kept pushing his lawyer to get the trial over with. Karl was sick of sitting in limbo. He wanted his name cleared.

Karl still had love in his heart for Christina and her family and he felt bad that all of them were being put through hell. This mess in California had been created because of a plea deal he should never have taken. Karl wanted to kick himself for that. It was all because of Levi.

"We all know what this case in California is about," Karl would later say. "It's all about what happened in New York. If it wasn't for New York, if I didn't put my foot in my mouth, I know one hundred percent, I wouldn't be out here."

"But the thing is, they kept coming after me time and time again, and they beat me up until I took a plea, which no way in hell would I ever do again," Karl insisted. "And now I can call myself Sir Asshole..."

The longer Karl waited, the angrier he got, but the wait ended when Judge Thomas Smith set a trial date for October 3, 2018. It was another chunk of time being taken out of everyone's lives, but was a relief to everyone, knowing this would finally come to an end.

But curiously, Scott Gross wasn't relieved, not at all. He'd put up a good front, he'd acted confidently and had thoroughly convinced Karl that they would win the case, but when the trial date was imminent, when it was time to go to war, Scott Gross asked to have a private conference with the judge.

A five-minute conference was held in Judge Smith's chambers the morning of October 2, 2018, with DA Barbara Yook and DDA Jeff Stone present. It was at the last minute, just one day prior to jury selection, that Scott Gross announced he would be recusing himself because of "a conflict of interest" that rendered him unable to represent Karlsen.

Following that private conference, prosecutors announced that the trial would be postponed until 2019, explaining that Scott Gross would have to be replaced by an attorney from the Public Defender's Office. It was a necessary evil, that last extension, because a new attorney would need at least six months to prepare the case from scratch.

Of course, the media, the family, and everyone in the community were stunned by the news. Erin and Kati had already flown in for the trial, as did Colette, and Arlene had made the two-hour trek to San Andreas, settling down in a motel with the rest of the family, all of whom had emotionally prepared themselves to do battle.

Suddenly, they were going home without answers, without justice.

The torture was never-ending.

It was Arlene who had the most patience. She became the person who kept the faith, who stood strong in her conviction that Karl Karlsen would pay for his sins. Arlene and her husband, Randy, ran a Christian Ministry in Sacramento called "PRAZ 2 HM."

Pulling out her *Bible* and turning to 2 *Timothy* 4:2, Arlene read scripture to her daughter and granddaughters: "Be ready in season and out of season. Rebuke, correct, and encourage with great patience."

But it was impossible, in the face of so many years of waiting and praying, for Erin and Kati and Colette, not to mention Art, to find the strength to summon more patience. Not in that moment. Not when the defense attorney pulled the plug. It was outrageous, this new stunt.

And whatever it was that Scott Gross was hiding, whatever secret he held, would eat at them.

It seemed questionable that Mr. Gross suddenly discovered, after two years of representation, that he had "a conflict of interest" and thus had to recuse himself from the case. And to make matters worse, his "notice of recusal" was filed "under seal" by the court.

Whatever created the conflict between Karl and his attorney...

Would forever remain a mystery.

## NINETY-FIVE

After a slew of new legal pleadings, the murder trial against Karl Karlsen finally got under way in January of 2020, a full 30 years after Christina Alexander Karlsen had perished. It had been an eternity for her family, "but I've been strong," Arlene told a reporter, "God's been with me."

On the first day of trial, January 14, 2020, Karl walked into the San Andreas courtroom unshackled, wearing a grey polo-style sweater and crisp new slacks. He would soon be turning 60, but he didn't look it. If anything, his salt-and-pepper hair made him look distinguished, not old, and before the judge entered, he looked around the courtroom, pleased that there was so much media attention focused on him.

There was something about him that seemed proud.

For a fleeting moment, there was a sly grin.

The old fox was back, ready to outsmart whoever stood in his way. Karl made it seem like he had a secret, like he had something up his sleeve that would be harmful and embarrassing to the prosecution. It was all just a game to him, and Karl knew how to win it. When it came time for the jury to file in, Karl stood at attention. He didn't think highly of any of these people, he would later call them "a bunch of stupid hicks" but he feigned a look of deference.

The first witness was Erin, now age 36, who told the court that she'd had suspicions about the fire all her life. "I HEARD MY MOTHER SCREAMING..." Erin testified, telling the jury that her father was moving slowly, that he wasn't answering her mother's screams.

Erin recalled seeing a gash on her father's forehead, nothing more, and testified that the only time her father showed emotion was in the ambulance. She described the moment when her father said that "Mommy had gone to heaven," explaining that, at age six, she didn't fully comprehend what that meant.

On direct examination, Barbara Yook asked questions about Erin's childhood experience in Murphys and Erin had nothing but glowing things to say about her mother. She recalled fond memories of baking cookies, learning to sew, and pressing leaves into waxed paper. It was a simple life, a beautiful life. Her mother's world centered around her children, Erin told the jury. Erin always felt she was loved.

But that idyllic life ended when her father relocated them to Upstate New York, Erin testified, asserting that after her mom died, there were countless incidents of violence perpetrated against her and her brother. "We were walking on eggshells," Erin told the jury. "My father's mood predicted how the day would go." And according to her testimony, it was *Levi* who suffered the brunt of their dad's rage.

"Levi would tell me that he had been hit with pipes or shovels, with electric cattle prods, and with pitchforks," Erin alleged.

"I watched my father take a four-inch cutting board and break it over my brother's backside for something he had done," she testified, "I watched Levi get beat by belts. Levi would come in from working on the farm with bruises on his chest and across his rib cage."

When asked why she never reported the abuse to any adult, Erin told the jury that she kept it to herself "because my father threatened to kill me if I told."

At an early age, both Erin and Levi had learned to suppress ugly things.

Especially Levi, who was adept at hiding his bruises.

He knew he had to, otherwise, he would pay dearly for it.

Karlsen's defense attorney, Richard Esquivel, had already come up with a plan to discredit Erin's version of the events that occurred on the day of the house fire. On cross examination, Esquivel suggested that Erin had a *distorted memory* of the fire, that her current recollections about what happened that day were quite different than what she'd told investigators back in 1991.

"You said here today that you heard your mother call out for help one time, is that correct?" Esquivel asked.

"Yes."

"But during the preliminary hearing, you testified that you heard your mother calling for help on three occasions, is that right?"

"I only heard her screaming once."

"You did not tell anyone that your dad moved slowly that day, did you?"

"I didn't understand the significance of it at the time."

"You remembered these facts at a later date?"

"I started to realize, with age, what had happened."

"Let me ask you, how do you feel about your father?"

"We don't have a relationship. It's complicated."

Throughout her testimony, Erin did what she could to stay strong, but on occasion, she broke into tears. However, nothing Erin said or did, seemed to move Karl in any way. He kept himself busy, with his head buried in paperwork, whispering to his defense attorney and shaking his head to signal that Erin was lying.

When the shapely redhead stepped off the stand, she looked directly at her father, but Karl turned away as if he didn't know her. Erin had an agenda, and from Karl's point of view, her tears were as fake as her new-found memory.

This was no longer his daughter.

This was the enemy.

## NINETY-SIX

Karl would later dismiss Erin's testimony as being "too jaded."
Who ever heard of a four-inch thick cutting board?
What Erin said up there was ridiculous.
The jury would see right through her.

But Erin's testimony, along with the list of firefighters and fire investigators who testified immediately after her, should have made Karl nervous. Instead, while the fire investigators testified, Karl shook his head in disbelief, trying to signal to the jury that these were a bunch of retired old men who were relying on faulty memories from decades past.

Karl was comfortable with that assessment.

He knew there was no physical evidence to back them up.

But things started looking bad when the prosecution's star witness took the stand. Karl hated this man, Ken Buske. He was full of himself, this forensic electrical engineer who supposedly determined the origin of the fire. Buske had no photos to show, he was nothing but hot air, Karl thought, but he would quickly learn that this expert had *kept a copy of the original report* he'd submitted to State Farm in March of 1991.

Buske was an expert's expert.

He'd not only saved a copy of his report, he'd saved a copy of the contemporaneous notes he'd written while at the fire scene.

The man was a perfectionist who had an impressive list of credentials. The jury learned that Buske's career had spanned over 40 years, during which time, he'd worked for the U.S. Navy, where he was in charge of 100 scientists, and the list went on from there. Moreover, Ken Buske still had a very active career, and was regularly called to the largest wildfire scenes in Northern California to offer his analysis.

He was a dignified gentleman who sometimes had to have his memory "refreshed" regarding the report he'd submitted to State Farm way back when, but it was all there in black and white. And while he testified, Karl stared straight ahead at him with steely eyes. Karl was sitting with his arms crossed, using his body language and facial expressions to signal defiance.

Buske had drawn an exact depiction of the 17 nails that held the plywood to the drywall in the bathroom, explaining that he'd been able to pull a corner of the plywood away from the wall, remarking that it would only take "twenty pounds of force" for that wood to be pushed out of the way.

Karl scoffed at that, turning to Esquivel's co-counsel, Leigh Flemming, openly laughing about the remark. How could Buske know that? *He wasn't there* when the house was burning. This man had no idea how hot that fire was. He had no idea how hot that screen was that covered the outside of the window. Whatever this expert was about to say – would be a bunch of garbage.

Buske testified that he'd looked at smoke patterns throughout the house to see if there were "witness marks" on the wall outlets, and finding none, he ruled them out as the source. He'd also examined the appliances, ruling out the washer and dryer, and he'd checked the exposed wires in the attic, ruling that out as well.

As for the electrical heater in the bathroom, which Karlsen hinted may have caused the fire, Buske testified that he scientifically proved it was not plugged in at the time of the fire.

As for the trouble light, which Buske had taken X-rays of and had examined under a microscope, that was indeed plugged in, however, Buske had experimented with it, trying to get it to ignite. In order to do that, he told the jury, he'd taken a carpet sample from Karlsen's hallway and had tried a variety of methods to see if it would catch fire while in contact with the trouble light. Buske testified that he'd set the powered light bulb on the carpet for 70 minutes, but under no conditions did it ignite.

At that point, Karl was giving Buske the stink eye.

There was no way this "expert" could prove that now, because the original carpet sample had been discarded. But as it happened, Karlsen's next door neighbor, Vic Lyons, had *the exact same carpet* installed in his house at the same time that Karlsen did, and Mr. Lyons allowed Buske to take a sample of his carpet so he could recreate an exact replica of the tests he'd performed on the carpet in 1991. And by using the duplicate of Karlsen's carpet, Buske was able to prove, conclusively, that the trouble light *did not* cause the fire.

When Karl heard Buske say that, he turned to Richard Esquivel and laughed. But then the next exhibit was presented. It was Buske's hand-drawn diagram of the fire scene, which was now being shown on the big screen for everyone to see.

From behind the defense table, Karl looked at the penciled sketch with disdain. It was crazy that this flimsy paper napkin was now being blown up onto a movie screen so that Buske could pick it apart. The prosecution was nitpicking, grasping at straws. Still, Karl's demeanor shifted. He became more attentive, putting on his eyeglasses to see exactly what Buske was pointing to.

It was a crude sketch of the layout of the hallway, the one Buske had drawn on a paper napkin when he'd met with Heather Gowen-Small to discuss the case. Now, from the witness stand, Buske was highlighting his drawing with a pink-colored marker, testifying that he was able to determine there had been two separate applications of kerosene which he'd determined by looking at the "wicking patterns" in the carpet.

"There had been a story that kerosene had spilled in this hallway previously," Buske testified, "and it looks like, yes, there had been a kerosene pour days prior, because it spread out and diffused itself throughout the carpet."

"When I further examined the carpet in the hallway, I determined that a second application of kerosene occurred just minutes ahead of the fire," Buske told the jury. "You can see the difference of the wicking of these patterns that I'm showing on the diagram here..."

Buske was tracing the U-Shaped pattern, highlighting a distinct horseshoe shape as he spoke. "This particular pattern had well-defined edges, which meant very little wicking occurred... And for very little wicking to occur, the timeframe has to be short."

In his final analysis, Ken Buske arrived at the conclusion that the fire was caused by *a human hand*. The ignition source was either a match or a cigarette lighter.

## NINETY-SEVEN

From day one of the trial, Colette had been sitting out in the hallway, holding her mother's hand, holding her nieces' hands, holding back the tears while waiting to testify. As a witness, she wasn't permitted inside the courtroom, but she knew all too well what was being presented in there. She'd been spared from the ghastly image of her sister's charred body, covered by soot and utterly unrecognizable.

Just the thought of the evidence the prosecutors were presenting, the video tape of her sister's burned-out home, the audio tapes of Karl trying to weasel his way out of culpability, the beautiful glamour shot taken of Chris on her 30th birthday, all of it made her feel sick to her stomach. Colette had always been a tough cookie. She'd served 23 years of active duty in the Air Force and was trained to know what to do when facing life or death circumstances.

But this was different.

The legal game of chess was fickle.

Anything could happen.

And Colette feared Karl might get away with it.

On January 24, 2020, Colette entered the courtroom to take the stand, and she tried to read the jurors, but they sat poker-faced. Justice would be lost if any one of them had a doubt... Once seated in the witness chair, Colette put on a brave face. She'd caught a glimpse of Karl's face from the corner of her eye, but refused to look in his direction.

The DA started with easy questions, asking Colette to describe her days as a child growing up in Murphys, and Colette described an idyllic childhood, telling the jury that she and her sister were "best friends." Colette brought her sister back to life, telling the jury how much fun they had as kids, telling them that Chris had a smile that lit up a room. As she spoke, the DA flashed a photo of Christina's innocent face, with a smile that was larger than life, for the jury to see.

But Barbara Yook quickly moved away from happy talk, asking Colette questions about what she observed in the days leading up to

Christmas of 1990, displaying the diagram of the house that Colette had drawn for investigators back in time.

The DA had Colette point to the location of the bedrooms, to the specific location of every piece of furniture that was there, having her mark the location of the windows in the bedrooms and the bathroom. Colette would testify that the last time she saw her sister was on the morning of Christmas Eve, at which time there were no broken windows in the house. She told the jury that the water pipes in the house were not frozen at all. While there, she'd taken a shower and had given both her kids baths, and the water ran just fine. There was no need to haul water into the residence from outside.

"Do you remember what you were doing on January 1st, 1991?"

"I was at home with my kids in Red Bluff and I received a call from my father that there had been a fire on Pennsylvania Gulch and my sister did not get out."

"Do you recall what happened when you arrived at your dad's that day?"

"I was met at the door by my niece, Erin. She said 'mommy is in heaven with Baby Jesus,' and said 'I heard mommy calling for daddy but daddy drove away.' And I just kind of absorbed the comment," Colette testified, "because I found it odd."

"Did you see the defendant in your father's house?"

"I did. I saw Karl, and I had a conversation with him. And I told him I wanted to see my sister."

"Did he say anything back to you?"

"He said I couldn't, and I asked him why not, and he told me she was all burnt up. He told me she was 'a crispy critter...'"

BOUSSON: KARLSEN CALLED HER SISTER A CRISPY CRITTER read the headline of *The Union Democrat* later that afternoon, and the public was flabbergasted. That Karlsen actually called his wife a *crispy critter*, that was incomprehensible. The public would learn that Karlsen had requested that his wife's body be taken directly to the crematorium, that he'd demanded a "direct cremation."

There would be no wake...

No casket...

No funeral...

"I suppose if I called her a crispy critter, which I don't think I did," Karl later said, "but *if* I said it, I must have been talking about the fact that she was already cremated."

But on the day Christina died, January 1, 1991, her body had yet to be removed from the hospital's morgue. The cremation process was not yet underway.

## NINETY-EIGHT

There's a general rule in the judicial system which precludes the "prior bad acts" of a defendant from being entered into evidence. To let a jury hear about  prior criminal allegations or convictions of a defendant, would create unfair prejudice. However, there are certain exceptions, and one of those relate to the defendants' modus operandi.

In Karlsen's case, because he used the same M.O. in the death of his son, the California jury would hear all the details regarding the murder of Levi Karlsen. John Cleere had flown in to testify, bringing with him two crucial items of evidence: a copy of the 9-hour video interview conducted with the defendant on November 23, 2012, and a copy of Karlsen's *Certified Record of Conviction.*

Cleere would testify that Karlsen pleaded guilty to the murder of his son, having taken a plea deal on November 6, 2013, at which time he was convicted of Second-Degree murder. Through John Cleere's testimony, the jury would learn that Karlsen had taken out a large insurance policy on his 23-year-old son, that he'd received a whopping $700,000 payout after his son's demise.

Karl tried to hide it, he tried to act cool, but inside he was furious that Cleere had been allowed to testify. He'd been told by his former defense attorney, Lawrence Kasperek, that there was "an understand-ing" between law enforcement in New York and California, that his guilty plea would not be entered into evidence if there was ever a trial in Calaveras County.

Karl's former attorney was a fraud.

As soon as the trial was over, he would get Kasperek disbarred.

Under the principal of modus operandi, the jury would then learn about the mysterious barn fire that occurred at the Karlsen farm which killed three of Karlsen's prized horses. They would hear testimony from William Ostrander, the investigator from Wayne Cooperative Insurance, who told them that Karlsen defendant purchased additional insurance on those horses just weeks before the blaze, and had received a $70,000 payout.

Also put into evidence was a page from Karlsen's military records, dated March 28, 1984, which described a fire incident that occurred during "a convoy departure back to the Strategic Missile Support Base." The official document praised AIC Karlsen for his act of bravery because he'd been able "to extinguish the fire before any loss of resources could occur."

When it was time for the defense to put on their case-in-chief, there was not much in the way of evidence to bring forth, nor were there many witnesses. Richard Esquivel called a total of two witnesses to the stand, one of whom was fire expert John Miller, who testified that Karlsen's version of the events on January 1,1991, were accurate, that Karlsen's claims "could be scientifically corroborated."

The second witness was Ken Buske, who Esquivel would hammer away at, reminding the jury that Buske didn't arrive to the fire scene until February 7, 1991, a full *five weeks* after the fact. Esquivel was able to rattle Buske, getting the expert to concede that the photo evidence was gone, the physical evidence was gone, implying that Buske's expert opinion was misleading.

Esquivel would later focus much of his effort on discrediting Buske during his closing argument, spending over an hour trying to tear the prosecution's expert down. The defense attorney called Buske "a big shot" who refused to acknowledge his mistakes. He argued that Buske's report was "filled with errors and inconsistencies," arguing that Buske's description of the fire scene did not match the images that were depicted in the video of the fire scene, telling the jury to study that closely.

Esquivel was courageous, he put on a closing argument that lasted for *three hours*, during which he concentrated his efforts on trying to prove three things.

*The fire scene had not been cordoned off by law enforcement.

*The fire scene had been tampered with.

*The fire scene had been contaminated long before Buske got there.

Richard Esquivel knew he only needed one juror to agree with that.

"Every bit of evidence was here for the DA in 1991," Esquivel told the jury, insisting, "It wasn't good enough *then*, and it's not nearly good enough now."

"They want you to ignore all the contradictions in their case because he killed Levi," Esquivel argued. "You can be repulsed by him for killing his son, but did he kill his wife? There needs to be proof!"

Esquivel's closing was given with tremendous passion, but it paled by comparison to the closing that Barbara Yook had presented the day before, and everyone in the courtroom knew it.

Barbara Yook had described the horror of Christina's final moments, accusing Karlsen of "building a coffin" for his wife to perish in. With a copy of the State Farm check that Karlsen received looming large overhead, Yook told the jury "It's time to tell the defendant that *life is more important* than money."

In front of a packed courtroom, Yook summarized every scintilla of evidence that had been presented and revisited the testimony of each key witness. She told the jury that "Christina Alexander Karlsen was so many things to so many people, but to the defendant, she was no more than a *piece of property.*"

The DA's closing took over two hours.

It was exhausting but brilliant.

"When you kill somebody for money, it's murder," Yook said before she left the podium. "It's time to tell the defendant that he will not get away with Christina's death any longer."

The following morning, after Judge Smith read the jury instructions, the 7 women and 5 men of the jury went into deliberations. The jury had to consider the testimony from 35 witnesses and had a substantial amount of evidence to comb through, but their deliberations only took a few hours.

On Monday, February 3, 2020, the exact date of Levi's birthday, the jury returned their verdict, pronouncing Karl Holger Karlsen guilty of murder in the first degree, having determined that Christina Alexander Karlsen was killed by an act of arson.

As the verdict was being read, people in the gallery gasped.

Family members cried.

But Karl sat there, motionless.

As cold as a marble statue.

## NINETY-NINE

On the date Karlsen was sentenced, March 17, 2020, the world had slowly been coming to a halt. The people of Wuhan, China, had already been put on lockdown. By March 17, the plague had spread to 114 countries. People were dying and there was no cure in sight.

COVID was a cosmic mystery.

All over the world, people hung onto their God.

By that date, the worldwide lockdown had not yet become a reality. COVID was transmitted in close quarters, people thought, particularly on cruise ships and airplanes. And although flights were still operating, travel was getting too dangerous. After waiting a lifetime to confront her father, Erin chose not to fly back to California for the sentencing. And she was not the only one. Kati had chosen to stay in place as well.

At that time, the spread of COVID was in its early stages, and since younger people seemed to be immune to it, Karl thought his daughters would be there. The courts in California were still in session, there were no restrictions, no zoom calls, no barriers, yet in place.

With the thought of having to face his daughters' impact statements, Karl knew it was going to be a rough day. But low and behold, at the last minute, the snake found a way out of its basket. By claiming he had a low-grade fever, Karl was able to duck out of the courtroom. The sniveling coward was placed in an adjacent holding cell where he could hide from his victims, where he could listen to their impact statements through a speaker.

"On January 1,1991, my life changed forever," Colette told the court. "My heart was broken, my spirit was shattered permanently. And while this trial is specific to my sister, I think it is important to address the murder of my nephew. The court must realize that Karl is an individual whose love for money far exceeds the respect for a human life. *Karl likes to kill.* I truly believe that if Karl Karlsen ever gets out of prison, he will kill again."

When it was Arlene's turn to speak, she directed her comments to the monster behind the curtain, saying "My Christina died in a mysterious house fire and *you Karl*, you walked away and left her to die. You have caused me to grieve, to hurt, and to cry. You need to be locked up for the rest of your life."

Kati had submitted a videotaped impact statement, her sullen face appearing on the large screen. Kati told the court that the trauma her father had caused her led her to "suicidal thoughts" and expensive counseling sessions. She described the years of pain she suffered, blaming not only her father for her troubled state of mind, but her stepmother as well.

"It was a Cinderella story with no prince charming, and help never came," Kati told the court. She claimed that she grew up in an abusive setting, stating that Child Protective Services had been to her home "many times."

During her hour-long statement, Kati blamed Cindy for her unhappy childhood, which shook Cindy to the core. Kati was the daughter she felt closest to, yet Kati sat in open court, telling the court that Cindy neglected her, implying that the neglect she felt was tantamount to child abuse.

It wasn't only a low blow.

It simply wasn't true.

Kati then spoke about how shocking it was to learn that her father had collected close to *a million dollars* from the deaths of her mother, brother, and cherished Belgian horses. "I will never be free from the damage inflicted," Kati told the court. "I ask that you give me the comfort of knowing that my father will never be released from prison."

But it was Erin's impact statement, which her Aunt Colette read aloud in the courtroom, that was the most damning of all. Erin had written a diatribe, an intense speech, blaming her father for "physically, mentally, emotionally" abusing her and her siblings, stating that the abuse she suffered "will haunt me for the rest of my life."

She talked about the horror of her mother's death, emphasizing that her mother didn't die quickly. "She had time to think," Erin had written, "she had time to understand that she would never see her babies again."

Erin pulled at heartstrings as she lamented about having "never gotten the chance to know my mother." She described how devasting it was to grow up without a mother, "without the genuine authentic love of a parent."

She hated her stepmother, Erin wanted to make that clear, and blamed her for the abuse she suffered at the hands of her father. "After Cindy joined the picture, my siblings and I became indentured servants," she wrote. "We maintained the home, we did the bulk of the cooking, and were even responsible for making the marital bed. And if one thing wasn't done to Cindy's liking, she would inform our father, and *it would be dealt with strictly*, usually physically."

Erin went on to talk about Levi's death, focusing on the $700,000 that her father and stepmother had "spent recklessly" after Levi's death. She accused them of taking away everything Levi's life insurance could have provided for his daughters, telling the court that her father and Cindy had "stolen the braces from their teeth, their first cars, and their college educations."

She called her father inhumane.

What he did was unforgivable.

"Thanks to the assessment of twelve complete strangers, I can move forward knowing that my mother and brother are together resting in peace, knowing that my father is in a place where he can no longer hurt anyone."

\* \* \*

For the loss that Kati and Erin suffered, Judge Thomas Smith would order Karl to pay restitution to his girls in the amount of $200,000, the amount he'd collected from the insurance payout after their mother's death. The judge also awarded each of Karl's daughters an additional $10,000 for their pain and suffering, money that could go toward their counseling costs.

Judge Thomas Smith would then sentence Karl Holger Karlsen to life without parole, to be served consecutively, after Karlsen finished the remainder of his prison time in New York for the murder of his son. Calling Karlsen a coward, the judge said he would have sentenced Karlsen to a harsher sentence if that were possible, but the death penalty was never on the table. In the end, the sentence provided the family with much needed relief, and some form of closure.

But Karl had only begun to fight.

He was innocent, and he would prove it.

His conviction would be overturned on appeal.

# ONE HUNDRED

No normal person understands murder, really. Even if there seems to be a clear-cut answer, questions will always linger.

What did Levi know? What did he see?

During the trial, there was testimony about Levi standing next to his father as they both watched the house burn. This well-kept secret came directly from Karl's mouth, who told Jim Roberts that when the fire first started, he ran back to the house and "Levi was suddenly standing next to me."

If that was true, the boy escaped on his own.

But Karl never told that detail to anyone else.

He remained steadfast in his assertion that he'd pulled Levi out through a burning-hot window, alleging that a fireball came toward them and blew them off the porch. But the problem was, Karl had no injuries that needed medical treatment. And neither did Levi.

"There's no dispute that Levi was not injured, and how is that possible?" Barbara Yook asked in her closing argument. "*I submit to you that Levi got out on his own and at that point, Karl was stuck.*"

Having purchased large insurance policies on Christina and his three children, Karlsen had a plan in place. He would solve his problems in one fell swoop. He would be free of his anchors and would collect a windfall of a half a million dollars when it was all over. Karl had ensured that outcome by moving a large dresser over his girls' bedroom window to prevent their escape.

And six-year-old Levi had to have sensed that.

Even if Karl's' version of the story was true, even if he did rescue his son as he claimed, wouldn't Levi have questioned why his father took the time to walk him out to the pickup truck? And it wasn't only Levi who was put in there separately, it was their Dalmatian puppy, Lydia, too.

Levi must have realized what his father's real intentions were.

Because he'd seen it with his own eyes.

His father had designed it so that all of them would be trapped.

His plan was to kill every one of them.

# EPILOGUE

*The statement of Cindy Best Karlsen, written in response to the allegations made against her for years, some of which were presented in court on Judgement Day, March 17, 2020:*

When I met Karl, I saw a man who tragically lost his wife and was struggling to raise three kids on his own. I married Karl because I loved him and I felt the kids needed me but it didn't take long to realize that these kids were greatly impacted by their mother's death. Levi seemed the most affected and we even sought counseling from the school and also outside counseling. That counselor discontinued the sessions since Levi would never open up to him. I realize now that it was probably because he was threatened by his father.

It is not easy being a step-parent because you are always under a microscope. Things that a biological mother would do that was acceptable, a step-mother was looked upon as being wicked and mean. The children grew up with a swimming pool, bikes, toys, sleds, hayrides, and birthday parties. They attended summer camps and vacation Bible school. They participated in sports and both girls were cheerleaders in their high school years.

Did I make mistakes? Of course, but I felt I did the best I could. I loved them and they loved me. Before she left to join the Air Force, Erin wrote me a letter that I will always cherish. "I'd just like to say thank you for everything you do for all of us!" she wrote. "We're all very lucky to have found you. If my mother had to have hand-picked someone, it would have been you." Erin ended the letter, saying, "I will miss you a lot when I leave, but I'll be back for visits."

I think that says it all. Erin's letter sets the record straight, but just to be clear, the children were never "indentured servants" nor did they touch our "marital bed." These are false claims which Erin made during her impact statement, and I don't know why. They all had chores to do but they were normal, healthy chores to teach them responsibility.

Another thing I want to set straight is that I had nothing to do with the insurance investments. I was a pawn, not just of Karl, but also of

Tony Crisci. After Karl was arrested in 2012, I wrote to a higher-up at New York Life, asking that Tony Crisci be criminally investigated. New York Life should have caught the red flags, but they didn't. Tony was later investigated by New York Life and the investigator came back to me and said that he agreed that Tony Crisci's actions were "unethical," but he said that Crisci hadn't done anything illegal. I still believe he should have been fired.

I have never used Levi's insurance money for my own benefit except for the time that Karl talked me into getting a facelift while at the same time that I was having surgery on my eyelids (which was medically necessary and was covered by my insurance). Karl had a motive when he talked me into borrowing from the interest on one of the accounts, promising to pay it back once the duck business was making money. I later learned that he did that so he could have an excuse to "borrow money" by holding the facelift over my head.

Any new cars that I had, I was making payments on and I can prove that. Any vacations we went on were mostly paid for by me by saving my $5 bills that I made waitressing. That added up to quite a lot of money. When we all took a family vacation to Disney in 2001, I used the money that I inherited from my mother's estate to pay for it.

Karl was spending the money like crazy and I knew he was going to spend it all. At that point I realized that this money was never intended for my granddaughters, that Levi did not set up those policies on his own. All along, Karl intended to collect this money for himself, to spend however he pleased.

The claim that I stole money is ridiculous.

When Karl was draining the insurance money, I knew that I had to try to get some of it before he spent it all because I needed to survive. I had to live on the run and had to set something up that would be secure for the future. I still had Alex to raise and get through college, that is why I made the investment of buying a house in Newark and then rented it out. I also needed the income because I knew that after we divorced, there would be nothing left for me, and I was right.

When Elletra turned 18, I sent her a substantial check. I've been waiting for the girls to reach legal age so *they* could be in control of it, not their mother. Ivy will also receive a check when she is 18 because I know that's what Levi wanted.

My cousin Jackie Hymel betrayed me by secretly going behind my back, telling law enforcement that I was being shady with the money. However, she was the one who was grabbing at me, borrowing $10,000 so she could bail her stepson out of jail. I guess she thought that was okay because she paid the money back? She acted like she was on my side, like she understood what I had to do, when all the while she was trashing me to the police.

I need to address the fact that law enforcement has taken all the credit for Karl's arrest, when the truth is, they had no evidence until I got Karl to confess about what he did to Levi.

Mike stated that he suspected Karl of setting the house fire, yet he did nothing. He also suspected him of setting the barn fire and did nothing. I believe there are other members of the Karlsen family who suspected that Karl set both of those fires and they did nothing. Why? The answer is that they didn't want to dirty the Karlsen name, because they felt they had a prominent standing in Seneca County.

In my opinion, they all have Levi's blood on their hands. None of their lives were ever at risk as much as mine, Alex's, and my grand-daughters' were. Their lives were safe since they all sat by and said nothing.

These years following Karl's arrest, life has not been easy for me and Alex. I was never living the "high life" as they have claimed. Karl spent most of that money, not me. I still waitressed for years after Levi's death and I still work hard at my job in sales to this day because I have to make a living.

When I needed to sell the farm, Kati and Mike offered to pay me $50,000 which was less than a quarter of what it was worth. They tried to prevent me from selling it to anyone else by calling the Code Enforcement Officer and getting the house condemned. I have *written proof* that the Seneca County Code Enforcement office was called by Mike Karlsen which shows that Kati had given him consent to act as power of attorney.

After the illegal inspection of my home was conducted, the code enforcement officer listed 67 violations that needed to be repaired or fixed. I was never aware of these violations until a year later, when the house was going to be put up for sale. The violations included many small things like weeds that were overgrown and garbage that was piled up in the backyard. Looking back at it, I believe that Mike used his "connections" in Seneca County to try to buy the house out from under me.

Luckily, I was able to sell the farm to a Mennonite family for $200,000 because the buyer realized that most of the violations were small or trumped up. Unfortunately, much of that money was used to pay off the liens on the house, in the amount of $169,000, which was the debt that Karl owed to his lawyers and to various banks.

I am saddened and flabbergasted by the turn of events. I didn't always make the right decisions by choosing to drown myself in booze, trying to erase away the pain. I currently have four years of sobriety and with that comes clarity. I am at peace with the knowledge that I helped put Karl behind bars because I think my granddaughters were going to be his next victims. I am grateful to Dave as he probably saved my life. It wasn't always easy for him and I still don't know why he stuck around, but he did, and for that I am grateful.

I am grateful to the few people who believed in me, especially Aphrodite, and perhaps I am grateful to Alex most of all because he not only supported me, he found a way to bring light back into my life. I am so proud of the young man Alex has become. He is now happily married to a beautiful young lady and I look forward to being a grand-mother to their children.

I love Elletra and Ivy and I will always have open arms for them should they ever want to have a relationship with me. It's sad that they were duped as well.

None of this was easy on anyone. I wish nothing but the best for my stepdaughters, who I will always love, regardless of what they've said and done to discredit me.


To Christina,

You were always a huge presence in our home. I sometimes asked myself when I was presented with a problem, "What would Christina do?" From what I learned about you over the years is that you were a fun-loving person and a great mom. I wish I had met you, I think we would have been great friends. May you and Levi rest in peace.


To My Dearest Levi,

Sweet little boy who loved tacos and strawberry cream cake every year on your birthday. I am sorry if I ever made you feel like I didn't love you and I'm sorry that I didn't tell you how proud I was of you in the months leading up to your death. I did, and I was. I'm sorry if I failed you. I take comfort in knowing that you are at peace in the arms of your mother and Jesus. You are forever in my heart, I love you always.

As for me, my judgement day will come before God and that is the only one that matters.

## ABOUT THE AUTHOR

**APHRODITE JONES** is a TV persona and bestselling author who knows the world of true crime firsthand. For over three decades, Jones has brought readers inside the darkest motives and emotional truths behind each tragedy, always focusing on the real-life victims. Jones is the host and executive producer of the hit ID series *"True Crime with Aphrodite Jones."* All six seasons are now available on Apple, Discovery+, Hulu, Amazon Prime and other streaming platforms.

Her bestselling true crime books have been the subject of highly acclaimed films, including the Academy Award-winning *Boys Don't Cry*, the ABC film *Betrayed By Love,* the hit Netflix series, *The Staircase,* and the Lifetime film, *The Staircase Murders.*

Her illustrious career as a crime writer includes her coverage of some of the highest profile cases of our time, including the trials of O.J. Simpson, Casey Anthony, Phil Spector, Scott Peterson, Michael Jackson, and Joaquin "El Chapo" Guzman, among others.

A recognized expert in the field of true crime, she has made regular appearances on both broadcast and cable networks, including appearances on Dateline NBC, ABC's 20/20, FOX News, CNN, and MSNBC. A graduate of UCLA , she holds a Masters of Philosophy from NYU where she completed the Ph.D. program in English and American Literature. The author encourages comments and questions and can be reached via her website, www.aphroditejones.com

WEB: www.aphroditejones.com

APHRODITEJONESBOOKS

Made in the USA
Las Vegas, NV
12 July 2024

92211328R00225